COMPARATIVE EUROPEAN POLITICS

General Editors: Max Kaase and Ken Newton

Learning Democracy

COMPARATIVE EUROPEAN POLITICS

Comparative European Politics is a series for students and teachers of political science and related disciplines, published in association with the European Consortium for Political Research. Each volume will provide an up-to-date survey of the current state of knowledge and research on an issue of major significance in European government and politics.

OTHER TITLES IN THIS SERIES

Learning Democracy

*Democratic and Economic Values in
Unified Germany*

ROBERT ROHRSCHNEIDER

OXFORD
UNIVERSITY PRESS

OXFORD

UNIVERSITY PRESS

Great Clarendon Street, Oxford OX2 6DP

Oxford University Press is a department of the University of Oxford.
It furthers the University's objective of excellence in research, scholarship,
and education by publishing worldwide in

Oxford New York

Athens Auckland Bangkok Bogotá Buenos Aires Calcutta
Cape Town Chennai Dar es Salaam Delhi Florence Hong Kong Istanbul
Karachi Kuala Lumpur Madrid Melbourne Mexico City Mumbai
Nairobi Paris São Paulo Singapore Taipei Tokyo Toronto Warsaw

with associated companies in Berlin Ibadan

Oxford is a registered trade mark of Oxford University Press
in the UK and in certain other countries

Published in the United States
by Oxford University Press Inc., New York

British Library Cataloguing in Publication Data

Data available

Library of Congress Cataloging in Publication Data

Rohrschneider, Robert.
Learning democracy : democratic and economic values
in unified Germany / Robert Rohrschneider.
(Comparative European politics)
Includes bibliographical references and index.
1. Democracy—Germany. I. Title. II. Series.
JN3971.A91R655 1999 320.943'09'049—dc21 98-54769

ISBN 0-19-829517-0

1 3 5 7 9 10 8 6 4 2

Typeset in Times
by BookMan Services
Printed in Great Britain
on acid-free paper by
Bookcraft Ltd
Midsomer Norton, Somerset

Preface

When the Berlin Wall fell in autumn 1989, the timing could not have been better for me. As a young assistant professor searching for a new research project after completing my dissertation, the collapse of socialism raised important questions about its legacy and the viability of democracies in eastern Germany and elsewhere in East-Central Europe. While there are several legitimate approaches to examining this subject, I was especially attracted to the question of how citizens' experience in a socialist state shaped their democratic values. I therefore designed a research project in the spring of 1990 exploring how the political experience of eastern and western Germany's political elites affected their democratic views.

Anybody who has conducted field research appreciates the surprises one encounters. Nothing illustrates this enticing quality more than my first conversation with a parliamentarian from eastern Berlin whom I phoned to set up an interview. Upon mentioning my name, the MP appeared very pleased to hear from me which I, naturally, took as a sign that he appreciated the significance of social science research. It turned out, however, that he had rented a small apartment from one of my distant cousins (who shares my last name) in eastern Germany during the 1980s—a branch of my family I vaguely remembered from conversations at the dinner table. The MP's enthusiasm about my call waned quickly when I explained the reason for it. This personal anecdote symbolizes Germany's tumultuous history—and illustrates the 'quasi-laboratory' context of Germany's post-1945 developments. Families sharing the same heritage, traditions, and customs were separated and exposed to two fundamentally opposed regimes. For a social scientist interested in the formation of democratic values, Germany's division and subsequent unification offers a unique opportunity to examine how political institutions affect democratic values. This book exploits this rare occasion by comparing mass and political elites' democratic values after 1989.

The MP mentioned above did grant me an interview, both in 1992 and 1995. I am indebted to him and all the other parliamentarians who took the time to answer my questions. I would like to acknowledge the support I received from the president of the Berlin parliament at that time, Hanna-Renate Laurien. She facilitated my access to the Berlin parliament and enabled me to conduct the interviews in an office in the parliamentary building. The parties' *Fraktionsvorsitzende* at that time also endorsed the project: Klaus-Rüdiger Landowski (CDU), Carola von Braun (FDP), Dietmar Staffelt (SPD), Sybill-Anka Klotz and Renate Künast (Bündnis '90/Greens), and Gesine Lötsch (PDS). Their support was crucial in establishing the project's credentials among parliamentarians.

Several researchers in Berlin made helpful suggestions throughout the fieldwork. At the *Freie Universität* Berlin, Niels Diederich, Dietrich Herzog, and Hilke Rebenstorf (now at the University of Potsdam) provided beneficial comments during the preparatory phase of the fieldwork in 1991. The hospitality extended to me by several colleagues at the *Wissenschaftszentrum* Berlin—Dieter Fuchs, Hans-Dieter Klingemann, Edeltraud Roller, and Bernhard Weßels—not only provided a stimulating intellectual environment, but also made my family's stays in Berlin very pleasant.

I also benefited from the suggestions I received from colleagues who read parts or all of the manuscript. I am grateful to Russell Dalton for his readiness to discuss the project on numerous occasions and for his insightful comments. Moreover, as my mentor in graduate school and through his own work, he has been an invaluable inspiration for which I am deeply grateful. Mark Peffley not only read parts of the manuscript, but provided moral support during our late-night conversations. Several others made helpful comments on parts of earlier drafts: Wilhelm Bürklin, Edward Carmines, Dana Chabot, Raymond Duch, Kathryn Firmin-Sellers, Clark Gibson, Robert Huckfeldt, Jeffrey Isaac, Robert Ladrech, Herbert Kitschelt, Andreas Sobisch, and the three readers for Oxford University Press. Samuel Barnes provided an opportunity to present parts of this research at a conference at Georgetown University. In addition to the colleagues at the WZB mentioned earlier, I would like to thank James Gibson, Ronald Inglehart, Markus Küppers, Elisabeth Noelle-Neumann, and Frederick Weil for sharing some of their data. Indiana University's political science data lab provided valuable technical assistance during the final phase of this research. Finally, I appreciate the interest of the series editors, Max Kaase and Kenneth Newton, in the project and the care with which Dominic Byatt and Amanda Watkins at Oxford

University Press shepherded the manuscript from submission to publication.

I am pleased to acknowledge the fellowship I received from the Social Science Research Council's Berlin programme. The fellowship enabled me to conduct the first round of interviews with Berlin parliamentarians in 1991–2. I would like to thank Herbert Kitschelt and the Institute for Social Sciences at Humboldt University for inviting me to spend one semester in Berlin in 1994–5 when I conducted the follow-up interviews with eastern Berlin parliamentarians. Indiana University's departments of Political Science and West European Studies also supported the project on various occasions. An invitation by the Bundespresseamt to participate in the 1998 election tour provided a valuable opportunity to study German politics up close. Without the financial support of these institutions, this book could not have been written. Finally, I am grateful to the International Social Science Council, the Candido Mendes University of Brazil, and the award committee of the ECPR for awarding the book the 1998 Stein Rokkan prize for Comparative Social Science Research.

There is really no commensurate way through which I could publicly acknowledge the contributions my family made to the project. Suffice it to say that my mother's confidence and father's pride in me set expectations I did not want to fail. Sarah-Elisabeth Rohrschneider, arriving between the two waves of interviews, rearranged my priorities and taught me things whose existence I was unaware of. My father-in-law, Earl Rovit, had the questionable pleasure of discussing many half-baked ideas and pointing out linguistic lapses in the manuscript. Throughout my conversations with him, I came to especially appreciate his unfailing belief in the democratic creed. My wife, Rebecca Rovit, accompanied the project from inception to publication. She bore the brunt of my disappointment when MPs cancelled interviews, my writing would not go as well as I had hoped, or when empirical analyses did not support my hunches. But her willingness to endure these frustrations pales in light of her steadfast confidence in my ability to complete the project and the high standards she set for me through her own scholarship. To dedicate this book to her can only be a token of my gratitude.

R.R.

Acknowledgments

Parts of Chapter 5 were previously published in 'Report from the Laboratory: The Influence of Institutions on Political Elites' Democratic Values in Germany', *American Political Science Review*, 88:4 (1994), 927–41. Parts of Chapter 6 were previously published in 'Institutional Learning versus Value Diffusion: The Evolution of Democratic Values Among Parliamentarians in Eastern and Western Germany', *Journal of Politics*, 58:2 (May 1996), 442–66. Parts of Chapter 7 were previously published in 'Pluralism, Conflict, and Legislative Elites in the United Germany', *Comparative Politics*, 29, pp. 43–67. Parts of Chapter 8 were previously published in 'Cultural Transmission versus Perceptions of the Economy: The Sources of Political Elites' Economic Values in the United Germany', *Comparative Political Studies*, 29:1 (Feb. 1996), 78–104.

I am grateful to the American Political Science Association, the University of Texas Press, Comparative Politics, and Sage Publications, respectively, for their permission to reprint the material.

Contents

List of Tables

List of Figures

Glossary of Party Names

CDU   Christlich Demokratische Union (Christian Democratic Union)

CSU   Christlich Soziale Union (Christian Social Union)

FDP   Freie Demokratische Partei (Free Democratic Party)

SPD   Sozialdemokratische Partei Deutschlands (Social Democratic Party of Germany)

Bündnis '90/Greens   The merger of the Greens and the Alliance '90.

PDS   Partei des Demokratischen Sozialismus (Party for Democratic Socialism), formerly the SED.

With love
to
Rebecca

1

Introduction

When Politburo member Günther Schabowski pulled a note from his sheaf of papers to announce new travel regulations during a press conference in Berlin on 9 November 1989, he inadvertently initiated the dissolution of the GDR. Originally designed to facilitate visits to the West, the new regulations quickly established a direction of their own, leading to the opening of the iron curtain in Berlin's centre. Tens of thousands of eastern Berliners visited the western part of the city during the night from the 9th to the 10th, only to return to the calmer sectors of eastern Berlin after they had spent a few hours in the capitalist oasis within the socialist state. The most visible consequence of Germany's defeat in 1945—the intra-German border—vanished almost by accident.[1]

It is a historical irony that this event occurred on 9 November, which also marks the dates of the Reichskristallnacht in 1938, the Hitler Putsch in 1923, and the pronouncement of the Weimar Republic in 1918. Despite the enthusiasm which the collapse of the authoritarian system generated, this coincidence symbolizes that Germany's unification also revives several questions about the future of its democracy—questions that analysts of western Germany had thought were resolved. Especially throughout the 1980s, scholars reached a consensus that the western German mass public and elites had developed a democratic political culture (Roth 1976; Conradt 1980; Baker, Dalton, and Hildebrandt 1981). But eastern Germans did not participate in the democratization project initiated in the West after 1945. Instead, the socialist state in important ways represented a continuation of Germany's anti-democratic past: one-party controlled, with few opportunities for either elites or the public to express their opinions freely (Ludz 1972; Schweigler 1975; Childs, Baylis, and Rueschemeyer 1989).

Germany's division and unification therefore raise several important questions which this book addresses. Given their exposure first to the Nazi regime and then to the socialist system, how able are eastern Germans to adhere to democratic rules? What are eastern Germans' democratic ideals? More generally, how democratic can a citizenry be given its fifty-year exposure to totalitarian rule? Finally, what does this legacy imply for the prospect of democracy in the unified Germany?

In order to understand the impact of eastern and western Germans' regime experience on their democratic values, this study suggests an *institutional learning* model which conceptualizes the micro-logic by which a nation's institutional framework shapes individuals' basic values. The core argument of the model maintains that the democratic citizenship-qualities—*democratic restraint, self-reliance,* and corresponding *societal ideals*—underlie several democratic and market-economic values. Because these citizenship-qualities are acquired primarily if citizens have a chance to practise them, a lack of this opportunity reduces citizens' support for several democratic values. As I will argue in detail in Chapter 2, a nation's institutional framework—the political as well as economic—is central in providing these opportunities. Consequently, political tolerance, for example, is likely to be a scarce commodity when individuals have mainly experienced an authoritarian system that does not restrain itself from outlawing political opposition. Conversely, political tolerance should be higher when individuals have mainly experienced a democratic system where opposing interests provided the foundation for public life.

This summary of the institutional learning perspective, however brief, already suggests one major expectation that is tested in this book: individuals' political and economic values reflect the ideological premises of the political and economic systems to which they are exposed. This prediction is far from trivial. In recent decades, the 'third democratic wave' has frequently been attributed to the spread of democratic values through the rapid expansion of electronic mass media (Huntington 1991; Starr 1991). This line of reasoning has been used to explain the democratic revolt of the eastern German populace in the autumn of 1989 and the surprisingly strong support of eastern Germans for democratic procedures revealed in public-opinion surveys after 1989 (Fuchs, Klingemann, and Schöbel 1991; Weil 1993; Dalton 1994). However, this argument conflicts with models which suggest that ideological values are developed over longer time-periods, spanning as much as one generation or more (Almond and Verba 1963; Kaase 1983; Eckstein 1988). From this perspective, it is unlikely that citizens in eastern Germany and other post-socialist countries developed democratic values. The following chapter explains that the institutional learning perspective helps to determine which democratic values diffuse across systems and which ones are developed primarily through exposure to a nation's institutional configuration.

The summary also contributes to an understanding of which values this study focuses on. Here I follow Almond and Verba's distinction between values that establish the community boundaries from those political values that manifest the ideological basis of a political regime (Almond and Verba 1963). Community-related values extend beyond the foundations of formal institutions by providing individuals with social identities. Ethnic group membership, regional attachments, and national boundaries exemplify such sources of one's identity. Identity-related values typically reach beyond the realm of the political system by separating individuals who enjoy all the privileges and obligations of a community from those who are denied these privileges. In contrast, regime-related values concern the ideological foundations of a nation's institutional framework. In essence, *ideological values express individuals' preferred political ideals and the procedural framework through which these ideals ought to be achieved.* This book focuses on the ideological values that manifested the major differences between the socialist and parliamentary regimes in the two German states between 1949 and 1989—democratic rights and ideals, political tolerance, pluralist views, economic processes and ideals.

Germany's partition after 1945 offers a fortunate opportunity to examine the influence of institutional learning on individuals' ideological values under 'quasi-laboratory' conditions. To test the implications of the institutional learning model, the book uses survey data at the elite and mass levels. The elite data stem from two waves of interviews I personally conducted with Berlin parliamentarians (called MPs for reasons of brevity). In the first wave, conducted in 1991–2 shortly after Germany's unification, I interviewed 168 parliamentarians—seventy-nine from the East and eighty-nine from the West. I also re-interviewed sixty-five eastern MPs in 1994–5 in order to examine whether—and if so, how quickly—eastern MPs have adjusted to the new institutional context. In addition to the East–West comparison, the study also examines potential mass–elite differences over ideological values. In particular, elites' higher education and their greater exposure to institutional norms may entail that institutional learning and diffusion processes affect eastern MPs and mass publics differently (Chapter 2). There are several public-opinion surveys in the public domain, conducted after 1989, which permit a comparison of most mass and elite ideological values this study focuses on.

To a surprising degree, eastern Germans' political values—among mass publics as well as MPs—continue to reflect their exposure to a socialist regime. For example, particularly eastern Germans born and raised after 1945 continue to espouse socialist *ideals*, even though they also agree that the collapsed socialist system was inefficient and un-democratic. In turn, eastern Germans' ideological values influence how citizens evaluate the existing institutions (e.g. parliament and the executive). Eastern Germans tend to be more critical of these institutions than western Germans, and socialist ideals generate negative attitudes about their performance.

The book contributes to several debates. On a practical level, it documents the difficulty of merging the two parts of Germany into one truly unified nation. Because it is the first comprehensive study to examine several democratic values that are vital to the operation of a democratic system and a market economy, the book indicates where Germans drifted apart and where they actually converged over time. Although western Germans dominate the vast majority of institutions in Germany (Bürklin 1996), the persisting East–West differences over ideological values have important consequences for the political process. The debate over constitutional changes at the federal and state levels displays these value differences, as does the success of the reformed socialist party—the PDS—in eastern Germany.

Although this study focuses on Germany, its theoretical implications also extend well beyond this nation. Because the findings frequently corroborate the institutional learning effect in eastern Germany, one may surmise that other democratizing nations in East-Central Europe also experience the continued legacy of socialism. Consequently, a substantial proportion of mass publics and elites in East-Central Europe most likely hold ideological values that are incompatible with a liberal democracy and a market economy. To the extent possible, the book will furnish evidence that the Germany-based results are generalizable to other post-socialist nations. In addition, because the institutional learning model synthesizes several approaches in the democratic transition literature—a point I will develop in Chapter 2—the study points toward fruitful ways of studying democratic transitions. Typically, when studies assess the stability of new democracies in East-Central Europe, they tend to scrutinize either citizens' ideological values or the performance of new democracies.

The institutional learning model suggests, however, that the *interactive* effect of ideological values and performance evaluations on existing institutions must be examined in post-socialist nations.

Finally, the book makes a contribution to the study of how public opinion forms. Rarely are social scientists in the position to distil the long-term effect of a nation's institutional context on citizens' ideological values. By focusing on a nation's institutional framework as an influence on ideological values, this research assesses the relative contribution of micro- and macro-level sources of citizens' ideological values. I develop these and other implications of the study in the concluding chapter, after I have established the theoretical arguments and documented the ideological differences across the former East–West divide.

The Plan of the Book

Chapter 2 develops the institutional learning perspective fully. It indicates why restraint, self-reliance, and corresponding ideals are developed together, and why a nation's institutional framework is crucial in providing the opportunities for individuals to develop these citizenship-qualities. The chapter also suggests two criteria for determining when the effect of institutional learning may be offset by the diffusion of values across systemic boundaries, both at the level of mass publics and political elites. The chapter then establishes the conceptual relationship between ideological values, citizens' performance evaluations of existing institutions, and their support for these institutions. Finally, the chapter suggests that the institutional learning perspective synthesizes separate strands in the democratic transition literature. Chapter 3 discusses the extent to which Germany's partition in 1945 and its formal unification in 1990 meet the quasi-laboratory conditions required to test the framework. Chapter 4 introduces two elite surveys and the available public-opinion surveys; and it discusses the political and social climate at the time when I conducted the fieldwork. The chapter concludes by addressing several methodological issues.

The empirical chapters (Chapters 5–9) follow a basic organizational structure. Each chapter first discusses how the institutional learning framework leads to several hypotheses. It then examines these predictions by presenting the results from the elite studies and compares them, when possible, to the views of mass publics. A chapter then presents cross-national evidence in order to link the Germany-based findings to other transition countries. While this book does not seek to present a fully fledged comparative analysis of ideological values, the objective is to indicate that the Germany-based patterns are not unique. A final section in each chapter summarizes the results and highlights the central implications with regard to an ideological value.

Chapter 5 begins to test the various predictions derived from the theoretical framework by analysing eastern and western Germans' democratic ideals and their views on democratic procedures. Like the succeeding chapters, it uses closed and open-ended questions to examine citizens' democratic ideals and their views about the democratic process. The chapter confirms several predictions of the institutional learning model. Eastern Germans are substantially more likely than western Germans to endorse socialist ideals, both at the level of elites and mass publics. At the same time, support for broad democratic principles is strong in western and eastern Germany, indicating the presence of a partial value diffusion. These basic patterns also emerge in other East-Central European nations. Chapter 6 continues to examine eastern and western Germans' commitment to democratic procedures by focusing on their willingness to extend democratic rights to unpopular political groups—political tolerance. Unlike Chapter 5, where I focus on citizens' evaluations of general democratic rights, this chapter assesses the depth of their commitment to the democratic process. The chapter also analyses MPs' reasoning about their willingness (or reluctance) to protect the rights of political minorities. While a majority of eastern and western Germans support democratic principles, eastern MPs are considerably less tolerant than their western counterparts. Indeed, the difficulty of developing democratic restraint is manifested in the large proportion of western Germans who would withhold democratic rights from ideological extremists. MPs' reasons for extending and denying civil liberties also displays their different institutional learning. A similar pattern emerges in a comparison of publics' political tolerance in the former Soviet Union and the USA. Chapter 7 examines views about another procedural value—the pluralist process. Like political tolerance, the acceptance of conflict and compromise represents a pillar of a liberal democracy. And like political tolerance, pluralist competition requires a considerable amount of restraint and self-reliance. This chapter again documents that ideological values based on these citizenship-qualities are not easily developed within an authoritarian system. Eastern Germans are substantially less likely than western Germans to endorse pluralist principles. In fact, eastern MPs' responses to the open-ended question to a surprising degree fit Ralf Dahrendorf's seminal analyses (1967) about the lack of support for the pluralist process in German society.

Chapter 8 shifts attention to the economic sector by analysing the economic values of eastern and western Germans. When the GDR collapsed, it was widely assumed that eastern Germans were dissatisfied with the inefficient command economy. They certainly were. But eastern Germans also continue to support socialist-economic values as an ideal. The analyses in this chapter also consider that the difficult economic situation in Germany may generate support for policies that cushion individuals from the difficulty of rugged market competition. The findings indicate that while individuals' economic situation influences their views about specific welfare policies, the institutional learning effect strongly shapes individuals' views about basic economic principles. Finally, cross-national evidence suggests that East-Central Europeans also view market economies sceptically.

Chapter 9 shifts the focus to the consequences of individuals' ideological values for a nation's institutional framework. The chapter directly addresses one controversial debate in the democratic transition literature: does there have to be a congruence between citizens' ideological values and existing institutions? Or is the performance of institutions the main source for political stability? This chapter studies the impact of ideological values *and* performance dimensions on citizens' institutional trust. It also moves the relationship between ideological values and individuals' performance evaluations into the centre of attention, thus suggesting a way of bridging separate strands in the democratic tradition literature. Evidence indicates that performance evaluations and ideological values jointly influence citizens' views about democracies, both in Germany and East-Central Europe.

The concluding chapter summarizes the main findings and outlines the implications of the study for German politics and society. It also discusses the study's theoretical lessons and highlights its practical implications for East-Central Europe.

2

Charting the Inquiry

The collapse of the iron curtain revives long-standing theoretical questions about the relationship between regime changes and citizens' democratic values. Analysts who assume that democratic values of publics and elites are required for a stable democracy are faced with a difficult question: what is the prospect for democracies given the absence of a prolonged democratic regime experience in East-Central Europe (Almond and Verba 1963; Almond 1980)? Some analysts would predict that socialist-authoritarian values must have developed in East-Central Europe over the past four decades (Verba 1965*a*, 1965*b*; Schweigler 1975; Almond 1983). If this assessment is correct, democratic systems may be destabilized because many citizens may reject the basic ideas upon which a democracy is based. Other value-focused studies maintain that a nascent democratic culture has developed in democratizing nations despite the authoritarian nature of socialist systems (Fuchs, Klingemann, and Schöbel 1991; Starr 1991; Gibson, Duch, and Tedin 1992; Dalton 1994). This view attributes to the collapse of socialism, in part, its failure to create a socialist ideological culture and is more sanguine about the prospects for democratic institutions. Yet, in spite of this disagreement over the precise reservoir of democratic values in East-Central Europe, this perspective suggests the importance of democratic values for the viability of democratic institutions.

In contrast to this value-based approach (*culturalists* for short), another group of scholars maintains that culturalists overrate the centrality of democratic values for the viability of democracies in East-Central Europe. These *institutionalists* believe that democratic institutions in East-Central Europe may survive within a 'hostile' political culture if elites endorse democratic institutions, and if the performance of a political system is adequate (Przeworski 1991; Geddes 1995). Some analysts focus on the role of political elites and the process of designing democratic institutions (e.g. Huntington

1984; O'Donnell and Schmitter 1986; Higley and Gunther 1992), while others focus on the performance-dimension of new institutions (Rogowski 1974; Przeworski 1991). Despite these variations, the unifying element among institutionalist analyses in the context of democratic transitions is the premiss that 'genuine democrats need not precede democracy' (Di Palma 1990: 30). Democratic values presumably follow, but do not have to precede, the establishment of democratic institutions which function well because—once established—they shape mass and elite ideological values.

Empirical evidence may be mustered for each of these conflicting perspectives. Those who maintain that socialist-authoritarian systems shaped individuals' values refer to studies that document the apparent viability of socialist values, the relatively low levels of tolerance, or the low level of religious values in post-socialist nations (Friedrich 1990; McGregor 1991; Finifter and Mickewicz 1992; Gibson and Duch 1993; Bahry, Boaz, and Gordon 1997; Fuchs, Roller, and Weßels 1997). Those who maintain that democratic values have diffused into socialist states refer to public-opinion studies, conducted shortly after the dissolution of the iron curtain, which document the existence of strong support for democratic rights in several of these nations (Gibson, Duch, and Tedin 1992; Weil 1993; Dalton 1994; Veen 1997). And those who maintain that values adjust to democratic institutions after a regime change refer to historical examples of successful democratic transitions where the performance helped to create a democratic political culture, such as in Spain after Franco's death in 1975 (McDonough, Barnes, and Lopez-Pina 1986) or in western Germany after 1949 (Barry 1970; Rogowski 1974).

Despite the empirical support garnered on behalf of each perspective, culturalist and institutionalist approaches both remain problematic. Culturalists, for example, provide us with little theoretical guidance about when institutions shape citizens' ideological values. Nor do these scholars alert us as to when diffusion processes may offset the presumed influence of a political system on values. Consequently, culturalists tend to use the learning and diffusion perspectives inductively, if not in a circular manner: when publics in former socialist nations espouse values that reflect the socialist system, such a finding is attributed to the exposure of citizens to the socialist institutions in Central Europe. If, in contrast, citizens' values in these nations are surprisingly democratic, values are said to have been diffused. In turn, institutionalists, who maintain that the proper values will develop as democratic institutions remain in place, frequently neglect to provide a micro-level model about the influence of institutions on values; neither do they supply the necessary evidence to buttress their claims about the presumed influence of democratic institutions on ideological values. Consequently, these studies also appear to be circular: the (in)stability of democratic institutions is taken as evidence that publics and elites (un)successfully moderated their ideological beliefs.

The unresolved institutions–values nexus in cultural and institutional studies of democratic transitions constitutes the point of departure for this research:

(1) To what extent do the ideological foundations and the operating procedures of a nation's institutional framework shape individuals' ideological values?

A second, related, question concerns the impact of value diffusion on individuals' ideological values:

(2) To what extent may the impact of a political and economic system on ideological values be offset by the diffusion of ideological values from the West into the East?

These questions, in turn, raise the issue of how individual values relate to citizens' support for existing political institutions:

(3) To what extent are ideological values and perceptions of the performance of institutions related to individuals' support for democratic institutions?

The first two questions are concerned with the 'institutions-to-values' causality: does a regime, given enough time, imbue individuals with those values that underlie institutions? In the context of post-socialist nations, did socialist systems imbue individuals with socialist ideals? Or was the exposure to information about western systems sufficient to develop democratic values? The third question shifts the perspective to the 'values-to-institutions' causality: how strongly are ideological values and the performance-dimensions related to individuals' support for existing institutions? Does there have to be, in Almond and Verba's (1963) terminology, a congruence between the type of political values citizens hold and the type of system that is in place? Conversely, are positive performance evaluations the key to citizen support for existing institutions, as institutionalists suggest?

Although the two processes—from institutions-to-values and from values-to-institutions—are closely linked, it is heuristically useful to distinguish between them for at least two reasons. First, democratic systems in East-Central Europe were established suddenly, so that there is a fairly sharp incision delineating the end of socialist regimes and the beginning of democratic systems. Consequently, it is possible to separate the two processes analytically and to examine them separately shortly after the regime transitions occurred. Once this distinction is observed, it leads to two sets of research questions. The institutions-to-values process raises questions about the effect of the old regime on citizens' values and about the ability of new democratic regimes to alter citizens' pre-existing values. The values-to-institutions perspective, in turn, raises questions about how citizens' ideological values and performance evaluations influence their support (or rejection) of democratic institutions. Secondly, the separation helps to clarify where culturalists and institutionalists disagree but also where they converge in their arguments and conclusions. The ensuing discussion suggests, for example, that the most serious disagreement concerns the values-to-institutions process, whereas there is some room for consensus with respect to the institutions-to-values process.

A systematic analysis of the three research questions requires a long-term 'experiment' in which individuals from one nation are systematically exposed to two different political systems. I will attempt to shed light on the first two questions by examining the extent to which eastern and western Germans have diverged over a range of ideological values after forty years of separation; the third question calls for an analysis of whether individuals' values and performance evaluations are related to their support for existing institutions. Germany's historical context provides an excellent opportunity to examine the relationship between regime exposure and political values. Germany's division in 1949 and its formal unification in 1990 create conditions which approach a quasi-experimental design (Chapter 3). Therefore, a comparison of eastern and western Germans' political views shortly after unification enables one to examine the influence of two fundamentally different regimes on individuals' political values. Further, since this study tracks the evolving attitudes of eastern Germans after the establishment of democratic institutions in 1990 (Chapter 4), there is the additional opportunity to examine the impact of a democratic regime change on political values in eastern Germany.

The overarching theme of this research thus focuses on the relationship between political institutions and ideological values. In addition, a sub-theme contrasts mass and elite political values in eastern and western Germany. Elites occupy a central position in the construction of democratic systems, and it is especially important to know the answers to the study's three central questions at the level of elites (Dahl 1971). Further, some of the processes, like value diffusion, probably operate at different rates at the level of mass publics and elites (a point I will elaborate below). Therefore, this study also incorporates mass–elite comparisons over political values.

The present chapter is structured in four parts. The first part situates the study within the context of the institutions–values nexus. This discussion demonstrates that culturalists and institutionalists tell us surprisingly little about the impact of regime exposure on political values at both the level of mass publics and political elites. The second part of the chapter presents a theoretical framework which suggests an integration of the various perspectives. The third part shifts attention to a central controversy between culturalists and institutionalists, namely the relationship between political values, perceived institutional performance, and institutional support. The fourth part discusses potential mass–elite differences as they relate to the theoretical framework.

THE INSTITUTIONS–VALUES NEXUS: EXPOSING A VOID

In the light of socialism's collapse, one may be tempted, like Fukuyama (1989), to conclude that communism as a viable ideological force has become obsolete. But such a conclusion would be premature, because cultural and institutional approaches provide us with precious little guidance in understanding the influence of regime exposure on political values. To elaborate on this assertion, this discussion suggests that (1) cultural and institutional analyses of democratic transitions do not examine systematically the impact of political institutions on individuals' political values, either on the level of elites or mass publics; and (2) that cultural and institutional approaches overlook the fact that they are often complementary, rather than diametrically opposed, in explaining the development of citizens' institutional support.

The Unresolved Institutions-to-Values Process. Ever since Gabriel Almond (1956) and Almond and Sidney Verba's (1963) seminal political culture studies, cultural analyses of democratic regimes have assumed that stable democratic institutions are moored in democratic orientations among a nation's citizenry. In the context of western democracies, Almond and Verba stipulate that the stability of democratic institutions increases if citizens hold a specific mix of democratic values, what has been called the 'congruence postulate' (Eckstein 1966). Although critics of *The Civic Culture* noted that the study underestimates the possibility that institutions imbue citizens with those values that institutions need in order to endure (Pateman 1972, 1980; Elkins and Simeon 1979), this critique is probably overstated because Almond and Verba acknowledge that institutions may shape values (Almond 1980; Lijphart 1980).[1] However, the criticism may have been prompted by the absence of a systematic analysis in *The Civic Culture* as to how institutional variation affects values. The main reason for this omission is undoubtedly the lack of proper cases where institutions and political values may be varied and measured, and where other influences on values can be adequately controlled for. Given the multitude of factors that vary across the five nations examined in *The Civic Culture* (Germany, Great Britain, Italy, Mexico, the United States), it is very difficult, if possible at all, to isolate the unique influence of institutional arrangements on the publics' ideological values in these nations.

More recent empirical public-opinion studies attempt to overcome the small case problem by collecting institutional data and information about citizens' orientations from public-opinion surveys of a large number of countries (Inglehart 1988; Bollen and Jackman 1989; Weil 1989; Inglehart and Abramson 1994; Muller and Seligson 1994).[2] Although extremely valuable, these studies must rely on relatively few indicators of citizens' values and thus do not provide detailed information on how institutions affect the content and structure of mass values. A closer approximation of the proper research design needed to examine the institutions-to-values process may be found in a series of reports on the evolving attitudes of the Spanish mass public toward democratic institutions after the collapse of the Franco regime in 1975 (Barnes, McDonough, and Lopez-Pina 1985; McDonough, Barnes, and Lopez-Pina 1986). Further, Robert Putnam and his colleagues (1993, 1983) use the creation of regional institutions in Italy in 1970 to analyse the link between political culture and the performance of these institutions.[3] Still, while these studies investigate the institution–culture linkage, especially Putnam's analyses, none of the cases offers the opportunity to compare directly the influence of two fundamentally different ideological systems on individuals' values. Like mass political culture studies, elite studies remain inconclusive about the impact of regime exposure on elites' political values. Cultural approaches highlight elites' professional norms as sources of parliamentary behaviour (Herzog *et al.* 1990; Searing 1994) and elite attitudes (Roth 1976; Aberbach, Putnam, and Rockman 1981); or they document the influence of elites' generational experience on elite polarization over such New Politics issues as environmentalism (Dalton 1987).[4] Institutional elite studies, in contrast, assume that the unique regime experience of elites within a given polity (e.g. political institutions) contributes to a similar outlook on core political values[5] (Higley and Burton 1989; Di Palma 1990; Higley and Gunther 1992). Particularly, analysts of regime transitions in Latin America and Southern and East-Central Europe suggest that once democratic institutions are established by 'pact-making' elites, democratic institutions presumably contribute to a moderation of ideological differences among various elite sectors (O'Donnell and Schmitter 1986; Przeworski 1991; Higley and Gunther 1992).

Despite the recognition that both cultural and institutional factors are important sources of elite values, these two perspectives have not yet been combined into a single study. Cultural analyses generally do not incorporate national-level factors into their empirical analyses of elites' values and frequently treat political values as an 'uncaused first cause' (Putnam 1973: 149). Institutional approaches, in turn, frequently do not provide evidence that pact-making elites indeed moderate their antagonistic outlook after democratic institutions are established.

Culturalists, Institutionalists, and the Congruence Postulate. While institutional and cultural approaches evidently acknowledge the importance of a nation's institutional configuration as a potential source of political values, differences between these two approaches become more pronounced in terms of the values-to-institutions process. Culturalists assume that ideological values shape support for existing institutions (the congruence postulate). Institutionalists, in contrast, maintain that this linkage is overstated. Earlier versions of this argument appear amidst critics of *The Civic Culture* who argue that the performance of a political system is a more important determinant of democratic stability than individuals' values (Barry 1970; Rogowski

1974). More recently, an important strand in the democratization literature focuses on the performance of newly established democratic institutions as the central determinant of their viability, discounting the importance of mass and elite values in democratic transitions (Di Palma 1990; Przeworski 1991).

Culturalists and institutionalists alike seem unaware, however, that they are addressing different aspects of the same question (i.e. what determines institutional support), and that they may complement, rather than counter one another. Institutionalists focus on how an institutions' (perceived) performance affects citizens' support for existing institutions, whereas culturalists suggest that institutional support depends mainly on political values. Clearly, it is plausible to suggest that both—political values as well as the perceived per-formance—jointly influence individuals' institutional support. I will discuss below the interaction between cultural and institutional factors in shaping individuals' trust in existing institutions (see also Chapter 9).

In sum, both cultural and institutional perspectives broadly suggest that a nation's institutional environment may shape mass and elites' ideological values. However, since neither perspective systematically develops a micro-logic about the impact of institutions on ideological values, it is relatively easy to overlook the similarity. Further, the lack of a micro-level model which explains how a political system affects citizens' political values also generates some of the aforementioned problems of each approach. For example, if such a model existed, it would be possible to determine when a political system shapes ideo-logical values, and when value diffusion may offset this learning effect. Likewise, such a model might be used to evaluate institutionalists' assumptions about the presumed influence of a political system on individuals' political values. One central task of this chapter, thus, is to develop this micro-logic about the institutions-to-values process.

A HEURISTIC FRAMEWORK: INSTITUTIONAL LEARNING

How, then, should one conceptualize the relationship between institu-tions, ideological values, and individuals' institutional support so that these relationships may be investigated on the individual level? This section first suggests a micro-logic by which a nation's institutional

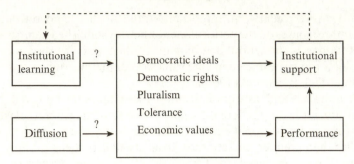

F IG. 2.1. Institutional learning: the central relationships

framework influences individuals' ideological values. I use the term
institutional learning when referring to the idea that citizens are
exposed to the values and norms underlying a nation's institutional
configuration. I then discuss the conditions under which the diffusion
of political values from the West into the East may offset individuals'
institutional learning. To facilitate this discussion, Figure 2.1 outlines
the basic conceptual relationships examined in this study. The figure
includes a question-mark from the two macro-processes to five ideological values (whose focus will be explained below), because it is still
uncertain how one should discriminate between diffusible and non-
diffusible ideological values at this juncture.

Democratic Citizenship

While *The Civic Culture* has sparked numerous empirical studies of
citizens' political values, there are few explanations, if any, about the
individual-level requirements of democratic citizenship. The lack of a
conceptual anchor led analysts to attribute a multitude of attitudinal
dimensions to a political culture, thus diluting the precision of this
concept. This conceptual stretching prompted one analyst to liken the
study of a political culture to nailing 'a pudding to the wall' (Kaase
1983).

To focus the following discussion of institutional learning, I suggest
that the democratic citizenship-qualities—*democratic restraint, self-
reliance*, and related *societal ideals*—are substantially shaped by one's
exposure to political and economic processes. The central argument is
deceptively simple. Citizens of different political systems are exposed

to different political processes and ideals. Some of these processes nurture democratic restraint, self-reliance, and democratic ideals, while others prevent the development of these democratic citizenship-qualities. Citizens who lack the opportunity to develop restraint, self-reliance, and democratic ideals are consequently less likely to endorse democratic values which reflect these democratic citizenship-qualities.

To elaborate this argument, consider that democratic systems focus on maximizing the opportunities for people to govern themselves through, for instance, participation and political competition (Dahl 1971; Held 1987). Although there is substantial disagreement over how best to achieve this (witness, for example, the debate over plebiscitarian versus representative models in western Europe throughout the 1980s), the debate centres on which political process, not outcome, ought to be established in order to maximize people's opportunities to participate in the political process (Held 1987; Dahl 1989; Chapter 5 below). This political process, where 'adversarial conflict becomes a normal and accepted aspect of political life' (Dahl 1989: 220), can function properly only if most, if not all, citizens accept as legitimate the fact that one's own preferences may be challenged and even be defeated by others who pursue their separate interests.

A first democratic citizenship-quality, then, is manifested by the notion of democratic restraint. Democratic restraint expresses the idea that citizens ought to accept diversity of political viewpoints, including those that conflict with one's own views. Democratic restraint is especially important when citizens are defeated in political competitions, because citizens must accept their status as losers. This is not to say that they may not try to change their status in the future. It does mean, however, that citizens reject methods which are outside of the set of competitive rules a democracy provides (e.g. violence) to change their present status. Democratic restraint is also called for when citizens are on the winning side of political competition. In this case, one must—if given an opportunity—refrain from changing political and economic rules in such a way that losers may not become winners in future competition. That this democratic restraint is difficult to realize is illustrated by the regrettable fact that 'the most commonplace way for a government to deal with its opponents is to employ violence' (Dahl 1966: p. xi).

Democratic restraint constitutes a central component of a democracy because it underlies several democratic procedures. In the realm of democratic rights, a citizenry exercises restraint by endorsing the right to free speech, the right to oppose one's government, or the right to demonstrate. Although it is relatively easy to endorse democratic rights in the abstract, the acceptance of these rights separates those citizens who endorse political diversity as an idea from those who seek to impose a fixed vision on a society. Relatedly, democratic restraint also requires one to extend democratic rights to those whose viewpoints one dislikes, and perhaps even despises. This does not mean that one unequivocally accepts any group, however violent. It does mean, however, that one's political sentiments alone do not constitute a reason to deprive others of civil liberties (Chapter 6). Within the realm of the democratic process, the notion of democratic restraint presumes that one is willing to compete peacefully for influence in the political process—one must accept pluralist competition.

The need for democratic restraint is not limited to the political sphere, but also applies to the economic domain. In fact, the nature of market competition requires an extraordinary amount of individual restraint. With its emphasis on economic competition, the logic of a market economy requires competitors to accept defeat and to re-enter the competitive market *peacefully*. That is, losers of economic competition must use precisely those rules to improve their economic status that led to economic defeat in the first place. Further, regardless of how heavy the losses are which one might suffer in economic competition, citizens must accept these losses and not use violence or other non-market rules (e.g. bribes) to change their lot. The acceptance of market competition therefore requires an extraordinary amount of restraint on the part of market competitors. Thus, as in the political realm, democratic restraint is manifested in the economic realm by accepting the possibility that one may suffer materially when one competes for scarce resources.

While processes that are based upon democratic restraint aim at guaranteeing citizens the opportunity of participating in the political and economic process, the notion of self-reliance stipulates that one must act on one's own behalf in order to exploit the opportunities which a democracy and a market economy offer. Democracies are unlikely to deliver goods if citizens do not become active on behalf of their preferences. Individuals and groups must lobby policy-makers for their goals in order to have these reflected in public policies, independent of whether these goals are based on self-interest or (presumably) serve the broader community. Like democratic restraint, self-reliance is not developed easily. Citizens must become knowledgeable, form opinions, and develop strategies that lead to the achievement of their objectives. Further, like democratic restraint, self-reliance is an idea that is complex theoretically. For example, to accept self-reliance means to limit the influence of political visions which claim to pursue the interests of the community as a whole.

The requirement of self-reliance is equally important in the economic realm. Most importantly, one must compete with others for scarce economic goods in order to improve one's economic standing, sometimes against much stronger economic competitors. Competitors must, for example, invest resources to collect information needed to arrive at a decision about a competitive bid or try to form an alliance in order to be more competitive than others. There is no guarantee that one's efforts will succeed. Still, competitors in the political and economic realm are asked again and again to rely on their own creativity and resourcefulness to receive desired goods. Democratic restraint and self-reliance, then, are intertwined elements of democratic citizenship: democratic restraint stipulates that a democratic citizen lets others pursue their preferences, while self-reliance presumes that citizens must act on behalf of their own preferred policies.

The demands placed on citizens when they are required to exercise restraint and self-reliance are considerable, because these ideas 'are complex, rooted in traditions of human history and political theory which are themselves difficult to grasp' (Sniderman 1975: 181). Consequently, restraint and self-reliance are developed primarily when citizens are given an opportunity to practise these qualities. A nation's institutional framework is crucial in providing these opportunities. Political and economic institutions establish behavioural prescriptions for citizens and reinforce these prescriptions through, for example, rewards and punishments. Particularly in a democracy, the behavioural prescriptions of institutions encourage the development of democratic restraint and self-reliance. Public debates, campaigns, and competition all expose citizens to a multitude of conflicting views. Cumulatively, this process conveys to citizens the message that the existence of diversity is good and the suppression of opponents is bad. Citizens who are exposed to a political regime that does not encourage the development of these citizenship-qualities are thus less likely to endorse political values—political as well as economic ones—that reflect restraint and self-reliance.

Up to this point, the discussion has focused primarily on the procedural dimension of democratic citizenship. Yet any political process is closely entwined with a set of societal ideals (Dahl 1989: 191). Societal ideals provide an understanding about the objectives of a specific political and economic order; and societal ideals supply a rationale for why one political process is preferable to its alternatives. For example, the western German system is a representative parliamentary democracy based on a canon of democratic values which places a premium on political equality. The basic goal of a democracy is to maximize individual political freedom. In contrast, a socialist system prioritizes social equality and maintains that political equality cannot be achieved within the framework of a market economy (MacPherson 1977; Chapter 5 below). Other models of democratic citizenship, in turn, emphasize plebiscitarian procedures (Barber 1984). Thus, the process through which democratic restraint and self-reliance are developed cannot be divorced from the societal ideals that underlie the political process in any given country. Democratic restraint and self-reliance provide the foundations for democratic procedures, while political and economic ideals provide a justification as to why and for what purpose these procedures are established. Since democratic restraint and self-reliance are not practised within a political vacuum, citizens are also likely to absorb the core political and economic ideals upon which institutional rules are based (see also Chapter 5). Cumulatively, this reasoning leads to the first basic premiss of the study:

• *The Institutional Learning Axiom*: political and economic processes substantially shape democratic citizenship-qualities; that is, democratic restraint, self-reliance, and related societal ideals.

The Pace of Value Change. Institutional and cultural studies would probably not quarrel with this institutional learning axiom and its underlying rationale. Sharper differences between the two approaches emerge, however, over the pace required until ideological values reflect the principles of a new set of institutions after a regime change. Most cultural analyses assume that ideological value change is primarily driven by *generational replacement*. In this model, any regime experience inherited from the previous regime weakens the influence of the institutional learning of a new political system (Almond and Verba 1963; Sigel 1989). After the establishment of a new regime, however, generational experience may become a 'major basis for subcultural differentiation' (Eckstein 1988: 798). Citizens who are born after a regime transition are only exposed to the institutional learning of new institutions, and should be more receptive to the citizenship-qualities of the new political process than individuals whose political views are shaped by a prior regime.

Institutionalists, in contrast, assume that the nature of ideological value change is substantially driven by *individual conversion*. From this perspective, all citizens, regardless of their prior predispositions, may adjust their ideological values to a new institutional framework. Over two decades ago Rustow succinctly stated the conversion argument when he noted that 'we should allow for the possibility that circumstances may force, trick, lure, or cajole non-democrats into democratic behavior and that their beliefs may adjust in due course by some process of rationalization or adoption' (Rustow 1970: 344). The notion of conversion is a central theme in several democratization studies which maintain that new institutions, once established, will moderate elite and mass behaviour within a relatively short time period (Huntington 1984; Higley and Gunther 1992).

Given the uncertainty in the literature with respect to the institutions-to-values causality, it is difficult to predict whether the conversion or replacement model is accurate. Although the logic of the institutional learning axiom suggests that the acquisition of democratic citizenship-qualities is difficult, this does not preclude a long-term conversion of individuals' values. Especially on the elite level, individuals may adjust to a new institutional configuration over a relatively short time period (see below). I will use the evidence amassed throughout this research to evaluate these conflicting predictions about the pace of ideological value change.

In sum, this conceptualization of institutional learning provides a way to understand how a nation's institutional framework shapes democratic citizenship-qualities, and it therefore provides a conceptual link between institutional and cultural approaches. In each chapter that follows, I will elaborate on the relationship between the citizenship-qualities and the five political values in Figure 2.1, but it is readily apparent that democratic citizenship-qualities are manifested in individuals': (1) support for democratic rights, such as free and periodic elections, freedom of the press, or the right to demonstrate; (2) willingness to extend basic political rights to political minorities, or what has been termed 'political tolerance'; and (3) support for a pluralist process where a range of individuals and groups compete for influence over the policy process. While the first three value domains directly reflect the procedural dimension of institutional learning in a democracy, the next two value domains also reflect the societal ideals upon which the political process is based, namely: (4) citizens' democratic ideals; and (5) citizens' economic ideals. Throughout this research, I refer to these five value domains collectively as ideological values.

Value Diffusion

The institutional learning axiom predicts that citizens with few opportunities to exercise restraint, self-reliance, and democratic ideals are less likely to support a range of democratic values. The institutional learning axiom is pertinent in light of numerous studies that emphasize the development of a nascent democratic and market culture in post-socialist nations. This diffusion perspective attributes the development of democratic rights in socialist-authoritarian systems to the growing availability of mass communication technologies which publicize the superior political and economic capacity of western democracies (Weil 1989; Mishler and Rose 1996). Such exposure to the West presumably enables citizens in authoritarian systems to compare their own plight with the rosier portrayal of market-based economies and democratic institutions. Mishler and Rose (1996), for example, suggest that citizens' negative evaluations of the collapsed communist regime provides a temporary reservoir of support for democracy. Socio-economic modernization and rising educational levels in East-Central European societies also increase the odds that individuals will be exposed to western-style values (Pye 1990; Inglehart 1997).

The diffusion argument is especially plausible in its capacity to explain the evolution of support for democratic rights in authoritarian contexts, such as in the former states of the Soviet Union (Gibson, Duch, and Tedin 1992), East-Central Europe (Fuchs and Roller 1994), and eastern Germany (Fuchs, Klingemann, and Schoebel 1991; Dalton 1994). However, the diffusion perspective is also problematic because it suggests that democratic values may be diffused independent of the extent to which democratic restraint and self-reliance underlie a value domain, or the degree to which democratic ideals conflict with socialist ideals.

In order to explain why certain values may diffuse across systemic borders while others are predominately shaped by institutional learn-

Democratic restraint/self-reliance

	Low	High
	Diffusion dominates Liberal-democratic rights	*Institutional learning dominates*
Minor revisions of socialist beliefs		
Democratic values require:	*Institutional learning dominates*	*Institutional learning dominates* Democratic ideals Political tolerance Pluralism Economic ideals
Major revisions of socialist beliefs		

FIG. 2.2. The contingent effect of institutional learning and value diffusion on ideological values

ing, consider Figure 2.2. I suggest that value diffusion across systemic boundaries is likely only if: (1) a low level of democratic restraint and self-reliance underlies a value domain; and if (2) the acceptance of democratic values requires few or no changes of pre-existing socialist ideals.

The first criterion directly flows from the institutional learning axiom: one would expect citizens whose regime experience is limited to authoritarian systems to exhibit less democratic restraint and self-reliance than individuals who were exposed to a political system that encouraged these qualities. For instance, political tolerance is widely viewed as a desirable and necessary characteristic of an established democracy. Yet to practise tolerance requires considerable restraint. Even publics in western democracies frequently express intolerant views (Sniderman 1975; Sullivan *et al.* 1982; Chapter 6 below). Further, pluralist competition embodies considerable uncertainty and risks, thus requiring substantial restraint on the part of individuals and groups, who must accept the possibility of political or economic defeat (Dahl 1971; Di Palma 1990; Przeworski 1991; Chapter 7 below). The paternalistic nature of socialist-authoritarian states inhibited the development of self-reliance, in the political process as well as in the economic realm (Chapter 8). From this perspective, it is unlikely that post-socialist publics will display tolerant views, value support for individual entrepreneurship, or evince enthusiasm for pluralist competition.

A second characteristic which influences the likelihood for value diffusion is the degree to which democratic values can be integrated into a socialist belief system without fundamental changes of socialist beliefs. Studies of individual belief systems indicate that modifications of one's values depend, in part, on the degree to which new information conflicts with pre-existing values (Jervis 1976; Fiske and Taylor 1991). As a general rule, the odds for the acceptance of democratic values in East-Central Europe should be greater, if the integration of these values into individuals' prior values does not require fundamental revisions of socialist beliefs. Socialism, for example, frequently presented a humanist façade by maintaining that it represented underprivileged minorities or defended individual freedom (Held 1987; Chapter 5 below). Democratic rights may therefore resonate with a familiar theme to eastern Germans. Equally important, one may theoretically envision a political ideology which maintains several elements of socialism (nationalized industries, for example) *and* respects basic political rights. Such a synthesis, after all, was attempted by Spanish and Italian Eurocommunists in the 1970s. In contrast, when the acceptance of democratic values requires individuals to abandon central components of socialist ideology, the odds for accepting democratic values are reduced significantly. For instance, it is impossible to advocate socialism (central to which is a restricted use of private property) *and* endorse market values which are based on the premiss that the unrestricted use of private property is by and large desirable. In addition, it would be difficult to support socialist and representative political ideals. The acceptance of democratic and market ideals thus requires significantly more revisions of socialist beliefs than the acceptance of democratic rights.

We now have two criteria to determine the likelihood that western values were diffused into the East during Germany's division:

- *The Diffusion Axiom*: value diffusion from democratic to non-democratic nations is possible if ideological values require little restraint or self-reliance and if they require few revisions of socialist ideals.

Perusing Figure 2.2 reveals that only democratic rights fall into the upper-left cell of diffusible values. These rights are relatively easily endorsed, since the expression of support for them does not require an insurmountable amount of self-restraint or self-reliance (Chapter 6). Further, support for democratic rights may be merged with core components of socialist ideals—nationalization of industries or social egalitarianism, for example—without fundamentally violating the premisses of socialism. This typology supplies the micro-logic to explain why analyses of mass values in post-socialist nations frequently detect a nascent democratic culture: these analyses focus on those values that require relatively little restraint and, in addition, are fairly easily reconciled with socialist values. In contrast, several other ideological values fall into the non-diffusible cell; they require a high degree of self-reliance and/or restraint. Further, these values require a considerable amount of changes in any pre-existing socialist belief systems. The odds that these ideological values will be diffused are substantially lower than the chances for value diffusion of democratic rights.

In sum, the institutional learning and diffusion axioms establish the expectation that eastern and western Germans' ideological values manifest their different opportunities to develop restraint, self-reliance, and related societal ideals. The central prediction of this argument is simple: citizens develop those citizenship-qualities that underlie a nation's institutional framework.[6] This institutional learning is offset by value diffusion only under a restricted set of conditions: those in which western values necessitate little restraint and self-reliance, and conflicts between socialist and democratic ideals are minimal.

The institutional learning and diffusion axioms therefore establish benchmark expectations which can be tested empirically. *If* institutional learning influences citizens' ideological values, one expects to find fairly strong support for several socialist values in the East when compared to the West. One advantage of this perspective, then, is that it provides a conceptual map against which empirical results can be assessed. This is not to say that there are no additional factors which may affect ideological values. If research found, for example, that ideological values were widely endorsed even though they required a substantial degree of restraint, the institutional learning model would be undermined and other explanations (e.g. unintended consequences of regime activities or counter-cultural developments) would have to be brought to bear. Even in this scenario, however, the axioms provide a conceptual yardstick, helping to define what constitute 'expected' and 'unexpected' results.

IDEOLOGICAL VALUES, PERFORMANCE EVALUATIONS,
AND INSTITUTIONAL SUPPORT

Neither culturalist nor institutionalist approaches are likely to take
exception to the institutional learning and diffusion axioms, although
these perspectives would clash over the pace required before values
adjust to institutions. Controversies between the two approaches,
however, are more intense over the relationship between ideological
values and the stability of political institutions—the values-to-
institutions nexus. Culturalists maintain that ideological values significantly influence individuals' support for existing institutions (Almond
and Verba 1963; Eckstein 1966). Although *The Civic Culture* establishes the congruence postulate at the aggregate level (see Chapter 9
below), the logic of the postulate suggests that one also should find
this relationship at the individual level: citizens who do not share the
societal ideals upon which a nation's institutions are based should
also be less likely to support existing institutions. If one defines a
legitimate political system as one where a populace believes that no
better alternative exists to the existing system (Linz and Stepan 1978:
16), the possible persistence of socialist ideals may reduce eastern
citizens' support for a democracy.

Institutionalists, in contrast, dispute the importance of values in
generating support for democratic institutions, because they focus on
two aspects of a system's performance as the key to institutional
stability. A first performance-based argument suggests that a system's
economic performance significantly influences the support it enjoys
(Barry 1970; Przeworski 1991; Welsh 1994). The logic is familiar from
earlier analyses of democratic transitions in the context of post-war
European nations (in particular, Italy and western Germany): citizens
who evaluate the performance of institutions positively, particularly
in terms of economic outputs, are expected to support institutions
more strongly than citizens who believe that institutions do not
perform well economically. Since East-Central European systems are
recent, these institutions must initially rely on strong economic
performance to generate acceptance. In the context of the unified
Germany, eastern Germans' support for representative institutions
ought to be more contingent upon positive performance evaluations
than western Germans' support for these institutions.

Another performance-based source of institutional support concerns the basic position of political groups relative to the political centre of a political system ('winners' versus 'losers'). This is primarily a group-based process, particularly on the levels of elites who represent significant societal groups (O'Donnell and Schmitter 1986; Di Palma 1990; Higley and Gunther 1992). This process implies a logic whereby elites who are not permanently excluded from occupying important institutional positions are expected, everything else being equal, to endorse new democratic institutions more willingly than elites representing groups whose political influence is permanently reduced by new institutions. Przeworski (1991: 32) succinctly states this possibility when he argues that 'those who expect to suffer continued deprivation under democratic institutions will turn against them'. Political 'winners' may support new democratic institutions even if these elites presumably do not hold democratic values (e.g. Romanian communists); and political losers may reject democratic institutions, even if losers presumably hold democratic values (e.g. marginalized members of the opposition groups in eastern Germany which helped to topple the socialist system).[7]

While the controversy over the relevance of ideological values for institutional stability represents the critical divide between culturalists and institutionalists, this debate overly emphasizes their differences and downplays the complementary character of these arguments. After all, it is plausible to suggest that both ideological values and performance evaluations shape institutional support. Thus, it is partly an empirical question as to which of these factors more forcibly determines institutional support. Equally important, one would expect that ideological values not only directly influence institutional support, but also define the yardstick which individuals use to evaluate the performance of political institutions in the first place. An ardent supporter of a free market is likely to accept a certain level of unemployment and may even regard it as necessary for a smoothly running economy if other economic indicators are acceptable (e.g. growth rates). In contrast, those with a social-egalitarian bent might find the same unemployment rates outrageous and advocate fundamental alterations in the economic and political process. It appears, then, that ideological values shape a citizen's yardstick which measures a system's performance. It would thus be inappropriate to treat ideological values and performance evaluations of institutions as independent dimensions when, in fact, they jointly affect citizens' evaluations of existing institutions. For this reason, Figure 2.1

includes a path from the 'values-box' to both the 'performance-box' and the 'institutional-support box':

• *The Ideological-Performance Axiom*: ideological values and the evaluation of institutional performance jointly influence individuals' support for existing institutional arrangements.

Finally, Figure 2.1 recognizes that strong institutional support, aggregated to the systemic level, may influence the length of institutional learning. Strong citizen support for an existing system surely increases the odds for systemic stability which, in turn, may prolong the institutional learning process. However, given the multiple levels involved, it would be as implausible to suggest that strong support for a system at the level of publics or elites automatically leads to stability, as it would be incorrect to argue that weak support necessarily leads to the collapse of a system. Because a systematic treatment of the effect of institutional support, aggregated to the national level, on the stability of systems goes beyond the scope of this book, the relationship is represented by a dotted line.[8]

In sum, the three axioms synthesize the micro-level implications of culturalist and institutionalist arguments with respect to the: (1) impact of a nation's institutional framework on ideological values; and (2) the influence of ideological values and performance dimensions on individuals' support for existing institutions. Together, these axioms would predict that: (1) Germany's division in 1949 created two ideological cultures; (2) that the development of a democratic culture in eastern Germany is limited to support for general democratic rights; and (3) that ideological values and performance evaluations influence citizens' institutional support.

INSTITUTIONAL LEARNING, VALUE DIFFUSION,
AND MASS–ELITE DIFFERENCES

The discussion of institutional learning and value diffusion up to this point has ignored any mass–elite differences that may exist over ideological values. However, the logic of institutional learning and value diffusion suggests that two elementary differences between the mass public and political elites—their education and intensity of exposure to institutional learning—shape the degree to which individuals develop democratic citizenship-qualities. In essence, in terms of political elites' disproportionate exposure to institutional learning, one expects them to be more likely than a mass public to absorb the citizenship-qualities conveyed by institutions, both in the East and the West. In terms of elites' higher educational background, the expectations are less clear in the post-socialist context. To disentangle the various possibilities, I first discuss potential mass–elite differences over ideological values in a democratic system.

From prior research on mass–elite differences in advanced industrial democracies, we know that elites' higher education and their intense exposure to the democratic process tend to *reinforce* each other. Higher education typically engenders an ability to deal with cognitively complex issues, such as being able to reconcile one's self-interest with the right of other individuals to pursue separate goals (Lipset 1959; Sniderman 1975). Further, in western democracies the content of education reinforces this tendency by emphasizing such values as individual liberty, political tolerance, or political pluralism (Hoffmann-Lange 1985; Weil 1985). Therefore, higher education in the West typically engenders democratic restraint, self-reliance, and democratic ideals. This tendency is reinforced by the routine of the legislative political process, where elites must accept political opposition and frequently reconcile diverging political interests. This exposure to institutional processes, like education, encourages the development of restraint, self-reliance, and the development of democratic ideals.

Given that political elites are better educated and more intensely exposed to institutional learning than mass publics, western political elites are typically more supportive of democratic values than the western public (Fig. 2.3). For the purpose of illustration, the left-polar end in Figure 2.3 represents strong support for democratic values while the right-polar end represents strong support for socialist values. The mid-point (M) represents weak support for either ideological position; it is not meant to reflect centrist ideological views. The proximity to M indicates the degree to which views are strongly held, while the location to the left or right of M indicates whether ideological values reflect representative or socialist ideals.[9] According to the logic just discussed, I position western elites closer to the left (WE) than the western publics (WP). Simultaneously, I position WP to the left of M because I expect the western public to endorse representative and market-based views, but less strongly than western political elites.

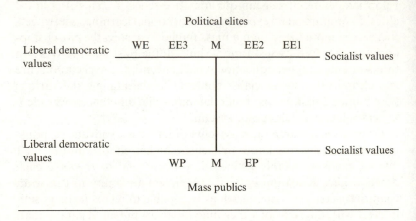

F IG. 2.3. Institutional learning, value diffusion, and mass–elite differences

Again, the position of WP reflects the conjecture that the western public is less supportive of democratic values than political elites, not that the public is more supportive of socialist ideals.

The expectations about mass–elite differences are less clear in a post-socialist environment because elites' higher education and intense exposure to institutional learning may *counterbalance* each other. In terms of eastern political elites' exposure to socialist values, the logic of institutional learning implies that eastern elites may actually be more supportive than the eastern mass public of socialist values and less supportive of democratic rights, political tolerance, or market-based processes. After all, eastern political elites, on average, tended to have been more intensely exposed to socialist values and norms than mass publics through, for example, their exposure to socialist institutions. Thus, the institutional learning axiom would suggest an approximate location of political elites at EE1 while the eastern public's relative location ought to be approximately at EP.

Contrary to this expectation, eastern elites' higher education may actually make them more receptive to democratic values than ordinary citizens even in a socialist context. While the educational content in socialist systems undoubtedly does not generate democratic citizenship-qualities (Weil 1985), the ability to reason in abstract terms may nevertheless increase individuals' willingness to accept alternative viewpoints or different ideologies (Sniderman 1975).

Higher education typically increases the diversity of information and intellectual traditions to which one is exposed. Likewise, higher education increases the odds that individuals are exposed to information about democracies. Exposure to such information, in turn, typically correlates with disproportionate support for democratic rights even within an authoritarian context (Gibson, Duch, and Tedin 1992). The diffusion of values may thus be felt more strongly at the elite level than on the mass level. To the extent, then, that higher education offsets elites' past exposure to the socialist process, one would expect eastern elites to be more supportive of democratic values than a public in a post-socialist environment.

The post-socialist context thus creates empirical ambiguities about expected mass–elite differences. On one hand, if the 'liberalizing' component of education is a predominant source of elites' ideological views, eastern elites are expected to be more supportive of democratic values than the eastern public and, perhaps, even the western public; eastern elites may be located in the vicinity of EE2 or EE3. On the other hand, if the institutional learning component is the predominant source of elites' views, then eastern elites may be more supportive of socialist values than the mass public (EE1). I will examine these conflicting predictions throughout this research by comparing mass and elite views where available data permits this comparison.

CONCLUSION

Culturalists and institutionalists are concerned with how one may increase support for newly established democratic institutions in East-Central Europe. Despite this shared goal, a lack of synthesis of their various arguments leads one to overlook the fact that these efforts converge to some degree, both in terms of where they are problematic and where they make complementary contributions. The logic of the institutional learning, diffusion, and ideological performance axioms bridges the gap between cultural and institutional approaches at several junctures. With respect to the institutions-to-values causality, the first axiom supplies a micro-logic as to the democratic citizenship-qualities which an institutional framework influences. This micro-logic helps explain why certain democratic values are expected to develop primarily in a democratic environment; and the framework delineates diffusible values from those that are primarily acquired through institutional learning. Further, in terms of the values-to-institutions process, the ideological performance axiom suggests that ideological values and performance factors jointly affect citizens' evaluations of institutional support. Finally, although this perspective does not define exhaustively which values should be attributed to a democratic 'culture', it does provide a conceptual anchor by requiring analysts to justify a particular value focus in light of the three citizenship-qualities. Together, the axioms suggest that one may not infer from the collapse of socialist systems that socialist values are absent. Instead, one must examine the impact of socialist regime experience on public and elite values, because the framework raises the explicit expectation that socialist systems engender socialist values. Therefore, an empirical test of the implications of the framework requires: (1) that multiple value domains be examined simultaneously in order to assess which values have been diffused and which ones are predominately shaped by institutional learning; and (2) that one systemic factor—the institutional framework—be varied while other background factors are kept constant.

3

Institutional Learning in Germany

This chapter summarizes the different historical trajectories of eastern and western Germany after 1945 in order to highlight the different institutional learning processes in eastern and western Germany. There are numerous historical studies about the period between 1949 and 1989 and my purpose is not to present a complete narrative of Germany's post-war developments. Rather, this chapter will focus on the degree to which the eastern and western German contexts provided the opportunities to develop restraint, self-reliance, and societal ideals.

INSTITUTIONAL LEARNING IN EASTERN GERMANY, 1945–1989[1]

The central objective guiding the Soviet occupation of the eastern zone was to co-ordinate all political activities under the leadership of the Soviet administration, called SMAD.[2] Shortly after Germany's capitulation on 8 May 1945 political activities in the Soviet zone re-emerged. Surprisingly to the western allies, party activities began earlier in the eastern zone than in the three western zones. The communist party—KPD—was founded on 11 June 1945, followed by the Social Democrats (SPD) on 15 June, the Christian Democrats (CDU) on 26 June, and the centrist LDPD in early July. The SMAD also permitted the establishment of several mass organizations, such as the centralized union (FDGB) and the Free German Youth organization (FDJ). Together, these parties and mass organizations tried to attract the ideological spectrum of eastern German society from the ideological left to the moderate centre. In May 1948 the Soviets also permitted the formation of the National-Democratic Party—NDPD—which admitted conservatives and former members of the Nazi party.

Despite the initial diversity of organizations, however, free party competition was never firmly established. For one reason, all parties as well as mass organizations had to co-operate within a so-called anti-fascist alliance. The alliance, in turn, was dominated by the KPD which made most of the important political decisions, along with the SMAD. Moreover, political parties were not independent political entities, but were closely supervised by the SMAD and the KPD. The lack of independence is clearly manifested by the fact that the SPD was forced to merge into one party with the KPD in 1946. SPD party members in a western Berlin referendum rejected the merger into a socialist unity party, called SED,[3] by an astounding 82 per cent, casting serious doubts on arguments that a majority of SPD members in eastern Berlin supported the merger. Another indication of the limits on parties to operate freely emerged during the local election in Saxony in September 1946. Although the SED won this first local election in the eastern zone, the non-socialist parties were disadvantaged because their names frequently did not appear on the ballot—indicating to citizens that openness, trust, and democratic competition were in short supply in the evolving eastern German political process. The SMAD quickly abandoned its 'experiment' with free elections when the SPD and the CDU received more votes than the SED in the first city-wide election in Berlin (October 1946). Whereas the western Allies increasingly loosened their initially tight supervision over political competition as time progressed in the years after 1945 (see below), the SMAD and SED tightened their political control over the eastern German political process during this time. These developments are consistent with a remark attributed to Walter Ulbricht, who said at a communist party meeting in 1946: 'Everything has to look democratic, but everything has to be controlled by us' (as quoted in Orlow 1995: 249). By the time eastern Germany became the GDR on 7 October 1949, the eastern German system had already established a institutional learning process which substantially reduced the odds that restraint, self-reliance, and liberal ideals would develop in the East.

Despite the growing control of the SMAD and SED over public affairs, the first constitution of the GDR actually contains several passages about liberal-democratic rights, the pluralist process, and the desirability of German unification. The party made these 'concessions' to the non-communist believers in eastern Germany to win them over for the socialist cause. Unfortunately, the 1949 constitution had little to do with how the actual political process operated, because of the SED hegemony in the political and economic process. Growing repression characterized the 1950s, and citizens began to realize that the constitutionally guaranteed liberties would be largely ignored. For instance, the SED purged about 200,000 former SPD members from its ranks in the years 1948–50 because they allegedly held democratic-socialist attitudes, not socialist ones. The uprising on 17 June 1953, crushed by Soviet tanks, also did little to foster confidence in the liberal-democratic rights listed in the 1949 constitution. Finally, the oppressive nature of the regime is reflected in its attacks on the churches in the middle of the 1950s. No profession escaped the totalitarian nature of the regime. Artists, for example, had to create expressions of loyalty to socialism; not only were they told what not to produce, but also what constituted works of 'Real Socialism'.

The SED legitimized its dominant position by referring to its role in spearheading the proletarian revolution. Since the SED represents the working class, and the working class ought to control the state, it follows in Marxist-Leninist logic that the SED legitimately controls state institutions. Consequently, the formal state structures, such as the eastern German parliament (Volkskammer), had little influence on important policy decisions, which were primarily made at the highest levels within the SED. One example manifesting the dominant role of the SED was the National Front. Founded in 1949 with the GDR, the National Front supervised the activities of all political organizations in the GDR. It controlled, for example, the recruitment of candidates on to unity lists which could be either accepted or rejected by voters in the general elections to the Volkskammer. The 1968 revision of the GDR constitution recognized the hegemony of the SED. It states, for example, that the 'GDR is the political organization of the urban and rural working people who are jointly implementing socialism under the leadership of the working class and its Marxist-Leninist party' (as quoted in Dennis 1988: 92). The National Front is also explicitly recognized as the sole legitimate organization of parties and mass organizations. Some civil liberties either disappeared entirely (the right to strike, for example) or were recognized to the extent that they were consistent with the principle of the new institutions (i.e. with the leadership of the SED). Clearly, state institutions helped the party to implement policies, but they did not decide policies.

This lack of opportunities to develop democratic citizenship-qualities was also manifested in other spheres. The military, sports clubs, and even social contacts were influenced by socialism's ideological and organizational characteristics. The dominance of socialism was especially visible in schools and universities. Because educational institutions generally influence personal and political values, and because of their special role in recruiting the future socialist elites, schools and universities constitute a central source of democratic citizenship-qualities. In the case of the GDR, however, educational institutions probably hindered their development.

Most importantly, the criteria used for educational advancement reduced the opportunities for students to develop restraint and self-reliance. As in any school system, individuals' abilities partially influenced their opportunities for professional advancement. However, because schools and universities played a central role in the selection of the future leadership of the GDR, political loyalty to socialist principles also shaped individuals' career opportunities (Glässner 1989; Watts 1994; Geissler and Wiegmann 1996). Students had to conform to political criteria, such as accepting the principles of Marxism-Leninism. Students also had to endorse the leadership of the SED and to accept the policies developed by the socialist party. Although there is no reliable statistic showing how many students endured professional disadvantages on political grounds, it is plain that criticism of the communist party or even its specific policies was undesirable. Personal biographies of opposition members published since the collapse of the socialist system illustrate the lack of educational opportunities for those who refused to be silenced.[4] In light of the institutional learning axiom, one would expect that the requirement to conform had an adverse affect on the development of democratic citizenship-qualities. For the experience in the educational process conveyed the message that the suppression of opposition is justifiable and that self-reliant activities in schools (and elsewhere) are undesirable.

The lack of opportunities, in turn, was explicitly legitimized by socialist ideals. The curriculum in the GDR was heavily structured by socialist ideals. Marxism-Leninism was a compulsory subject for most students. History and the social sciences were predominately concerned with the role of the working class, and egalitarian principles. These courses emphasized the role of property relations in shaping capitalist societies and explained the leading role of the working class and the socialist party. Consequently, the socialist curriculum did not establish a separate field of study for the political system. This results from socialism's premiss that the political and economic spheres are interdependent and cannot be examined separately. Unlike in a democratic system, which attaches considerable importance to citizens' opportunities to scrutinize the political process, citizens were exposed to the notion that the control of those holding political power is secondary in a socialist state. Similar restrictions of citizens' opportunities can be found in the economic sphere (Kopstein 1997). Voluntary associations, such as independent unions, wage-bargaining, or conflict resolution on a voluntary and contractual basis were unknown in the centralized command economy.

On the whole, those arenas that nurtured democratic citizenship qualities in the West—for example, free, fair, and secret elections, the opportunity to participate in genuine party competition, or voluntary participation in interest groups—were largely absent in eastern Germany from the very inception of the GDR. The SED, for example, closely supervised elections, which were not free. Candidates either belonged to the SED or were members of parties and mass organizations closely affiliated with the SED. And voters who used a voting booth were suspected of being 'hostile forces' opposing the socialist system. From the inception of political organizations in 1945–6 until the collapse in 1989, eastern Germans increasingly experienced the dominating force first of the SMAD and then the SED. The growing restrictions thus reduced eastern Germans' opportunities to participate in political competition, practice fairness in elections, or internalize the ideals that legitimize restraint and self-reliance.

Establishing a Socialist Economy. In addition to rooting the SED firmly in power, one central task for the SED was to rebuild the shattered economy. This turned out to be a monumental task that was never fully accomplished. Initially, the Soviets almost immediately began to nationalize industries. The most important goals of the Soviet Union were to extract as much in reparation payments as possible and to nationalize the key industries.[5]

The nationalization of large parts of the economy and the drain of resources made an economic recovery in eastern Germany exceedingly difficult. Another reason for the slow economic recovery was the fact that a central planning commission made most economic decisions. This commission developed target norms for aggregate outputs which various industrial sectors had to meet. Regional and local planning commissions co-ordinated the implementation of economic norms at the regional and plant level. The central economy was chronically unable to meet the two objectives which eastern German planners pursued simultaneously: to meet demands for consumer goods and to invest sufficiently in heavy industry in order to promote growth. Consequently, economic planners vacillated between these two basic objectives. In the early 1950s the central planning commission emphasized heavy industry. While the increase in economic growth during this time was considerable, it also created a shortage for consumer goods during these early years. The increased production norms in early 1953 led to the workers' uprising on 17 June 1953. Although these protests were initially limited to a demand for reduced work norms, they quickly turned into a general call for free and parliamentary elections, until Soviet tanks crushed this protest. After these events the leadership paid more attention to consumers' needs. In order to deal with the continuing economic problems, the GDR leadership even tried a new economic system whereby plant managers were given greater responsibilities in making economic decisions. This system was introduced in 1958 and initially appeared successful, although shortages remained. By 1960, for example, living standards were still about 40 per cent lower than in West Germany, labour productivity about 25 per cent lower than in the West, and food had to be imported (Orlow 1995).

As a result, hundreds of thousands of young people fled the GDR during the 1950s. Doctors, engineers, nurses, construction workers, and farmers simply packed their belongings and travelled westward across the still-unfortified border. The GDR was to lose the core of its industrial workforce. In 1959, for example, over 143,000 individuals fled—and these were frequently well-educated citizens with skills vital to the economy. Because people continued to flee, despite pleas by the political leadership, the Berlin Wall was erected on 13 August 1961. Thereafter, few people could cross the hermetically sealed border.

In spite of constructing the Berlin Wall, however, the GDR only partially succeeded in blocking the flow of information from the West into the East. For example, most areas in the East could receive western television. Although it is impossible to assess precisely how many eastern Germans preferred western television over eastern television, studies suggest that the primary source for information was western television—including information about events that occurred in the GDR (Hesse 1990; Dohlus 1991). Further, older eastern Germans (over 65) were permitted to visit the West, while western Germans received visas to enter the GDR. In 1985, for example, 6.7 million western Germans visited the GDR. These contacts and the dissemination of information through western electronic media undoubtedly informed eastern Germans about the shortcomings of the socialist system. At the same time, eastern Germans' exposure to the western German system was based on hearsay, not personal experience.

Erich Honecker, the architect of the Berlin Wall, replaced Ulbricht in 1971. Honecker turned to nationalizing those industries that were still privately owned, notably independent artisans and small-scale contractors. By 1972 99.4 per cent of all industrial workers worked for state-owned enterprises; and state-owned enterprises produced almost the same percentage (99 per cent) of total industrial production. Nevertheless, economic problems actually worsened, and food still had to be imported in order to raise the living standards during the 1976–80 five year plan. The economic stagnation had severe consequences for those living in the GDR. Whereas the average income of a household in the GDR in 1970 amounted to 64 per cent of a comparable household in the West, this proportion was reduced to 46 per cent by 1983. By some accounts, eastern Germany was bankrupt by the early 1980s and saved from economic collapse only by loans from western Germany (Kopstein 1997).

Opposition in the GDR. In addition to the growing economic malaise, the SED leadership also had to confront the growing dissatisfaction of the eastern German population about economic shortages.[6] To varying degrees, the GDR always had to cope with the presence of some regime opposition. Over time, however, the objectives of the opposition groups changed from rejecting the system to aiming at a reformed socialism. In the 1950s the SED encountered a considerable lack of enthusiasm for its socialist appeals. Workers, for example, openly left public demonstrations for socialist goals, party functionaries were accosted by angry citizens, and more or less open resistance occurred at the workplace. These were mostly isolated incidents without the support of a broader network, which partly explains the overall failure of these protests to change the socialist regime. In addition, the violent suppression of 17 June 1953 also indicated to eastern German citizens that neither the SED leadership nor the Soviet Union was willing fundamentally to change existing political and economic structures.

The Protestant Church was of particular importance for the long-term growth of the opposition in the 1980s. According to historian

Mary Fulbrook (1995), open hostility characterized the church–state relationship in the 1950s and 1960s. Shortly after Germany's defeat, the SMAD dissolved religious schools in 1946. After establishing the GDR, the SED in 1951 obliged teachers in state-sponsored schools to follow Marxist-Leninist principles, thus reducing the role of Christian values in public education. Further, the state established the so-called *Jugendweihe*—a secular version of the Protestant confirmation—in order to reduce the influence of the Protestant Church on the moral values of the eastern German public. By the early 1970s, however, a change of functionaries at both state and church administrations, along with the growing consensus that the GDR was to be permanent, led to a reconciliation. This *rapprochement* culminated in the church–state agreement of 6 March 1978, where the church conceded to the state the predominance of socialism in eastern Germany. Meanwhile, the state conceded some organizational independence to the church to deal with its internal affairs.

The partial autonomy of the church in the East proved to be of enormous significance for the growth of a small, but tenacious, group of regime opponents. This opposition which—unlike its predecessors in the 1950s—did not want to eradicate socialism but to reform it, found a sanctuary within the organizational compounds of the Protestant Church. Since the state conceded to the church independence in managing what were called 'hostile-negative' forces (read protestors), the church maintained autonomy over how to discipline—or not to discipline—those who opposed the state. Because the church was less inclined to crush opposition to the state than the state itself, almost all organized opposition in the late 1970s and early 1980s was expressed through the church, such as the *Friedensdekaden* or the peace demonstration in Dresden's Frauenkirche in February 1982. At the same time, the state hoped that it might control this opposition through the church because it maintained close contact with leading church officials.

The early 1980s thus witnessed the growth of church-affiliated activities which to some degree expressed a disagreement with the policies of the GDR, such as in the context of the deployment of Soviet medium-based missiles. Mikhail Gorbachev's ascent to power in the Soviet Union in 1985 and his reform course further fuelled the organization of individuals who wanted to reform, but not abandon, socialism in eastern Germany. For example, in January 1986 the Initiative für Frieden und Menschenrechte (IFM) was founded with the aim to establish such civil liberties as the rule of law, independent courts, or the right to strike in eastern Germany. Significantly, the IFM was the first opposition group organized largely outside of the organizational reach of the church—and thus more difficult to control by the despised secret police, the Stasi.[7] Other new organizations quickly arose, such as the Umweltbibliothek (environmental library) in 1986. Although the Soviet Union continued to pressure eastern Germany to reform its rigid system, international developments quickly isolated the GDR, making it very difficult to maintain its hard-line policies toward reformers. In particular, the Hungarian government dismantled its border fortifications with Austria in the late summer of 1989, enabling eastern Germans to reach the West through Hungary. The rigged May 1989 local elections reaffirmed the ruling Politburo's unwillingness to liberalize eastern Germany. Pressures on the ruling class mounted during the autumn of 1989, when regular Monday demonstrations in Leipzig called first for a liberalization of the GDR and then for Germany's unification.[8] The abdication of Honecker on 9 October and his replacement by Egon Krenz meant too little reform too late. With the announcement of new travel regulations on 9 November 1989, eastern Germans simply took it upon themselves to decide when they visited the West—the Berlin Wall fell.

The time between the fall of the Wall and Germany's formal unification on 3 October 1990 witnessed a rapid succession of events that left most politicians and observers struggling to keep abreast of the historical developments. Early December 'round-table' talks among various political groups began to shape the future of the GDR, and free elections to the eastern German parliament (Volkskammer) ensued. These took place on 18 March 1990 and led to a victory for the 'Alliance for Germany', consisting of the CDU, the Democratic Awakening, and the German Social Union. Because eastern Germans continued to move to western Germany, a monetary, economic, and social union between the GDR and western Germany came into effect on 1 July, bringing the Deutschmark to eastern Germans. After Germany's borders were established in the so-called '2 plus 4' talks and several weeks of negotiations between Germany and the former occupational powers, the GDR 'entered' a political union with western Germany on 3 October 1990.

The continuous opposition to the eastern German system indicates that the socialist system was never fully legitimized. Undoubtedly, economic shortages contributed to its collapse, as did the presence of the western German system whose superior economic capacity could be observed daily on the evening news. However, the fact alone that parts of the eastern German public opposed the socialist state cannot be taken as evidence that socialism as an idea disappeared. The post-communist experience therefore provides an especially intriguing context against which one may examine the validity of the institutional learning model. For if eastern Germans espouse socialist ideals, for example, it would result from their exposure to a rejected political system.

Historians and political scientists will debate for years to come why the iron curtain shattered and what led to the demise of the eastern German system; I do not purport to contribute to this eminently important question. Rather, the discussion has tried to show that: (1) the eastern German political system was authoritarian; (2) a centralized system made most economic decisions; and (3) eastern Germans were frequently exposed to the western German system through visitors and the western mass media. Thus, both the political and economic processes provided few opportunities to develop restraint, self-reliance, and an appreciation for liberal-democratic ideals and market models. At the same time, access to western media provided a visual, but not experiential, alternative political and economic order to the socialist reality.

INSTITUTIONAL LEARNING IN WESTERN GERMANY, 1945–1989

Like the SMAD in the eastern zone, American, British, and French occupation forces began to rebuild the political and economic systems in the three western zones. The political and economic reconstruction of what was to become western Germany initially proceeded at a slower pace than in the East, partly because it was more difficult to co-ordinate the activities of the three Allied forces. While the British and the United States, on the whole, shared many ideas about how to re-structure western Germany, the French authorities especially insisted on a strict separation of its zone from the other ones, which slowed the reconstruction of *one* political system in the early years of western Germany's occupation. But the most important difference between the eastern and western zones concerns the long-term objectives of the occupying powers. While the SMAD quickly moved to establish the SED as central decision-makers, the western forces first reconstructed the political system locally and then extended it to the state and national level, reflecting the different objectives.[9] While the SMAD wished to concentrate power in the SED, the western allies wanted to disperse power across different levels to avoid the re-emergence of an all-powerful centre.

Political activities in the SPD began under the leadership of Kurt Schumacher as early as 1945. In the first post-war decade the SPD heavily favoured the nationalization of key industries in western Germany, because it viewed capitalist enterprises as being highly instrumental in Hitler's ascent to power during the 1930s. However, the SPD also committed itself to a parliamentary democracy, contrasting sharply with the objectives of the SED. The West CDU was founded shortly after the eastern CDU. It emphasized the firm integration of western Germany into a western alliance structure partly because Konrad Adenauer, who was to become Germany's first chancellor in 1949, believed that Germany's unification with the East could only be negotiated with the Soviets from a position of strength (see below). The CDU favoured a parliamentary democracy and a federal structure which continued the regional tradition of German politics. The CDU also staunchly advocated a social market economy, although it favoured some nationalization of key industries shortly after the war. Finally, the liberal party—the FDP—emphasized liberal economic policies.

Because the western powers wanted to assure that supporters of activists in the Third Reich were barred from obtaining a politically prominent position in the new democracy, they resorted to several measures to control access to higher positions. They started what became known as denazification. This resulted in the removal of thousands of leading political, social, economic, and military elites from their positions. In addition, anybody who wished to occupy a leading position in the new western Germany had to complete a questionnaire concerning their political views. By the end of 1945 the US administration had already collected over 1.6 million responses. The ambitious goal to eradicate Nazism from Germany was scaled down considerably, however, when the need to rebuild a strong Germany as a buffer against the emerging socialist bloc began to outweigh the desire to democratize it fully. Consequently, only a fraction of chargeable activities committed during the Nazi era was actually prosecuted (Merritt 1995: 184), and many who had sympathized with the Third Reich were employed again—frequently at high levels in the fledgling democracy.

In order to re-establish a new leadership, the western allies began to permit local and state elections during 1946. Further, economic competition broadened across occupational zones when the Bizone—the merger of the British and US zones—was created in January 1947 and became the Trizone in the spring 1949 with the addition of the French zone. Despite the slower evolution of a national political structure in the West, however, the central difference from the eastern zone concerns the movement toward competitive elections. In 1946 voters elected state legislatures which, in turn, elected delegates to a parliamentary council in June 1948. It was charged to draft a federal constitution. Although several western German leaders were initially reluctant to institutionalize Germany's division permanently—the term Basic Law (*Grundgesetz*) supposedly endowed the new system with a more temporary character—the Berlin blockade signalled to the western world that a free and unified Germany was unlikely to become a reality. Thereafter, all western state legislatures except Bavaria accepted the Basic Law, and by 23 May 1949 western Germany had a parliamentary democracy.

A number of factors shaped the institutional features laid out in the Basic Law (Dalton 1992). A first goal was to establish a democratic system that avoided the pitfalls of the Weimar democracy. The framers of the constitution, for example, agreed that they did not want to repeat the mistakes of the Weimar Republic and establish a politically weak presidency. In addition, it was assumed that the 'irrational' mass public helped to topple the Weimar democracy. Plebiscitarian procedures, therefore, do not occupy a central position in the Basic Law. The authors of the Basic Law also envisaged a political system that dispersed political power across regions and across various political and social strata. This is manifested in the strong second chamber of the national parliament, the Bundesrat, which injects a significant regional element into the national political process.

In contrast to most prior constitutions in Germany, the new system thus permitted the expression of a range of interests. The Länder (federal states) are able to assert their interests through the Bundesrat. Party competition was established, thus providing citizens with opportunities to participate in the political process. Perhaps the most important effect of these institutional arrangements was that western citizens were exposed to the logic of democratic competition in local, state, and federal elections. The decentralization of political power institutionalized civil liberties listed prominently in the first section of the Basic Law. Political opposition was not only allowed but encouraged, and the framework of the representative democracy provided the means to express one's interests in the political process.

The school system adopted a leading role in re-educating the German public. In contrast to the eastern German system, however, the task was to instil democratic ideals and develop support for the democratic process. One manifestation of this difference concerns the process by which educational policies are made (Fuchs and Dornemann 1992). While the eastern system put centralized authorities in charge of education policies, the Basic Law allocated responsibility for educational policies to the federal states.

The western Allies, along with the emerging democratic elites, moved quickly to change the content of school curricula. In light of Germany's authoritarian past, schools stressed the advantages of the new democratic institutions. Initially, access to the higher educational institutions was restricted to a small proportion of the German population, limiting their potential to re-educate the broader public. However, beginning in the 1960s, demands by the mass public opened institutions of higher education to a larger segment of the population. For example, students criticized the hierarchical university structures and demanded more participation in intra-university affairs, resulting in a reform of universities.

The pluralist character of the educational framework also influenced what was actually taught in classes (Fishbein and Martin 1987). There was a multitude of textbooks, varying from state to state; parents have a growing influence on what was taught; teachers are at some liberty in selecting material, especially in the academic high-school track, the Gymnasium. This pluralist framework initially coexisted with a conservative approach to teaching, where students were mainly expected to follow teachers' instructions rather than being active participants in the learning process. However, the student revolution of the 1960s helped to reduce teachers' authoritarian role in the classroom. As a result, schools increasingly adopted a different teaching style throughout the 1960s and 1970s which, in addition to conveying knowledge, also taught democratic skills, such as independent thinking and the development of critical ideas. The experience in schools clearly represents one arena where German pupils not only learned about democracy, but also increasingly practised it. The school system contributed to the development of democratic citizenship-qualities and ultimately led to the western German public's acceptance of democratic ideals and processes (Conradt 1974; Baker, Dalton, and Hildebrandt 1981).

Other spheres also contributed to the development of citizenship-qualities. For example, the right to bargain in the economic sphere also made a substantial contribution to the development of restraint and self-reliance. This is not to say that all spheres of political and economic life were fully democratized; there were backlashes which may have had a detrimental influence on the development of democratic citizenship-qualities. In addition, the high degree of bureaucratization of German society may also have slowed the development of, for example, self-reliance (Chapter 7). Overall, however, the institutional learning process in the West offered substantially more opportunities to develop democratic citizenship-qualities than the one in the East.

There were limits to the constitutional freedoms, however. Because the founders of the Basic Law wanted to prevent democratic freedoms from abuse by ideological extremists, the Basic Law stipulates that those who wish to topple the democratic order, no longer may enjoy basic civil liberties and political rights (Ellwein 1983: 422). This stipulation was especially crucial during the founding years of the western German democracy, when authoritarian views persisted and when Germans were still inexperienced with the actual operation of a liberal democracy. The constitutional court reaffirmed on various occasions that certain right- and left-wing extremist organizations might be outlawed. However, these restrictions also had unintended—and unfortunate—consequences for how citizens in contemporary Germany view the civil liberties of extremist groups (see Chapter 6). Further, the tension between individual liberty and democratically responsible behaviour led to a controversial debate, especially throughout the 1970s when the SPD-led government under Willy Brandt began to monitor the political views of those who applied for positions in the civil service. Despite these restrictions, however, the western parliamentary democracy turned out to be remarkably successful, exposing western German citizens to the rules of liberal-democratic and market-based competition.

The democratic institutional learning initiated in 1949 was sorely needed. Public-opinion surveys conducted after the Second World War indicated that the western German public continued to hold authoritarian views. For example, many citizens regarded Hitler as a great statesman well into the late 1950s (Boynton and Lowenberg 1973; Merritt 1995). The initiation of the democratic institutional learning was crucial if the western German democracy was to be firmly implanted in western Germany. Through revamping the political and educational systems, the Allies hoped to reform Germany's authoritarian culture. A few incidents during the early decades of the Federal Republic reflected the lack of democratic practice in the early decades of the Federal Republic. For example, the *Spiegel* affair in 1962 represents an important moment in German post-war history. *Der Spiegel*, a weekly news magazine, published documents about the lack of readiness among some German army units. The minister of defence, the Bavarian Franz-Joseph Strauss, ordered the arrest of the magazine's responsible journalists with Adenauer's knowledge. This raised a storm of protest and led to the resignation of Strauss; the journalists were released, and Adenauer retired a few months later. The emergency laws passed in 1968 and the success of the right-wing party (NPD) in several state elections throughout 1969 also generated fears that the authoritarian streak in German society might be revitalized. At the same time, the formation of the Grand Coalition in 1965 signalled a turning-point in the dominance of the CDU/CSU in shaping post-war governments. A few years later the first successful change in government control in 1969 to the SPD demonstrated that democratic mechanisms were functioning as intended. By most accounts, western Germany's democracy was working reasonably well and, by the early 1970s, Germany had become a respected member of the international community.

Stabilizing a Democracy: Foreign Policy and Economic Miracles. One reason for the stability of Germany's new democracy was undoubtedly its integration into the emerging western Alliance structure, especially into what is now called the European Union and NATO. The remarkably fast integration into the western camp contributed to Germany's political stability at a time when a substantial proportion of citizens still held authoritarian views. Adenauer's broader foreign policy goals consisted of three closely related objectives. First, he sought to improve Germany's relations with the three western Allies, because he believed that a firm integration of western Germany into the western alliance structure was a prerequisite for achieving international sovereignty. For similar reasons, he favoured Germany's integration into a

European-wide supranational institutional framework. The last goal was to manage the problematic relations with the Soviet Union. Adenauer made significant progress toward regaining Germany's international recognition between 1949 and 1955. In 1952, for example, the Allied powers substantially revised the conditions for their occupation of Germany in the *Generalvertrag* (General Treaty). The emergence of greater international independence is even more clearly reflected in the 1954 *Deutschlandvertrag* (Germany Treaty) which returned its sovereignty to Germany; and Germany became recognized as the sole representative of the German people. Germany's integration into the West culminated in 1955 when it became part of NATO—barely ten years after the defeat of the last military units of the Third Reich, a new western German army was founded.

Equally important in stabilizing the fledgling democracy was the enormous success of western Germany's economy in improving material conditions, especially during the 1950s and 1960s. Initially, the task appeared daunting, particularly in the West. For example, the loss of 'productive capacity [in the East] has been estimated at approximately 15 percent, compared with 21 percent in the West' (Fulbrook 1991: 153). Furthermore, western Germany had to absorb about 10 million resettlers from the eastern territories. Despite these economic and social problems, some Allied planners initially favoured a reduction in Germany's capacity to rebuild a strong economy, on the grounds that a revitalized economy would unduly increase Germany's potential to build a strong army (e.g. the Morgenthau Plan). However, the evolution of the cold war and the enormous economic cost of supporting a weak economy made it infeasible to keep the German economy from developing to its full potential. This strategic change is manifested in the Marshall Plan, which required a firm commitment to a market economy before these resources could be used. By the time the French merged 'their' zone with the Bizone in the spring of 1949 the basic principles of a market system had been established.

Ludwig Erhardt's programme of combining market competition with social legislation proved to be highly successful. Market competition was encouraged but generous social policies cushioned the undesirable consequences of unfettered competition. These policies were—and still are—popular with the German population (see Chapter 8). This mix of welfare policies and market elements became known as a 'Social Market Economy'. The economy did so well that a shortage of labour developed during the 1960s. This led the various governments to invite so-called guest workers (*Gastarbeiter*), primarily from southern Europe and Turkey, to work in Germany. When Willy Brandt became chancellor in 1969, millions of guest workers had become integrated into the German economy.

One important development during Willy Brandt's chancellorship (1969–74) is the consolidation of western Germany as a stable democracy within the western alliance structure. But he also sought to normalize relations with the East—what became known as *Ostpolitik*. The Moscow Treaty of 1970, the Polish Treaty in December 1970, and the Basic Treaty concluded among the western allies in 1972 collectively recognize the status quo in Europe. This meant that the social-liberal coalition effectively acknowledged the shift of borders after the Second World War. The CDU/CSU in particular rejected this policy and argued that the Polish and Moscow treaties were unconstitutional, a view that was not shared by the constitutional court which upheld the treaties. The social-liberal coalition was returned to office with an overwhelming victory in 1972. Despite Brandt's popularity, however, his chancellorship ended in 1974 when one of his aides turned out to be an undercover agent for the GDR.

While the preceding governments successfully established Germany's new political system, Helmut Schmidt's (1974–82) chancellorship is characterized by a defence of this newly gained status as a stable democracy. Schmidt's government had to address several issues. It had to cope with the energy crises which threatened Germany's unparalleled economic growth in the post-war decades. Schmidt favoured a greater reliance on nuclear energy in order to reduce Germany's dependence on oil imports. But this strategy generated strong intraparty opposition within the SPD and fuelled the growing environmental movement among the German public. When Schmidt dealt with the threat emanating from Soviet medium-range missiles stationed in eastern Germany by calling for the deployment of US missiles in western Europe, he also revitalized Germany's peace movement. And in 1982 frictions with the FDP emerged over how to handle the economy, resulting in a constructive vote of no-confidence which voted Schmidt out of office and installed Helmut Kohl as his successor. The Kohl government quickly initiated a variety of cost-cutting measures to deal with growing unemployment and the growing strains imposed by welfare services on the federal budget. But it was only partially successful: economic growth rates increased, but unemployment rates were not reduced. The renewed emphasis on economic policy problems strengthened the Green party in both federal and state elections. Further, given the economic problems, guest workers, who represented almost 10 per cent of western Germany's population in 1989, were less welcome than in the 1960s. Nevertheless, it is a sign of the stability of western Germany's democracy that these problems did not lead to significant and widespread opposition to the political system itself during the 1970s and 1980s.

The growing success of western Germany's smooth-running democracy is reflected in the attitudes and behaviour of, especially, western Germans born and raised after the Second World War (Baker, Dalton, and Hildebrandt 1981; Dalton 1992). A growing proportion of citizens who did not experience an authoritarian system increasingly supported the institutions of the Federal Republic. The evolving democratic maturity of younger western Germans in particular is also reflected in the growing democratic *behaviour* of the post-war cohort. The first evidence emerged during the student revolts in the late 1960s. Although some participants became members of a terrorist organization—the Baader–Meinhof Gang, later called the Red Army Faction —most students participated peacefully in demonstrations against traditional university structures. Equally important, many western Germans from different social strata began to participate in environmental, peace, and women's movements. By the 1980s there were as many members in traditional political parties as in grass-roots organizations outside established parties. Not only did supporters of these latter groups advocate new policy priorities—environmental protection was valued as much or more than economic growth, for example—but this voluntary participation in grass-roots organizations indicated that western Germans became increasingly self-reliant in expressing their political views independent of the dominant elite views. On the whole, by the time of Germany's unification in October 1990 most observers agreed that western Germany had become a mature and viable democracy.

CONCLUSION

Both the East and the West attempted to make the ideological views of citizens conform to the operations and ideological premises of the political system. However, unlike the eastern German system, the political order and economic system in western Germany provided opportunities for citizens to develop restraint, self-reliance, and liberal-representative ideals. Undoubtedly, the opportunities for western Germans were also limited in important respects; historical reasons, for example, led to the restrictions of civil liberties of ideological extremists (Chapter 6). At the same time, the range of opportunities for citizens to advance their interests was undoubtedly greater in the West than in the East. Germany's post-war context thus offers a unique opportunity to test the institutional learning and diffusion axioms under quasi-experimental conditions. By examining a range of ideological values in Germany, it is possible to determine where eastern and western Germans diverged over ideological values, as the institutional learning axiom predicts, and whether they converged, as the diffusion-axiom predicts.

4

Research Design

The naturally-occurring 'crucial experiment' is, of course, a change in regime. If the political culture alters *afterwards* (e.g., in Germany after 1945, towards a 'civic culture' type), this strongly supports the view that it is a more or less accurate reflection of the current political reality.

(Barry 1970: 52)

A cross-national study design in testing the axioms would have the disadvantage that it is difficult to attribute the cause of one difference (ideological values) to another (political institutions). Fortunately, Germany's unification makes this nation a most appropriate test case for the theoretical arguments because its formal division and unification in 1949 and 1990, respectively, have created quasi-laboratory conditions in a natural setting (Przeworski and Teune 1970). Until Germany's division after the Second World War, the East and the West shared a broad range of social, political, and cultural characteristics. The previous chapter highlights that the most important difference between eastern and western Germany during the partition concerned the political and economic systems. If institutional learning affects individuals' ideological values, then one would expect to find systematic East–West differences over basic political and economic values, reflecting different opportunities to develop democratic citizenship-qualities. If, by contrast, value diffusion affects individuals' ideological values, one would expect to find traces of the diffusion process in eastern Germany, where most citizens had access to western German television. Most eastern Germans also received information about the West through their personal contacts with visitors from western Germany. Thus, when Germany became formally unified in October 1990 it presented an appropriate case to examine several issues relevant to the democratic transition literature.

One central aim in this study is, therefore, to determine how different eastern and western Germans' ideological values were shortly after Germany's unification. In addition, since this project examines the extent to which eastern Germans changed their ideological values in the years after unification (see below), this dynamic view provides evidence about the impact of democratic institutions on eastern Germans' values. A third major issue concerns the role of ideological values and performance evaluations in transition countries (the values-to-institutions process). By comparing the influence of these factors in a fairly well-established and new democracy, one may examine whether the relationships are mediated by the age of democratic systems.

COLLECTING THE DATA

Two surveys of Berlin parliamentarians, which I conducted personally, provide the data at the level of political elites. The first survey took place from October 1991 and lasted through June 1992. During this period, I interviewed 168 parliamentarians—seventy-nine from the East and eighty-nine from the West. During a second survey I reinterviewed sixty-five of the seventy-nine eastern MPs between November 1994 and April 1995.[1] The focus on Berlin increases the quasi-experimental nature of the analyses, because MPs represent urban constituencies only. Consequently, other structural variations at the federal level, which may influence federal MPs' views, remain constant (e.g. differences between urban and rural constituencies). In addition, many MPs grew up in Berlin. Finally, the focus on Berlin made it feasible for one individual to interview a fairly large number of MPs, without having to travel to remote constituencies. Where available, this book discusses evidence that the results from the Berlin study are generalizable to the federal political elite.

In order to measure the concepts discussed in Chapter 2, I prepared a structured questionnaire which contains both closed-ended and open-ended questions. The closed-ended questions are mostly derived from prior research on political and economic values. These are widely tested measures of basic political and economic predispositions and will be discussed in detail in the various chapters. I also included ten open-ended questions in the context of each value domain, for two reasons. First, political elites are frequently cognitively sophisticated individuals who often feel uncomfortable about indicating their views in pre-formulated response formats. Secondly, when I began to prepare the questionnaire during the spring of 1991 very little was known—and still is known—about the effects of individuals' regime experience on their ideological values. By giving political elites the opportunity to express their views outside the constraints of fixed responses, I expected to get more complete information about their ideological views than closed-ended questions alone would yield. I coded the responses to the open-ended questions on the basis of detailed interview notes.

A first draft of the questionnaire underwent close scrutiny before the fieldwork was carried out. First, I conducted a pre-test of the questionnaire in October 1991 with two party leaders from local district parliaments in East and West Berlin. In addition to conducting the formal interviews, I discussed the questionnaire with them. Secondly, I discussed the questionnaire with several elite researchers at the Free University and the Wissenschaftszentrum Berlin.

I started the field research for the first survey in the summer of 1991, shortly after Germany's unification on 3 October 1990. By this time the first national 'unity-elections' had taken place (2 December 1990), along with the first election to the unified Berlin parliament, held on the same day.[2] The dramatic historical events in the aftermath of the fall of the Berlin Wall dominated these elections. The national electorate credited Helmut Kohl with designing Germany's unification, which undoubtedly helped him to win the federal election. His promise of a quick economic reconstruction of eastern Germany was also better received by voters than Oskar Lafontaine's dire, but accurate, predictions about the difficulty of rebuilding eastern Germany's economy (Klingemann and Kaase 1994). These events also influenced the election to the first unified Berlin parliament; the CDU turned out to be the strongest party in the Berlin parliament. However, unlike at the national level, the strength of the PDS and the Bündnis '90/ Greens in Berlin led to the formation of a Grand Coalition between the SPD and CDU. After the election campaigns were over, the euphoria over the dramatic fall of the Berlin Wall gave way to consideration of the problems involved in merging two countries.

The fieldwork thus began as the excitement over Germany's unification dissipated. The mood in Germany in the summer of 1991 was less jubilant than during 1990, as Germans began the nitty-gritty work of merging the two former states. Phone-lines were laid, new local and regional administrative structures began to emerge, a new legal system was implemented—the unification process had moved from high diplomacy to mundane tasks. During the summer and autumn of 1991 citizens in the East and the West began to develop a realistic sense of the enormous dimension of the 'unification-project'. Despite the reduced enthusiasm, few voices openly blamed western Germans for the difficulties emerging in the East. To be sure, party groups, such as the PDS—the successor party to the SED—harshly criticized the perceived 'colonization' of the East by western Germans. On the whole, however, a sense of realism, not cynicism, developed during the first interview period about the prospects of a painless merger.

By the time I returned to Berlin in the autumn of 1994 to conduct the second survey the climate had changed significantly. It had become evident that the almost complete economic collapse in eastern Germany represented a long-term problem which could not be solved within a relatively short time period. The press candidly portrayed the gravity of the situation, and many politicians publicly complained about the lack of progress toward unification, both in the East and the West. Most eastern MPs did not express any more sympathy for the collapsed GDR than they had during the first wave of interviews. But many expressed more vocally than three years earlier the view that western German politicians had made several mistakes, such as providing little protection from rough market competition for eastern German companies during a time of transition. Despite this more pessimistic assessment of economic and social problems, Helmut Kohl's government won the 1994 autumn election, partly because economic forecasts appeared to signal brighter economic prospects for 1995 (Rohrschneider and Fuchs 1995). The second wave of interviews thus took place amidst an atmosphere of greater scepticism, sometimes even cynicism, about the successful completion of the unification project within the foreseeable future.

Interviewing MPs. The newly elected Berlin parliament had barely begun its work in 1991 when I sent a letter to Berlin parliamentarians in the early summer of 1991 before my departure for Germany. After describing the general aims of the project, I announced my intention to meet with all legislators for a personal interview about a range of topics. Upon my arrival in Berlin, I met with the president of the Berlin parliament to familiarize her with the project. Her support enabled me to use an office in the parliamentary building in which most of the interviews were conducted. Given the relatively centralized party structures in Germany, I also met all party leaders (*Fraktionsvorsitzende*) to obtain their consent to the study. They agreed to ask MPs from their parliamentary group to participate in the project.[3] Simultaneously with the official endorsement, I sent a second letter to all MPs, this time requesting a specific interview time. Although relatively few MPs responded to this request promptly, all had by this time become familiar with the project.

I scheduled most interviews during the biweekly parliamentary session, during which I contacted those MPs who had not responded to the previous requests for an interview. In addition to the aforementioned letter, I tried to contact all MPs at least three times when parliament was in session. Not all MPs could be contacted, despite repeated attempts, and a few refused to participate in the project. On the whole, however, MPs were so co-operative that I interviewed 168 MPs (about 70 per cent of all parliamentarians).

When I contacted MPs upon my return to Berlin in 1994, most of them remembered the first interview and were willing to grant a second one. The president of the parliament again provided me with an office in the new parliament (the Preussische Landtag) where I conducted all the interviews. Resignation from parliament, death, and scheduling conflicts reduced the number of reinterviewed MPs from the original seventy-nine to sixty-five in the second wave. The actual interviewing period lasted from November 1994 through April 1995.

Table 4.1 contains the proportion of MPs, by party, in the parliament and in the two surveys. The first two columns display information about the entire parliament. For example, there were 101 CDU-MPs in the parliament in 1992 (41.7 per cent of all MPs),[4] of whom I interviewed fifty-seven (33.9 per cent of the entire sample). The next two columns divide parliamentarians into the eastern and western parliamentary groups. There were twenty eastern CDU-MPs in 1992 (20.4 per cent of eastern MPs in parliament), of whom eighteen were interviewed (22.8 per cent of the eastern sample). I also reinterviewed fourteen CDU-MPs in 1995 (21.5 per cent of the 1995 sample). Finally, thirty-nine CDU-MPs (43.8 per cent of the western sample) were interviewed.

On the whole, the proportion of party groups in the sample closely mirrors the size of party groups in the entire parliament. Smaller par-

TABLE 4.1. *Partisanship of MPs in Berlin, sample and entire parliament*

	Berlin MPs (1992)		East Berlin MPs			West Berlin MPs	
	Data	Parliament	Data		Parliament	Data	Parliament
			1995	1992			
CDU	57	101	14	18	20	39	81
	33.9%	41.7%	21.5%	22.8%	20.4%	43.8%	56.3%
SPD	56	76	22	26	36	30	40
	33.3%	31.4%	33.9%	32.9%	36.7%	33.7%	27.8%
FDP	16	18	5	6	6	10	12
	9.5%	7.4%	7.7%	7.6%	6.1%	11.2%	8.3%
Bündnis '90/	18[a]	20[a]	6	8[a]	9[a]	10	11
Greens/ UFV	10.7%	8.3%	9.3%	10.1%	9.2%	11.2%	7.6%
Neues	4	4	4	4	4	—	
Forum	2.4%	1.7%	6.2%	5.1%	4.1%		
PDS	17	23	14	17	23	—	
	10.1%	9.5%	21.5%	21.5%	23.5%		
(N)	(168)[a]	(242)[a]	(65)	(79)[a]	(98)[a]	(89)	(144)

[a] One replacement MP is included in this count. That is, one parliamentary seat was occupied by two individuals for the purpose of this project. Therefore, the total N for the East Alternative movement and the total N of the sample and the entire parliament is increased by 1. Throughout this research, the 4 MPs from the Neues Forum are merged with those of the Bündnis '90/Greens.

ties are slightly over-represented because the project, once introduced, was visible among, say, fifteen to twenty MPs of smaller parties, so that it was easier to schedule appointments. For example, party leaders of smaller parties often jokingly encouraged their party members to participate in the study ('Have you had your turn yet?'), which helped to achieve almost complete coverage among smaller parties. Among larger parties, the main deviation between the sample and parliament occurs among western CDU-MPs, who are under-represented in the sample (56.3 per cent in the parliament compared to 43.8 per cent in the western sample). However, western CDU-MPs in the sample closely mirror the key-characteristics of all western CDU-MPs, such as gender, seniority, and the occupation of leadership positions. In addition, where appropriate, analyses control for party-membership so that the under-representation of western CDU-MPs in all likelihood does not affect the results of this study.[5] Finally, because of the small number in the Neues Forum (four MPs), I included them in the Bündnis '90/Greens party group in the party-based analyses in the succeeding chapters. The four MPs from the Neues Forum were elected to the Berlin parliament on the same party list as MPs from the Bündnis '90.

In addition to the two Berlin MPs surveys, the study will examine the ideological values of mass publics in eastern and western Germany. By now there are several public-opinion surveys in the public domain that include valuable information about the ideological values of the eastern and western publics, such as their views about socialist ideals, economic values, and political tolerance. Specifically, I frequently use the Allbus 1991, 1992, and 1994 (the German version of the GSS) surveys, which contain several indicators about publics' views about socialism, the pluralist process, and the welfare state. Furthermore, I incorporate public-opinion data about citizens' democratic ideals from the Allensbach surveys and the 1995–7 wave of the World Values surveys. Although I do not have access to the original data, published data, along with information I obtained from the principal investigators, permit a systematic comparison of democratic ideals across the East–West divide. Finally, I occasionally use the Eurobarometer and Social Justice surveys when indicators in these sources match the conceptual questions this book examines.

Three Possible Caveats. This project uses the opportunities which Germany's historical heritage offers to social scientists who are interested in the institutions–values nexus. Undoubtedly, Germany does not provide the conditions of a perfect laboratory; its historical legacy represents a natural quasi-experiment, not a genuine one. Consequently, a sceptic might note that there is some lack of control over additional variables which, perhaps, affect citizens' ideological values. For example, one may point to intra-German variation in political and cultural traditions which differ systematically across the East–West divide (e.g. the liberal tradition in the South-West and a lack of a comparable tradition in the East). However, given the logic of the three axioms developed in Chapter 2, such intra-German variations appear unlikely explanations for any systematic East–West differences over ideological values. For one thing, as this book will make plain, the patterns revealed throughout this study are best explained by the approach developed in Chapter 2 both on conceptual (lack of a better alternative model) and empirical grounds (e.g. cohort differences within the East cannot be explained by regional peculiarities in the West). In addition, by focusing on Berlin's political elites, the study further enhances the quasi-experimental character of the empirical analyses by controlling for most intra-German variations outside of Berlin. Certainly, one may not unduly stretch the notion of a quasi-experiment. But with appropriate caution, it is possible to utilize Germany's post-war legacy to examine the theoretical questions laid out in Chapter 2.

It would also be implausible to claim that a three-year panel study resolves the conversion versus generational replacement debate once and for all. Some individuals will undoubtedly adjust their ideological values after that period. For this reason, one would ideally reinterview the same individuals periodically to establish an even longer time series. Equally important, however, is the fact that analysts who subscribe to the conversion argument frequently provide no evidence at all or, at best, supply evidence from one time-point only. A panel study spanning three years therefore provides more evidence than has been previously available. In addition, the panel study focuses on political elites, who are intensely exposed to the institutional learning process. If *they* are slow to adjust their ideological values to the democratic system, it would provide substantial evidence for the slow pace at which ideological values change after institutions change.

Finally, it is important to forestall any unclarity about the level of analysis in this study. Clearly, the processes of institutional learning established by an institutional framework and the diffusion of values are located at the systemic level. The subsequent focus on individuals as the main level of analysis means that the observations are removed a considerable distance in time and space from the actual processes. Consequently, the different levels of analysis require considerable caution as the arguments progress from the macro-level (political processes and diffusion) to the micro-level (institutional learning) and, ultimately, back to the macro-level (system's stability). Yet, given Germany's division and unification, one may conceptualize the impact of these two macro-processes on citizens' political values, and then derive empirical predictions based upon this conceptualization. In short, this study suggests that the conditions created by Germany's division and unification have narrowed the gap between the macro-factors and individuals' values sufficiently that it is possible to investigate the confluence of these macro-processes on Germans' ideological values.[6]

THE RULES OF INFERENCE

Germany's 'quasi-laboratory' conditions allow one, with due caution, to attribute East–West differences over political and economic values to the different systems, provided that the institutional learning axiom predicts these differences. The historical synopsis highlights the centralized and authoritarian nature of the GDR and describes the democratic system in the West. Consequently, if a majority of western Germans, for example, strongly support democratic rights (e.g. free speech, the right to demonstrate) while a majority of eastern Germans does not endorse such rights, it would document the effect of institutional learning. Such a finding would also provide little support for the diffusion of values. If, in contrast, relatively strong support for democratic rights emerges in the East, it is plausible to conclude that democratic values diffused into the East. These hypothetical examples —and there are many more conceivable combinations—illustrate that East–West differences, along with the absolute levels of support for a value domain, provide important evidence needed to test the institutional learning and diffusion axioms. Two central rules of testing these axioms can thus be summarized as follows:

(1) Support for the institutional learning axiom emerges if substantial East–West differences emerge at both mass and elite levels and a large majority in the West supports a democratic value while only a small minority in the East does.

Conversely,

(2) Support for the diffusion axiom emerges if negligible East–West differences emerge at both mass and elite levels and if a large majority in the West and the East support a democratic value.

Of course, rarely do the empirical patterns neatly fit only one of these scenarios; it is more likely that the evidence reveals components of both. Given my theoretical aims, it is still useful to remember these two broad decision rules in the ensuing chapters, because the criteria direct attention to the most relevant evidence. The institutional learning axiom leads us to expect that East–West differences are large and also stresses the absolute support for a value domain. The diffusion axiom predicts small East–West differences and also stresses the absolute level of support for democratic values. Thus, detecting East–West differences is only the first step in validating the institutional learning axiom. It is possible, for instance, that a majority of citizens in the East and the West *reject* a democratic value, but that eastern Germans do so more strongly than western Germans (political tolerance is a case in point; see Chapter 6). Such evidence would clearly point to the lack of successful democratic institutional learning in the West. Conversely, it is possible that East–West differences emerge and that a majority of respondents supports a democratic value, but more strongly in the West than in the East (general democratic values represent an example; see Chapter 5). In this case, there is evidence for diffusion, but also for institutional learning.

The comparison of mass–elite values within the East and the West provides a different angle to test the institutional learning and diffusion axioms. If diffusion processes dominate the formation of individuals' political and economic values, eastern elites are expected to be more supportive of democratic values than the eastern mass public (see Chapter 2). In contrast, if institutional learning is the strongest effect on individuals' ideological values, eastern elites are expected to be more supportive of socialist ideological values than the eastern publics. To simplify the formulation of this decision criterion somewhat—and to anticipate a central result of the ensuing chapters —I focus the third decision criterion on the evidence for diffusion:

(3) Support for the diffusion axiom emerges if eastern elites are more democratic than the eastern public.

In addition to testing the central arguments, the analysis of mass values also helps to overcome one potential problem in examining the diffusion axiom exclusively at the elite level: it is possible, indeed likely, that any convergence of eastern elites' values toward those of western elites may in part be due to the selective recruitment of the most democratic individuals within the East. Because western German political parties exercised a heavy hand in the selection and nomination of candidates for political office in the East, candidates who had close ties to the GDR had fewer chances to be elected than citizens who were politically 'untainted'. I cannot completely eliminate this problem. But the parallel analyses of ideological values at the elite and mass level reduces it for two reasons. First, if East–West differences are small at the mass and elite levels, selective recruitment of democratic elites, naturally, cannot explain any East–West similarity at the mass level. Instead, one may plausibly conclude that value diffusion led to a value convergence among elites and mass publics (assuming that aggregate support for democratic values is strong; see the second rule).[7] Secondly, if mass–elite contrasts are similar in the East *and* the West, the unique recruitment process in eastern Berlin alone is an unlikely cause for the similar mass–elite contrasts. Instead, this would also point to the cognitive sophistication of eastern elites—and thus their greater exposure to diffusion processes—as one important factor in why they are more democratic than the eastern German public.[8] Clearly, none of the evidence alone can rule out entirely that selective recruitment of democratic elites leads to a value-convergence at the elite level. I do suggest, however, that the cumulative evidence from these various analyses will show that diffusion processes are partly responsible for any value convergence across the former East–West divide.

Fortunately, the over-recruitment of the democratic spectrum in the East also has an unintended beneficial effect as far as the validity of the conclusions from this study are concerned. If one finds, as I do for most value domains, that substantial East–West differences emerge at the elite level, it would attest to the effects of institutional learning *despite* the selective recruitment of the most democratic elite in the East.

Thus, the three decision rules help us to focus on the most relevant aspects of the multitude of empirical findings encountered in this research. This study, in sum, uses the two Berlin surveys and available public surveys to examine: (1) the degree to which East–West differences exist at the elite and mass level; (2) the absolute support for a value domain at both levels; and (3) whether mass–elite differences over ideological values are similar within the East and the West.

5

Democratic Ideals

I think entirely in dialectical terms.
(An eastern CDU-MP explains how he evaluates political issues:
R 52)

Every institutional framework relies on preconceptions about those values which a society ought to emphasize. These values also prescribe the process by which a community may achieve these goals. Western democracies, for example, are predominately founded on the premiss that individual liberties are best realized by solving societal conflicts through representative institutions. Representative democracies also favour a market economy because market systems presumably maximize individual freedoms. In contrast, a socialist system emphasizes economic equality before political liberties and rejects an economic order that emphasizes private property relations. In short, diverse ideological systems cast key concepts differently, such as the meaning of democracy or the relationship between individual liberty and economic equality.

This chapter uses the systemic variations existing in Germany between 1949 and 1989 to examine the validity of the institutional learning and diffusion axioms. Did the socialist system instil socialist ideals into eastern Germans? Do western Germans hold representative-parliamentary ideals? How do eastern and western Germans evaluate liberal-democratic procedures? How do citizens evaluate plebiscitarian procedures? In order to answer these questions, this chapter first discusses the basic logic of representative, socialist, and plebiscitarian democracies. Such a thumbnail discussion must necessarily omit many variations within different political traditions; however, I wish to accomplish two objectives, namely: (1) to summarize the essential features of the ideological foundations within two different systems in eastern and western Germany; and (2) to describe the rationale that lies behind the institutional features (e.g. why socialism favours social equality over political liberty). This discussion is useful because the in-depth interviews with MPs provide ample material to examine whether the rationale underlying alternative political orders is reflected in elites' reasoning about alternative political ideals. On the basis of this discussion, the next section applies the institutional learning and diffusion axioms to the context in eastern and western Germany to develop eight testable hypotheses. The third section presents the empirical evidence from the two elite surveys and public-opinion data. A fourth section discusses the democratic ideals of East-Central Europeans. Finally, the conclusion highlights the main implications of this chapter for Germany and the two axioms.

THREE MODELS OF DEMOCRACY

Over the centuries, such political philosophers as Rousseau, Locke, and Madison developed a variety of democratic ideas. As these theorists strove to design a political system that provides political rights and makes effective public policies, each theorist made a distinct contribution. Despite the breadth of democratic theory, it is useful to take three basic democratic traditions as the point of departure— representative, social-egalitarian, and plebiscitarian traditions—to outline the foundations of the eastern and western German political systems.[1]

Representative Democracy. Until the seventeenth century, the Athenian model exemplified democratic conceptions in which no distinction existed between representatives and those represented. In classical Athens, men who qualified as citizens—slaves and women, for example, were excluded from enjoying full political rights—met regularly in order to decide Athenian affairs. In order to maximize citizens' control over their lives, the office terms of elected officials were limited, frequently lasting only one year, and officials were often barred from re-election (Held 1987: ch. 1). This direct-democracy model defined what democracy connoted until the evolution of the nation-state required the establishment of political systems that extend political equality to all citizens of large territorial units (Dahl 1989: ch. 15). Liberal theorists developed the perspective that nation-states are best governed by representative institutions in which the elected officers 'undertake to represent the interests and/or views of citizens within the framework of the "rule of the law" ' (Held 1987: 4). The central objective of liberal-representative theorists was to guarantee individual liberties while simultaneously providing the nation-state with those means needed to secure trade, commerce, or defence (Held 1993). Liberal-democratic theorists subsequently focused on developing a set of rules—checks and balances, for example—which would balance the demand for equal political treatment of all citizens with the need for political procedures which would make effective public policies. The idea of political representation thus represents an important advance in institutional design which meets this demand. On the one hand, citizens select leaders—a mechanism providing the populace with a voice in the political process. On the other hand, actual decisions are made by a relatively small representative body, enabling it to debate issues and make public policies.

Proponents of representative democracy regard several attributes of representative systems as advantageous (Cronin 1989: ch. 2). Representative systems moderate societal conflicts by channelling citizens' interest into deliberative institutions, such as a representative parliament. Citizens may influence the political process through elections or membership in parties and interest groups, but they are barred from directly deciding public policies. The quality of the political process, in this view, is enhanced by the removal of publics from the immediate decision-making process, because political elites posses the education and skills needed to solve complex problems. Likewise, representative institutions provide for greater stability in public policies since the political process is removed from fickle public sentiments. Defenders of representative democracy often question the ability of ordinary citizens to decide governmental affairs. For example, Sartori argues the superiority of a representative system by noting that 'democracy is terribly difficult. It is so difficult that only expert and accountable elites can save it from the excesses of perfectionism, from the vortex of demagogy, and from the degeneration of the *lex majoris partis*' (Sartori 1967: 119). By the twentieth century, when universal suffrage became a widely accepted democratic standard in the West, representative democracy came to be associated with such elements as free, fair, and universal elections, civil liberties, parliamentary democracy, and associational autonomy (Dahl 1971).

In order to maximize individual political liberties within large territories, proponents of representative systems also favour an economic order based upon private property (MacPherson 1977). This presumption directly flows from the premiss of liberal theorists that citizens ought to make as many decisions as possible without the restraining influence of governments—including those that concerns one's market position:

> The claim that the liberal-democratic society maximizes individual utilities (and does so equitably) may be reduced to be an economic claim. It is in substance a claim that the market economy of individual enterprise and individual rights of unlimited appropriation, i.e., the capitalist market economy, with the requisite social and political institutions, maximizes individual utilities and does so equitably. (MacPherson 1977, 6).

Undoubtedly, this 'classical' view of liberal theories about the benevolent nature of unfettered market-competition underwent significant revisions, especially from the nineteenth century onwards. Not only does socialism argue that uneven economic resources may have undesired effects for the equity of individuals' political equality (see below), but liberal theorists themselves seek solutions to the negative repercussions of market forces within a liberal-democratic framework (MacPherson 1977; Dahl 1989). For example, in the context of European welfare states, the provision of basic social needs helps to temper the undesired repercussions that the lack of economic resources may have for individual political liberties. Yet, in juxtaposition to socialism, representative democracy continues to prefer a market economy over alternative economic orders because such systems produce the maximum amount of political liberty for the greatest possible number of individuals.

In sum, central to a liberal democracy are the assumptions: (a) that liberal-democratic rights must be extended to all citizens of a community; (b) that liberty and democracy primarily connote a system where political procedures maximize individuals' political and economic opportunities, but without providing economic security; (c) that participation in politics is limited to selecting leaders and to influencing politics through intermediate organizations; and (d) that a market-based political order is the most appropriate economic system to assure civil liberties.

Socialist Democracy. Representative-democratic conceptions and their institutional corollaries have been challenged, especially by the socialist critique of a representative democracy. Socialist ideology evolved in reaction to the desolate conditions of many individuals during the period of industrialization in the nineteenth century. Two intellectual fathers of contemporary socialism, Karl Marx and Friedrich Engels, criticized liberal-representative perspectives for disregarding the close connection between political liberty and economic equality. In particular, Marx argued that 'man is not an abstract being squatting outside of the world. Man is the human world, the state, society' (*The Critique of Hegel's Philosophy of Right*, as quoted in Held 1987: 106). One central element of individuals' environment which shapes their political opportunities is the economic order. In juxtaposition to many liberal-representative proponents, Marx maintained that individual liberty is impossible to attain within the context of market-based economies because the potential for vast differences of economic resources leads to uneven opportunities in influencing the political process. Those who own capital, land, and machines are in a much better position to influence political affairs, and therefore ultimately have more individual freedoms, than those who have only their labour to sell under increasingly competitive market conditions. In short, how much political liberty a person enjoys depends largely on the economic resources one commands. Although contemporary advocates of the welfare state (who frequently endorse representative systems) also acknowledge the linkage between political opportunities and economic resources, a major difference separates these advocates from socialist proponents. Socialism promotes the abolishment of the right to own private property in order to resolve the uneven influence of resource-rich competitors on political decisions, whereas proponents of the welfare state seek to ease economic inequality within the framework of a *social* market order which maintains the right to own private property.

The close bond between economic equality and political liberty in socialism—or the connection between type of economic system and type of political system—entails that socialism rejects the notion of a neutral liberal political state. The liberal-representative tradition (e.g. Locke, Hobbes) views the state as a neutral arbiter between competing social groups. But, according to Marx, the liberal state cannot be neutral because it already sides with a particular economic system —the chief task of the liberal state is to preserve a capitalist system. 'The state in a capitalist society, Marx concluded (a conclusion which became central to his overall teachings), cannot escape its dependence upon that society and, above all, upon those who own and control the productive process' (Held 1987: 117). Thus, socialism is based on the premiss that a representative-democratic system cannot function as a neutral mediator between contending societal interests because those with strong resources are better served by these institutions than those with fewer economic resources (see also Chapter 7). In contrast, contemporary welfare proponents attribute to the political realm an independent capacity to regulate economic conflicts, thus accepting the idea that these institutions may serve as arbiters among contending economic interests.

Given this view on the link between a market-based economic order and liberal-representative institutions, Marx rejected representative-parliamentary institutions and instead favoured the direct participation of individuals in the political process. Although Marx did not develop specific institutions to be implemented after the predicted revolution occurred, his observation about the Paris communes suggests that he favoured a pyramid direct democracy structure (Held 1987: 130; Dahl 1989). Thus, for my purposes at this point, it is important to note that socialism emphasizes the close connection between the political and economic spheres, and the impossibility of resolving economic interests satisfactorily within representative, market-based institutions.

In sum, without attempting to chart a complete history of socialist ideology, it is reasonable to state that socialism: (1) supposes the existence of a close connection between political liberty and social equality; (2) views private property relations as the main cause of political inequalities; (3) rejects representative institutions; and (4) rejects the notion of a 'neutral' liberal state.

Direct Democracy. A second challenge to liberal-representative institutions derives from the Athenian model of a direct democracy. This early democratic model is also called plebiscitarian democracy which, in its generic form, is a 'system of decision making about public affairs in which citizens are directly involved' (Held 1987: 4). This classical model of a democratic system assumes that citizens must decide their own affairs directly in order to attain personal liberty and self-determination. Consequently, contemporary proponents of plebiscitarian procedures argue that existing representative institutions in advanced democracies should be supplemented with direct democratic procedures in order to increase the influence of citizens in the political process (Pateman 1970; Barber 1984).

A number of assumptions unite both contemporary and classical models of direct democracies (Cronin 1989: Chapter 7). Proponents of a direct democracy believe that self-government and political liberty require citizens to be extensively involved in deciding their affairs. In contrast to representative perspectives, this view contends that participation in periodic elections is not enough to democratize a political system. This assumption reflects a belief that citizens are capable of finding reasonable solutions to public problems.[2] While contemporary proponents of direct democratic procedures concede that citizens frequently lack the expert knowledge to make public policy decisions, they also contend that there are safeguards within a direct democratic framework against abuses from a presumably fickle and uneducated citizenry (Barber 1984). Further, direct democratic procedures may actually enhance the political sophistication of citizens by increasing their involvement in political discussions (Pateman 1970). For example, direct democratic procedures, such as national referenda, may increase trust in governmental institutions among citizens.

It must be noted that both representative and plebiscitarian democratic variants aim to maximize the political liberty of citizens; these models do not represent diametrically opposed views on the ideal-typical democracy. This is reflected in the work of such advocates as Pateman and Barber who wish to supplement, not replace, representative institutions with plebiscitarian components. Despite this similarity in terms of their long-range objectives, however, both views envisage rather different political realities. In contrast to a representative system, a plebiscitarian democracy assumes that: (1) plebiscitarian procedures approximate the democratic ideal better than representative procedures; (2) these procedures allow for greater self-determination than representative institutions; (3) direct democratic procedures are likely to have positive repercussions for citizens' political sophistication; and (4) these procedures ultimately increase the legitimacy of a political system.

In sum, the three models of democracy differ significantly in terms of their ideological premises. Proponents of a liberal democracy suppose that societal conflicts are best resolved by periodically elected elites who reconcile diverging societal interests within the framework of representative institutions. Advocates of plebiscitarian procedures, in turn, wish to supplement representative institutions with the direct involvement of citizens in order to enhance individuals' political liberty. And socialist conceptions of a democracy focus on the economic basis of political liberty, arguing that economic equality must be established to attain political liberty for the populace.

Predicting Democratic Values and
Ideals in Eastern and Western Germany

What predictions about democratic ideals may be derived when one applies the institutional learning and diffusion axioms to eastern and western Germany? Are the ideological foundations of socialism and parliamentarism reflected in the democratic values of citizens in the East and the West? To begin with, a liberal-democratic system requires the existence of basic freedoms, such as freedom of opinion, free elections, the right to oppose a government, or the right to demonstrate—characteristics that Dahl (1989: 222) and others view as essential elements in a liberal democracy. Based on the institutional learning axiom, one would expect eastern Germans to be less likely to support liberal-democratic rights. In contrast, the parliamentary democracy established in 1949 ought to be reflected in support for democratic rights in the West:

- Hypothesis 1: *Eastern Germans are less supportive of liberal-democratic rights than western Germans.*

Furthermore, western Germans born after the end of the Second World War were exposed to the institutional learning of a parliamentary system, whereas the pre-war generation in western Germany also experienced the authoritarian influence of the Third Reich. In contrast, pre-war and post-war eastern Germans were exposed to authoritarian systems only. Therefore, the institutional learning effect —if driven by generational forces—should reflect cohort differences within western, but not eastern, Germany.

- Hypothesis 2: *Post-war cohorts are more supportive than pre-war cohorts of liberal-democratic rights in the West, but not in the East.*

The institutional learning axiom would thus predict that eastern and western Germans diverged over liberal-democratic rights during Germany's division. However, the diffusion axiom conflicts with these predictions by suggesting that liberal-democratic rights may have developed in eastern Germany despite the authoritarian political process. The diffusion axiom stipulates that value diffusion from the West into a socialist environment is possible if: (1) democratic values require little restraint and self-reliance; and (2) if the acceptance of democratic values requires only minor revisions of socialist beliefs.

Since support for general liberal-democratic rights meet these criteria (Chapter 2), the next hypothesis is:

- Hypothesis 3: *East–West differences in terms of liberal-democratic rights are small.*

As a further test of the presence of diffusion effects, consider that its effects should be felt differently across age-groups in the East. The diffusion perspective, combined with the notion of generational change, predicts that the democratic values of eastern and western Germans are 'pushed' toward convergence. Because the onset of the diffusion process falls into the post-war era (Pye 1990), its force should be felt primarily among the post-war generation of eastern Germans. In contrast, if institutional learning constitutes the dominant influence on younger MPs' evaluations of democratic principles, they should not be more supportive of democratic rights than citizens born before the Second Word War (H2). This hypothesis helps to determine whether diffusion affected ideological values because small aggregate East–West differences alone may also be attributed to the dispropor-tionate recruitment of democratic elites in the East. In the West, one would expect that MPs born after 1945 would be more democratic than MPs born before the war because post-war cohorts predominately experienced a democratic political system (Baker, Dalton, and Hildebrandt 1981; Eckstein 1988):

- Hypothesis 4: *Post-war cohorts in eastern and western Germany are more supportive of liberal-democratic rights than pre-war cohorts.*

With regard to democratic ideals, the institutional learning axiom also predicts that the ideological premises of socialist and parliamentary systems are reflected in citizens' democratic ideals: eastern Germans are expected to value social-egalitarian ideals. The generation-based expectation, which underlies several cultural models, also predicts that eastern Germans born after 1945 in the East especially espouse social-egalitarian ideals. In contrast, western Germans, especially those born after 1945, are expected to endorse represent-ative ideals, such as associational autonomy or party competition. These expectations are summarized in the following two hypotheses:

- Hypothesis 5: *Eastern Germans, especially those born after the Second World War, primarily endorse social-egalitarian democratic ideals.*

- Hypothesis 6: *Western Germans, especially those born after the Second World War, primarily endorse representative-democratic ideals.*

The final two hypotheses focus on eastern and western Germans' views on direct democratic procedures. There are two reasons to believe that eastern Germans are more likely than western Germans to support plebiscitarian procedures. First, the extensive involvement of citizens during the 1989 revolution undoubtedly sensitized eastern Germans to the importance of citizens' involvement in politics. Had it not been for the so-called Monday demonstrations of ordinary citizens in eastern Germany in 1989, the upheavals in 1989 may have taken a different course. Secondly, while socialist systems did not endorse independent involvement of masses in politics, socialist ideology did endorse the direct mobilization of masses for socialist goals (Held 1987). While I will not be able to disentangle the relative importance of these processes, the logic of these arguments provides the basis for the seventh hypothesis:

- Hypothesis 7: *Eastern Germans are more supportive of plebiscitarian procedures than Western Germans.*

Finally, the generational model predicts that while all citizens in eastern Germany experienced the collapse of their political regime, post-war elites should be particularly affected by this experience because younger citizens are more likely to be shaped by this monumental event than older cohorts (Nagel 1994). In western Germany, the post-war cohort also ought to be more supportive of plebiscitarian procedures than pre-war ones, but for a different reason. The enormous transformation of western German society in the post-war decades led to the evolution of postmaterial values which fundamentally shaped the political preferences of western citizens, especially if they were born after the Second World War (Inglehart 1990; Dalton 1992). The central characteristic of postmaterialists is their greater emphasis on such non-material goals as individual self-fulfilment, participation in politics, or a cleaner environment. In contrast, materialists prioritize such political values as economic growth, traditional gender roles, or participating in politics through orthodox channels in parties and interest groups (Inglehart 1977). This transformation is manifested, for example, in the evolution of social movements in the 1970s and the success of the western German Green party. Since the emergence of postmaterial values especially affects the post-war cohort, post-war citizens in western Germany should be more supportive than pre-war elites of plebiscitarian procedures (Inglehart 1990; Dalton 1992). Therefore,

• Hypothesis 8: *The post-war cohorts in eastern and western Germany are more likely than pre-war cohorts to endorse plebiscitarian procedures.*

These eight hypotheses provide the analytical grid for the ensuing analyses of democratic ideals in eastern and western Germany.[3]

DEMOCRATIC IDEALS IN EASTERN AND WESTERN GERMANY

Let me precede the analyses with a brief note on the structure of the empirical section in each chapter. I proceed by first presenting eastern and western German views about the value in question—democratic rights and ideals in this chapter—after which I examine the degree to which individual MPs changed their views between 1992 and 1995. A third part, for reasons discussed below, analyses East–West differences within parties. A fourth part examines whether East–West differences persist as other potential causes of East–West differences over ideological values are held constant. Finally, to the extent possible, a fifth part will present evidence from other countries in order to show that the Germany-based findings are not unique.

Liberal-Democratic Rights. In discussing democratic rights in Germany, I asked MPs:

In order to get a comparable picture of the distribution of opinion with earlier studies, I am now using a standardized format to simplify matters a little bit. I am aware that these statements capture your views only incompletely. Nevertheless, would you tell me for each of the statements whether you agree or disagree?

MPs were shown a card containing a seven-point agree (7, 6, 5)–disagree (1, 2, 3) scale, where a neutral middle category (4) represents undecided views. To measure MPs' support for liberal-democratic rights, I asked them to evaluate the statements presented in Table 5.1. The first two statements measure MPs' commitment to democratic rights, while the other four pose a conflict between democratic rights

TABLE 5.1. *MPs' support for democratic rights* (%)

Democratic right	East		West
	1995	1992	1992
Per cent agreeing			
A. Every democracy requires a political opposition	98.5	100.0	100.0
B. Every citizen has the right to demonstrate	93.9	100.0	97.8
Per cent disagreeing			
C. A citizen forfeits the right to demonstrate and to strike when s/he threatens the political order	63.1	53.2	60.9
D. It is the primary duty of the political opposition to support the government, and not to criticize it	73.9	72.2	66.7
E. Freedom of opinion and discussion must be limited by moral and ethical considerations	24.6	27.1	43.7
F. The freedom of political propaganda is not an absolute freedom, and the state should carefully regulate its use	49.2	57.0	70.1

Note: See Appendix A for exact recodes.

and the public order (C, D, E, F) (Kaase 1971; Putnam 1973). Evidently, there is nearly unanimous support for democratic principles among MPs when these principles are evaluated without reference to a specific context (A, B). Contrary to the first hypothesis, eastern Germans are as supportive as western MPs of important liberal-democratic pillars. Support for democratic principles is significantly reduced when they conflict with another goal, such as moral or ethical considerations (D), or the stability of the political order (E). This reduction occurs in the East and the West and reflects the tendency for individuals to be less supportive of democratic rights when these conflict with order-related objectives (see also Chapter 6). There is some evidence that eastern MPs are more willing than western MPs to curtail individuals' democratic rights when these clash with other goals. However, the differences are fairly moderate, and eastern MPs are as supportive of democratic rights in 1995 as they were in 1992. On the whole, while eastern MPs are slightly less supportive of democratic rights than western MPs, both elite sectors demonstrate substantial support.

Considerable support for democratic rights also exists at the level of mass publics (Table 5.2). Although the response format in these

TABLE 5.2. *Publics' support for democratic rights* (%)

Democratic right	Western Germany						Eastern Germany					
	1990	1991	1992	1993	1995	1996	1990	1991	1992	1993	1995	1996
Per cent agreeing												
A. Every democracy requires a political opposition	93	95	95	92	92	93	95	96	93	90	96	92
B. Every citizen has the right to demonstrate	90	94	95	92	90	92	92	96	94	91	94	93
C. Everyone should have the right to express their opinion	92	97	97	93	90	98	98	98	96	94	96	94
D. Every democratic party should have a chance to govern	91	92	94	92	85	89	91	95	95	95	91	91
Per cent disagreeing												
E. A citizen forfeits the right to demonstrate and to strike when s/he threatens the political order	28	31	26	34	30	27	32	33	31	42	32	36
F. It is the primary duty of the political opposition to support the government and not to criticize it	39	41	39	47	39	40	42	33	41	38	41	47
G. In a democratic society, some conflicts require violence	79	86	87	81	n/a	n/a	88	78	81	82	n/a	n/a

Source: 1990: German idendity survey; 1991, 1992: Allensbach surveys; 1993: Russell Dalton (1994: 478); 1995 and 1996: Max Kaase (1997: 6).

public-opinion surveys lacks the neutral category used in the elite surveys, the empirical patterns indicate the near-unanimity with which the eastern and western public endorse democratic procedures (indicators A through D). Mass support for democratic rights is reduced substantially, however, when a democratic right conflicts with an order-related public good (statements E and F). As at the level of elites, East–West differences are fairly small, which suggests a broad consensus over basic political procedures in Germany after unification.

More variations emerge when the responses of mass publics are compared to those of MPs. This comparison reveals that political elites are more democratic than mass publics in the West *and* the East. For example, 40 per cent of the western public disagree in 1996 that the primary duty of the opposition is to support the government, whereas 66.7 per cent among western MPs disagree with this un-democratic proposition in 1992. The corresponding percentages are 47 per cent among the eastern public and 72.2 per cent among eastern MPs. Likewise, while 53.2 per cent of eastern MPs and 60.9 per cent of western MPs disagree with the notion that citizens lose the right to demonstrate when public order is threatened, these percentages are considerably lower among the eastern and western public in 1996 (36 and 27 per cent respectively). Indeed, because of the absence of a neutral response category in the mass surveys, these figures actually represent conservative estimates of mass–elite differences.[4]

The similarity of mass–elite contrasts in the East and the West indicates that the institutional learning process in the GDR has not substantially shaped eastern elites' evaluations of liberal-democratic rights. Eastern elites' strong endorsement of democratic rights cannot have been generated by their parliamentary experience which, at the time of the first survey, had at most lasted about one year. Instead, eastern elites' higher education—reflecting greater analytical skills and greater exposure to information from the West—apparently compensates for eastern MPs' lack of opportunities to practise democratic restraint during the reign of socialism. Just as the diffusion hypothesis predicts, eastern and western Germans endorse in principle, if not in practice, the democratic process; and eastern elites, who are more likely to be exposed to the diffusion of democratic values than the eastern public, are more democratic than the eastern public. Indeed, eastern MPs are considerably more likely than the *western* public to endorse liberal-democratic rights.

Still, it is important to recall that the mass–elite contrasts in the

East may, in part, be generated by the selective recruitment of the most democratic individuals in eastern Germany. Therefore, in order further to analyse the diffusion model, I examine whether cohort-related differences corroborate the generational (H2) or diffusion perspective (H4). If the acquisition of liberal-democratic values reflects one's generational experience, support for these rights should be about the same among pre-war and post-war cohorts in the East, because all eastern Germans lived in an authoritarian system since 1933. In contrast, if the diffusion process predominately shaped the acquisition of liberal-democratic rights, younger eastern Germans should be more supportive of liberal-democratic rights than older ones (H4). If H4 is confirmed, it would provide evidence for the effects of value diffusion, because such cohort differences cannot have been generated by the disproportionate recruitment of democratic elites. To test this prediction, I constructed a summary indicator based upon the statements presented in Table 5.1 and correlated this indicator with MPs' ages. This indicator was coded so that a high value represents democratic views. Indeed, younger eastern MPs are more supportive of liberal-democratic rights than older MPs ($r = -.24$). Relatedly, when an equivalent indicator at the mass level based on the 1990 German identity survey (see Table 5.2) is correlated with age, younger citizens among the eastern ($r = -.16$) and western ($r = -.14$) public are more democratic than older Germans; a result that parallels the result of a study by Russell Dalton about citizens' democratic views (Dalton 1994: 488).[5] Contrary to H4, however, support for democratic rights is unrelated to western MPs' age ($r = .01$). It appears that age-related differences, which may have existed among western MPs at the beginning of their parliamentary career, diminish because of their intense exposure to the parliamentary process (Rohrschneider 1994).

Overall, the strong support for liberal-democratic rights especially among younger eastern Germans is inconsistent with the hypotheses derived from a generational model of institutional learning (H1; H2) but corroborates the diffusion axiom (H3; H4).[6] Evidently, eastern Germans' inability to practice democratic restraint did not hinder the development of support for liberal-democratic rights, especially among younger eastern MPs. The central reason for the acceptance of democratic rights is undoubtedly eastern Germans' exposure to the western German democracy, which provided a viable alternative to the disliked socialist reality in the East. The mass–elite differences combined with the cohort analyses within the East further suggest that value diffusion affected mass and elite values in addition to the disproportionate recruitment of democratic elites in the East.

Egalitarian-Democratic Ideals. In spite of the agreement among eastern and western German publics and elites over democratic rights, it would be premature to conclude that eastern and western Germans essentially hold the same democratic *ideals*. One shortcoming of closed-ended questions that focus on the democratic process is that they may mask considerable differences in elites' democratic ideals. Accordingly, I asked MPs to define the core elements of a democracy in their own words: 'The term democracy is frequently used without further specifications these days. What seem to you personally to be the essentials of a democracy?'

This open-ended question elicited a wide range of responses, but the basic patterns can be summarized as indicated in Table 5.3. (Appendix A contains the original code categories and recodes used for this table). The table displays the percentage of MPs mentioning at least one democratic component. Because I coded up to six components, the percentages total more than 100 per cent.

A large number of MPs began this discussion by mentioning at least one civil right (individual liberty, freedom of expression, etc.) as an important component of a democratic system, both in the East (64.6 per cent) and the West (73.0 per cent). The following response by a western SPD-MP exemplifies this type of discussion:

First, government by the people. That is, any political activity is legitimized by the people, either directly or indirectly. Second, a present minority should have the opportunity to become the majority . . . This means that basic civil liberties are guaranteed, such as the right to participate in politics—now I am going to mention a litany of civil rights. (R10)

Another western MP also started her discussion by referring to civil liberties (to preserve the anonymity of MPs, I refer to even-numbered interviews with a male and odd-numbered ones with female pronoun):

Checks and balances, free elections, the rule of law and, of course, the freedom to organize groups, and more generally individual liberties. (R7)

Within the East, pre-war MPs are more likely to mention civil rights (77.1 per cent) than post-war MPs (55.9 per cent), whereas there are no clear age differences among western MPs. Further, a quarter of eastern and western MPs mention at least one 'government by the people' component (e.g. popular control). Finally, eastern MPs

TABLE 5.3. *MPs' conceptions of democracy, by cohort* (%)

Democratic component	East		West
	1995	1992	1992
Government by the people	13.9	26.6	25.8
Pre-war	20.0	24.4	26.1
Post-war	6.7	29.4	25.6
Social equality	46.2	35.4	7.9
Pre-war	40.0	28.9	10.9
Post-war	53.3	44.1	4.7
Active participation	6.2	17.7	12.4
Pre-war	8.6	13.3	13.0
Post-war	3.3	23.5	11.0
Direct democracy	35.4	25.3	2.2
Pre-war	25.7	13.3	0.0
Post-war	46.7	41.2	4.7
Equality of opportunity	1.5	3.8	7.9
Pre-war	—	2.2	4.3
Post-war	3.3	5.9	11.6
Civil rights/limited government	80.0	64.6	73.0
Pre-war	77.1	77.1	69.6
Post-war	83.3	55.9	76.7
Institutions	56.9	40.5	60.7
Pre-war	57.1	51.1	58.7
Post-war	56.7	26.5	62.8
Political competition	9.2	20.3	30.3
Pre-war	11.4	22.2	32.6
Post-war	6.7	17.6	27.9
Societal competition	4.6	17.7	19.1
Pre-war	8.6	17.8	15.2
Post-war	—	17.6	23.3
Citizens' responsibility	18.5	8.9	7.9
Pre-war	28.6	6.2	13.0
Post-war	6.7	11.8	2.3
(N)			
Both cohorts	(65)	(79)	(87)
Pre-war	(35)	(45)	(44)
Post-war	(30)	(34)	(43)

Note: Entries are percentages mentioning one or more democratic component. Multiple responses were allowed. See Appendix A for details on the question wording and recodes.

mention civil liberties more frequently in 1995 than in 1992; this conversion is especially noticeable among post-war MPs in the East. Consistent with the results from the analysis of closed-ended indicators, eastern and western parliamentarians associate civil rights and popular control of a government with a democracy.

Despite this overarching consensus on the importance of civil liberties, MPs differ with respect to the social equality component. Specifically, eastern MPs are substantially more likely than western MPs to link social-egalitarian guarantees to an ideal-typical democracy. The following quotations illustrate the social-egalitarian bent of eastern MPs. One eastern SPD-MP argues:

A democratic system requires that everybody has a basic right [*Grundrecht*] to a job. Everybody should also be guaranteed the provision of basic material needs. (R26)

Another eastern MP from the Bündnis '90/Greens questions the relevance of political liberties when a democracy does not guarantee basic social services to its citizens:

A government should have far-reaching goals which include the right to work and to housing. I just think that nobody should be without shelter. To be sure, I don't want to abolish civil liberties. But how valuable are civil liberties, when one doesn't enjoy the protection of a social safety net? (R46)

And one eastern SPD-MP firmly argues that a bourgeois democracy cannot be a genuine democracy because:

the political system that exists now [in Germany] is not a real democracy. Parties pretend to represent the people, but they are actually controlled by big capital. (R138)

These are not isolated criticisms of market-based political systems. Over one-third of eastern MPs argue that guaranteeing a just standard of living or providing social security for everybody should be an important obligation of a democracy; and this proportion exceeds 44 per cent among MPs born in the post-war years. In contrast, only 7.9 per cent in the West mentions this component. It is not that western MPs reject the notion of a welfare state; many of them are as supportive as eastern MPs in providing the needy with basic material goods in case of personal emergencies (see the evidence presented about welfare views in Chapter 8). However, unlike eastern MPs, the provision of these goods is not linked to western MPs' ideal-typical conception of the *political* framework. Thus, unlike liberal-democratic rights, which tend to be supported especially by younger eastern MPs, the prevalence of social-egalitarian ideals among post-war MPs attests to the absence of diffusion of liberal ideals from the West into the East. Instead, the results corroborate the institutional learning axiom and are consistent with the generational model (see Bürklin 1996 and Welzel 1997 for similar evidence about national elites in Germany).

Surprisingly, social-egalitarian ideals are even more important in 1995 than they were in 1992—a clear indication that the conversion of MPs toward liberal-democratic ideals does not follow a linear path. Almost half of eastern MPs interviewed in 1995 mention at least one social-egalitarian component. Further, as discussed below, I find the same tendency with respect to plebiscitarian ideals and other value domains (see Chapters 6 and 8). This aggregate dynamic, then, suggests a modest, but systematic, movement *away* from liberal ideals over the three-year period.

Do mass publics in eastern and western Germany share MPs' egalitarian preferences? In a series of public-opinion surveys conducted after the fall of the Berlin Wall, citizens in the East and West chose from a list those components which they associate with a democracy (Table 5.4). Since the list contains liberal-democratic, egalitarian, and plebiscitarian components, the responses gauge respondents' democratic ideals. One drawback of this measure is that respondents were permitted to select any number of statements. The response format inflates the frequency with which components are chosen because citizens were not asked to weigh the relative importance of each component. This response format also limits the comparability of results from the mass and elite surveys, because the open-ended format in the elite survey encourages MPs to mention those components which figure prominently in their ideological thinking. However, the public-opinion surveys do provide an opportunity to analyse whether East–West differences over democratic ideals also exist at the level of mass publics.

As at the elite level, eastern and western publics link liberal-democratic rights to their understanding of a democracy; civil liberties, party competition, and a strong opposition are mentioned as key components of a democratic system. This emphasis parallels the strong support of both publics for liberal-democratic rights. Furthermore, a large proportion of respondents mentions these components at all three time-points. As on the elite level, considerable support for democratic rights exists among the eastern and western public. In the

TABLE 5.4. *Publics' conceptions of democracy* (%)

Democratic component	East			West		
	1990	1991	1992	1990	1991	1992
Political liberties						
Freedom of the press and opinion, that everyone can freely express their political opinions	92	83	90	91	89	94
That one can choose from several parties	85	70	82	87	85	91
That free elections with secret ballots are held regularly	84	66	78	83	82	84
Independent courts that judge only according to the law	76	62	78	74	77	78
That everyone can freely practise their religion	83	60	71	79	71	72
That one can travel freely anywhere in the country	76	53	65	78	69	76
A strong opposition that keeps the government in check	70	62	62	65	66	62
That no one is disadvantaged because he belongs to an extreme party	39	31	27	39	35	31
Economic/social equality						
That business firms may be privately held	—	45	47	—	62	61
That income differencees are not very great	44	44	38	22	26	25
That employees may participate in decision making at the workplace	73	62	58	60	54	54
Nobody suffers from want	72	61	52	50	54	45
Citizen participation						
That citizens can decide about important issues in referenda	75	68	71	52	57	57
That citizens can participate in many government decisions	68	57	58	55	57	57
The right to strike for higher wages and more jobs	—	67	63	—	63	61

Sources: For 1990 and 1991: *Allensbacher Jahrbuch der Demoskopie* 9: 558–9. The 1992 data, also based on a Allensbach survey, were provided by Frederick D. Weil.

context of these rights, then, support for the diffusion hypothesis is strengthening.

However, as on the level of elites, differences across the East–West divide emerge regarding social egalitarianism. Two statements in the surveys approximately tap individuals' egalitarian predispositions, namely: (1) business firms should be allowed to be privately owned; and (2) income differences should not be very great. These indicators focus on establishing a ceiling for income differences, and link the political order to a market economy. Less than half of the eastern public associate a market-based order with a democracy even at the end of 1993 (the last survey was conducted in December 1993), whereas almost two-thirds of the western public make this connection. Further, almost half of the eastern public associate a 'true' democracy with income differences that are not too great, whereas this proportion hovers at around 25 per cent among western Germans. Over three years into Germany's unification, eastern citizens continue to base their vision of an ideal democracy on social-egalitarianism. The greater egalitarian emphasis of the eastern public parallels the basic tendency found at the level of elites: liberal-democratic rights are valued by the eastern and western public, but eastern Germans tend to place them within an egalitarian context.

How do ordinary citizens evaluate socialist and liberal ideals when they clash? One important difference between a socialist and parliamentary democracy is the different emphasis assigned to individual freedom and social equality. Although freedom and social equality may be reconciled to some degree within a parliamentary democracy— this synthesis, after all, is manifested in European welfare traditions— socialist systems curtail individual liberties in order to promote social equality (e.g. nationalize private industries). In contrast, parliamentary systems accept some degree of social inequality as the price to be paid for individual liberties (e.g. the right to own private property). One measure of eastern and western Germans' views toward democratic ideals, therefore, consists in the relative priority which citizens attach to these partially conflicting goals.

In a series of public-opinion surveys conducted by the Allensbacher Institute for Public Opinion research, eastern and western Germans were asked to choose between freedom and social equality:

Two people are talking about what is ultimately more important, freedom or as much equality as possible. Would you please read this and tell me which of the two comes closest to saying what you also think?

A. 'I think that freedom and equality are equally important. But if I had to choose between the two, I would say personal freedom is more important; that is, for people to be able to live in freedom and not be restricted in their development.'

B. 'Certainly both freedom and equality are equally important. But if I had to choose between the two, I would consider as much equality as possible to be more important; that is, for no one to be underprivileged and class differences not to be so strong.'

These statements explicitly recognize the desirability of both goals; and they pose a conflict between them so that respondents must choose one or the other. Since liberal and socialist democracies provide different solutions to reconciling political liberty with social equality, the responses to this question tap an important component of eastern and western publics' democratic ideals.

There is a clear tendency among eastern Germans to emphasize social equality over political liberty (Fig. 5.1). With the exception of the first time-point (March 1990), eastern citizens select social equality as the more important goal. In fact, the percentage choosing social equality increases until about the end of 1992 and stabilizes at that level. Although there is a slight reduction by 1995, this decline does not indicate a reversal toward a greater emphasis on political liberties in the East as the increase by the end of 1997 documents. Seven years into Germany's unification, a majority of eastern Germans not only value social equality, but *prefers* it over political freedoms. In stark contrast, western citizens are considerably more likely to select political freedom over social equality. Although the emphasis on social equality increases slightly in the West, political freedom is undoubtedly the more important value among the western public. At the same time, there is a moderate but steady decline in the proportion selecting freedom over equality in the West. It is too early to tell whether the persistent economic problems erode the western public's commitment to political freedoms. This trend, therefore, ought to be monitored in future surveys. On the whole, however, these results parallel the different emphases found at the elite level. Equally important, the persistence of social-egalitarianism in the East undermines the conversion model at the mass level. Evidently, eastern Germans would prefer a socialist system infused with political liberties.

This conclusion about the persistence of socialist ideals is strongly buttressed by eastern Germans' summary evaluation of socialist ideals when these are divorced from the way socialism was practised in the

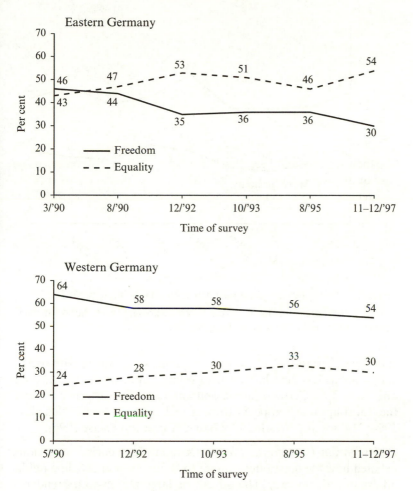

FIG. 5.1. Freedom versus equality among the Eastern and Western publics
Source: Noelle-Neumann (1995; 1998).

GDR (Fig. 5.2). When asked, 'Do you think that socialism was a good idea that was badly implemented,' a considerable majority of eastern Germans believes that these ideals were poorly implemented, not that the idea itself was wrong-headed. The percentage of respondents that continues to believe in the virtues of socialism reaches almost 70 per cent in 1997. Just as the institutional learning axiom predicts (H1), a

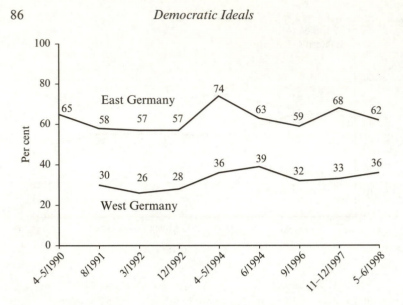

FIG. 5.2. 'Socialism is a good idea which was badly implemented'

(*Note*: Entries are percentages of respondents who agree with the statement.)
Source: Allensbacher Institut für Demoskopie.

substantial proportion of the eastern public sympathizes with socialism, whereas less than half of the western public holds this view. As
one student of German public opinion notes, for eastern Germans,
the 'third approach appears to be a real option' (Noelle-Neumann
1994: 218; see also Westle 1994; Bauer-Kaase and Kaase 1996).

Plebiscitarian-Democratic Ideals. Democratic theorists have long
debated how the mass public ought to be involved in deciding public
affairs in a democracy. The advent of large nation-states rendered
the Athenian model impractical, but there is a significant debate in
western democracies about devolving decision-making powers from
representative institutions to the broader public (Barber 1984; Cronin
1989). For example, social movements began to demand a greater involvement of ordinary citizens in the political process throughout the
1970s and 1980s; a development in the West that is attributed to a
transformation of advanced democracies and the resulting postmaterial value-change (Inglehart 1977; Dalton and Küchler 1990). The
Green movement in western Germany has been a persistent advocate
of widening the role of citizens in the political process through, for

example, direct democratic procedures. Eastern Germans, in contrast, were less exposed to the forces of advanced societies. But the distrust of socialism in representative bodies and the role of ordinary citizens in the 1989 revolution may have generated an appreciation of the ability of ordinary citizens to make important contributions to the political process. Therefore, to understand the institutional preferences of masses and elites in contemporary Germany, it is crucial to know how eastern and western Germans view citizens' proper role in politics.

The open-ended question about democratic ideals provides important information with respect to both elites and publics' evaluations of plebiscitarian ideals. As the institutional learning axiom predicts (H7), about a quarter (25.3 per cent) of eastern MPs mention at least one direct democracy procedure, whereas only 2.2 per cent in the West mention such an element (Table 5.3). One member of the eastern German opposition movement, for example, argued in 1992—and repeated the same theme in 1995—that:

citizens should be able to participate in political decisions in various ways. One possibility would be to give them the right to recall politicians, including ministers, at any time. Frequently, decisions are made against the interests of citizens . . . Basic civil liberties then run the danger of becoming meaningless. (R14)

Another eastern PDS-MP concurs when he suggests that:

Democracy in its original meaning means rule by the people. A bourgeois democracy pretends to represent the interests of the people through elections. In my view, democracy means simply that people really rule . . . Some details have to be decided by politicians . . . but only during a transitional period, until a full plebiscitarian democracy has been established. A representative parliament should exist only during a transitional period. (R32)

Further, a member of the eastern opposition movement, who also prefers a social-egalitarian democracy, argues in 1995:

Citizens should be able to participate in political decisions between elections through the possibility of participating in the legislative process. Citizens, for instance, should have the right to apply for permission to speak [in the federal parliament] during the formal legislative process. (R46)

The central difference between eastern and western Germans with respect to citizens' direct participation is that western Germans frequently prefer active participation within the framework of a representative democracy, because western MPs for the most part assume that representative institutions are superior decision-making bodies which are guided by expertise and rationality. In contrast, eastern MPs frequently hold a deep distrust in the ability of representative institutions to represent citizens adequately in the political process and frequently wish to replace, not supplement, these institutions.

These different assumptions about the sophistication (or lack thereof) of citizens emerged with particular clarity when MPs evaluated whether the issue of political refugees should be decided through a referendum. This issue constituted a pressing problem at the time of the first interview period (October 1991–June 1992), when skinhead attacks on foreigners caught international attention and when the debate over so-called 'asylum-seekers' took on emotional overtones. Against this backdrop, most western MPs were against submitting this issue to a referendum (11.5 per cent supported a referendum), whereas almost one-third of eastern MPs (29.9 per cent) supported a referendum. This is a minority in the West and the East, but given the heated and controversial nature of the issue, the proportion of eastern MPs supporting a referendum is surprisingly large. More important for my purpose, at this juncture, are the reasons behind eastern and western MPs' decisions to favour or oppose a referendum. MPs' reasoning frequently could have been copied from a textbook on democratic theory. Consider the following accounts by a western MP from the SPD when she explains why a referendum would not be a good idea:

That's a difficult question . . . because the issue is so emotional. I am afraid that citizens would decide on the basis of these emotions and would not consider the objective factors . . . I am principally for trying to integrate citizens beyond representative institutions. But not in the context of this issue. (R27)

Another western MP from the CDU concurs:

I believe in involving citizens in the political process. They should be able to express their opinions so that these views can then be translated into policies by competent politicians. But I would be against a referendum because citizens would decide with their emotions and not consider the objective situation. (R 25)

The following western CDU-MP also rejects referenda categorically:

I am basically for a parliamentary democracy. Despite the problems that exist with this type of system, it is the best democratic form. I think that it is much better to make decisions through a representative system than involving citizens directly. (R18)

Just as western Germans tend to argue for the superiority of a representative system of decision-making, so several eastern Germans argue with equal fervour that citizens can be trusted to arrive at reasonable decisions. One leading eastern MP of the SPD, for example, alludes to the minimal role citizens had in the political system of the GDR when explaining why he prefers a referendum:

It is absolutely necessary. Because this issue involves important fears and concerns of the population. And that's why the population should be directly involved through a referendum, for example, in solving this problem. I would prefer this over deciding policies once again without regard for the concerns of citizens. (R20)

Clearly, eastern MPs are not oblivious to the dangers inherent in direct-democratic procedures. The following dialogue with a leading member of the eastern German opposition movement exemplifies the concern proponents of plebiscitarian procedures may have, even though this MP supports a referendum to solve this issue:

'Principally, I am for it. But in the context of the specific issue, I am afraid that eastern Germans would decide against foreigners because eastern Germans are, for historical reasons, not particularly open to foreigners.'
[Interviewer: 'But you would still support a referendum?']
'It is difficult, very difficult indeed. It will have negative repercussions for Germany's image in other countries. But if one wants to remain credible as a democrat . . .'
[Interviewer: 'Why would a referendum hurt Germany's image?']
'Because I think I know how a majority of the people would decide this issue. But what can you do?'
[Interviewer: 'Why would you still be for a referendum?']
'I have to be for it. I also supported having elections, even though I anticipated that a majority would support the CDU and that many things would subsequently go down the drain. I believe that democracy must begin with a reliance upon the value of one's own argument. One really should stop telling people what they have to think and do . . . If one denies people the right to decide how one should treat foreigners only because one is afraid that people would arrive at the wrong decision, by God, we will never have a democratic society. On the other hand, I also see the danger that we won't have a democratic society because people will be against a democratic solution with respect to foreigners. It's better you don't ask me about this. You see, I am torn.' (R5)

These views about the need to involve citizens directly in the political process illustrate how different mindsets exist in the East and the

West, attesting to the power of institutional learning. All MPs discussed a highly emotional and controversial issue. All focused on the question of citizens' sophistication and the importance of the issue. However, eastern MPs are considerably more likely than western ones to trust citizens' judgement, whereas western MPs frequently view representative institutions as superior bodies of decision-making. Even when eastern MPs doubt the wisdom of publics (as did R5), they are still more likely than western MPs to see the benefits of plebiscitarian procedures. These are not just differences of degree over the desired involvement of citizens in the political process. Instead, eastern MPs, especially the post-war cohort, frequently advocate abolishing representative institutions in order to establish some form of direct democracy.

MPs' plebiscitarian ideals are not simply abstract statements without relevance to the political process. Their ideals have practical consequences. Eastern MPs are substantially more likely than western MPs to support specific direct-democratic procedures (Table 5.5). Because these questions were also contained in two surveys of the western German Bundestag (federal parliament) and the East German Volkskammer (the eastern German parliament elected in March 1990 and dissolved in October 1990), one may also compare Berlin MPs with national-level MPs. The first two procedures are non-binding referenda, whereas procedures C through F would oblige legislators to act in accordance with the outcome of a referendum. Eastern MPs on the national level and in Berlin are considerably more likely to support plebiscitarian procedures, especially when the procedures obtain legally binding status. In fact, eastern Berlin elites frequently explained their rejection of the first two options by disagreeing with the non-binding nature of these procedures. The proportion of elites supporting all four procedures (32.9 per cent in East Berlin, 9.0 per cent in West Berlin) reflects the different democratic visions that exist in East and West: in the West, plebiscitarian procedures are frequently seen as undermining democratic systems, whereas in the East they are often viewed as being the only way to establish a true democracy. These sentiments have not been abandoned in favour of more representative views over time. If anything, plebiscitarian preferences, like egalitarian ideals, have become more important to eastern MPs in 1995 than in 1992 (Table 5.3).

How do mass publics view their own role in politics? Overall, they prefer a democratic system that provides them with more particip-

TABLE 5.5. *MPs' support for direct democratic procedures* (%)

Measures	East			West	
	Berlin 1995	Berlin 1992	Volks-kammer	Berlin 1992	Bundes-tag
A. A legally non-binding referendum initiated by the parliament	29.2	35.4	35.0	18.0	12.0
B. A legally non-binding referendum initiated by the executive	27.7	19.0	22.0	10.1	5.0
C. A referendum initiated by a minority in parliament	53.9	49.4	26.0	24.7	10.0
D. A referendum initiated by a majority in parliament	69.2	60.8	67.0	33.7	16.0
E. A referendum initiated by the executive	56.9	45.6	35.0	19.1	6.0
F. A referendum initiated by the people	75.4	78.5	71.0	64.0	40.0
Support C through F	35.4	32.0	n/a	9.0	n/a

Note: Entries are percentages viewing each procedure as meaningful. See Appendix A for question-wording and exact response categories.

Sources: Berlin data are from the Berlin surveys; Bundestag data are published in Herzog *et al.* (1990): 130; Volkskammer data are published in Werner (1991): 431.

atory opportunities than they are given at the present time (Table 5.4). In fact, the proportion of *both* publics endorsing plebiscitarian procedures seems to suggest the existence of discordant views among the western public and elites. Both publics associate the direct involvement of citizens with a 'true' democracy, but the eastern public is more likely to support referenda than the western public. About 50 per cent of the western public mention citizens' participation in deciding important issues as a constitutive component of a democracy, while this proportion reaches over 70 per cent among the eastern public. Although the absence of a comparable response format at the mass and elite levels precludes a comparison of responses across the two levels, eastern Germans' support for direct-democratic procedures broadly parallels eastern MPs' trust in the ability of citizens to reach rational decisions. Apparently, the people's revolution in 1989 and socialism's aversion to representative ('bourgeois') institutions imbued eastern Germans with an appreciation for mass involvement in politics. In the West, in contrast, the mass–elite differences suggest the presence of serious disagreement over the proper role of citizens in politics. These partially different visions at the western mass and elite levels are likely to reflect the heated debates throughout the 1980s concerning the proper role of mass publics in politics and to corroborate analyses which diagnose a greater willingness among the western public to challenge elites outside of conventional modes of political participation (Barnes and Kaase 1979; Kaase 1990).

Summary. This analysis of democratic ideals reveals a diverse blend of democratic components. While eastern and western Germans agree on the importance of civil rights and political liberties, a substantial proportion of eastern Germans primarily value direct democracy and egalitarian components, whereas western Germans predominately specify (representative) institutions and competition among political and social groups. The differences emerge particularly between post-war cohorts, which suggests that both political systems and the people's revolution of 1989 shaped individuals' values. In the context of democratic rights, then, the evidence on the whole is more consistent with the hypotheses derived from the diffusion axiom than the institutional learning axiom. In the context of democratic ideals, however, the evidence clearly corroborates the hypotheses derived from the institutional learning axiom.

Another key result concerns the mass–elite contrast. In the context of liberal-democratic rights eastern elites are more supportive of these rights than the eastern *and* western publics. Apparently, the liberalizing component of eastern elites' education is a stronger influence on their evaluations of democratic rights. Undoubtedly, the disproportionate recruitment of democratic elites in the East is one important explanation for the greater support of democratic rights among elites than among mass publics in the East. Additional evidence, however, does point to the effect of value diffusion: elites *and* mass publics strongly support these rights, and cohort differences are consistent with the hypotheses derived from the diffusion axiom. It is more difficult to evaluate mass–elite differences in the context of egalitarian and plebiscitarian ideals, because of the lack of a comparable question format across these levels. But it supports the institutional learning axiom that the basic East–West differences found at the mass level over democratic ideals broadly parallel East–West differences found at the elite level. Evidently, both mass publics' and elites' democratic ideals are substantially shaped by their institutional learning.

Overall, individuals' institutional learning is partially offset by the diffusion of values in the context of general democratic *rights*, especially among younger citizens, but institutional learning dominates the formation of democratic ideals at the mass and elite level.

The Stability of MPs' Democratic Ideals: Conversion versus Replacement

The previous analyses document the persistence of social-egalitarian ideals between 1992 and 1995 at the aggregate level and would seem to endorse the generational model. According to this model, which underlies cultural approaches, ideological values change relatively little within short time-spans. However, in order to examine whether the evidence presented is rooted in individual-level stability as the generational perspective predicts, it is vital to know how much change actually occurred at the individual level. A substantial proportion of eastern MPs may have converted to liberal-democratic views while an even larger proportion of eastern MPs adopted social-egalitarian or plebiscitarian ideals. If changes between different democratic ideals occur at the individual level between 1992 and 1995, it may indicate the presence of significant confusion among eastern MPs—a profile that is inconsistent with the prediction of stability within the generational model. If this dynamic occurs, it might signal the reorientation of eastern MPs amid the new political context and might be interpreted as evidence for the conversion model advocated by institutionalists. If a conversion toward liberal-democratic orientations occurs, it ought to be measurable among parliamentarians, because they are intensely exposed to the liberal-democratic process.

I therefore classified eastern MPs' ideals in 1992 and 1995 into three groups, namely: (1) those who mention a component in 1992 but not in 1995; (2) those who either mention or do not mention a component at both time-points; and (3) those who do not mention a democratic component in 1992 but mention it in 1995. The second group represents MPs with stable democratic ideals, while the first and third group represent eastern MPs whose ideals changed.

The highest percentage of eastern MPs is without exception concentrated in the 'stability-bar' (Fig. 5.3). The largest group of MPs is represented by those who gave the same response in 1992 and 1995, although some changes occur. For example, there is a net conversion toward associating democratic institutions with a democracy (32.3

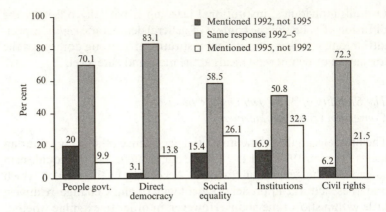

F IG. 5.3. The stability of democratic ideals among MPs, 1992–1995

per cent as against 16.9 per cent); and more MPs mention civil rights
in 1995 than in 1992. This dynamic lends some support to institutionalists' conversion argument. At the same time, there are more
eastern MPs expressing egalitarian ideals than there were in 1992.
However, despite these changes over time, eastern MPs' ideals do not
reflect a broad conversion toward liberal-representative ideals; neither
do they reflect the scale of instability which might be interpreted as an
initial movement toward western-democratic ideals. Although some
conversion toward liberal ideals occurs, the overarching stability is
more consistent with the generational than the conversion model.

Democratic Ideals and Party Groups

Up to this point, I ignored any difference that might exist with respect
to democratic ideals across the parliamentary group spectrum because the institutional learning and diffusion axioms apply equally to
all eastern Germans. But there are compelling reasons—theoretical as
well as practical ones—to examine East–West differences *within*
parties. Theoretically, the institutional learning axiom predicts that
eastern Germans' proximity to the socialist regime is reflected in their
democratic ideals. MPs who actively promoted socialist ideals in the
GDR ought to be more likely to espouse these ideals, independent of
whether individuals genuinely believed in socialism or only pretended
to endorse these ideals for opportunistic reasons. After all, the

premiss of the institutional learning axiom is that those who are most intensely exposed to these ideals are likely to harbour them regardless of why somebody became intensely exposed to the socialist process in the first place. In operational terms, one might expect parliamentarians of the reformed socialist party (PDS) to be especially supportive of socialist ideals (Norpoth and Roth 1996). Practically, the intra-party analyses illuminate whether basic ideological differences are organized so that they predominately occur within or between parties. That is, do East–West differences occur because the PDS is an eastern German party whose presence in eastern Germany generates the aggregate East–West differences?

The verdict is unequivocal: East–West differences exist within all parties (Fig. 5.4). Social-egalitarian ideals are not limited to MPs from the socialist PDS, although these MPs are more likely than others to link social egalitarianism to an ideal-typical democracy—62

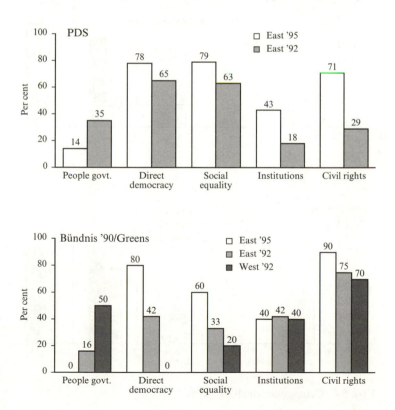

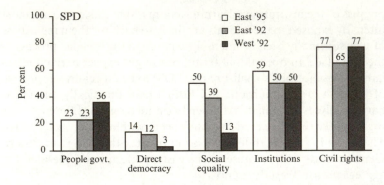

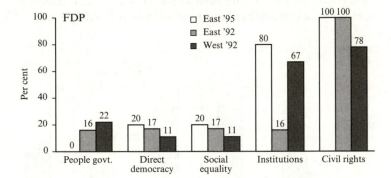

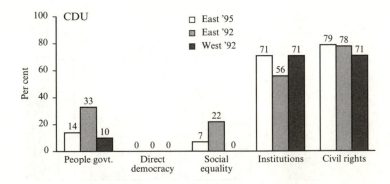

FIG. 5.4. Democratic ideals, by party

per cent of PDS-MPs mention egalitarian ideals in 1992 (Falter and Klein 1994). Equally important, however, is the fact that a significant proportion of eastern MPs within the Bündnis '90/Greens (33 per cent), SPD (39 per cent), and even the CDU (22 per cent) mention social-egalitarian ideals in 1992, whereas this proportion is substantially lower among western MPs in all parties. The conversion of MPs' ideals away from liberal ideals further accentuates intra-party differences by 1995, with the exception of the CDU. Similar intra-party differences emerge at the mass level (Fig. 5.5). Almost all voters of the PDS in the East continue to believe in socialist ideals, but so do partisan supporters of other parties. For example, 71.4 per cent of eastern CDU-supporters responded in 1994 that socialism is a good idea! Finally, MPs from the East and the West are also divided over the plebiscitarian dimension, except within the CDU where all parliamentarians favour a representative system. (No comparable data is available at the mass level.) Overall, the party-based analyses indicate that important East–West differences tend to be reflected within parties, both at the level of mass publics and political elites.

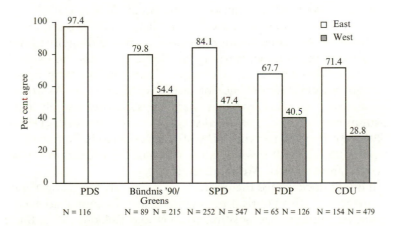

F I G. 5.5. 'Socialism is basically a good idea that was badly implemented' (by party, 1994).

(*Note*: Entries are proportion of party supporters who agree with the statement. Non-German respondents are excluded from the analysis, as are 'Don't know' and 'No answer' responses. The N was too low to compute this figure for western PDS partisans.)

Source: Allbus survey (1994).

THE PATTERN OF SUPPORT FOR DEMOCRATIC IDEALS

The institutional learning axiom attributes these East–West differences to the different societal ideals and operating procedures of the socialist and parliamentary systems, but there are other potential causes as to why eastern and western Germans disagree with respect to democratic ideals, such as the greater religiosity among western Germans (Dalton 1992). The existence of potentially confounding factors at the individual level call for a multivariate analysis where the effect of the eastern and western institutional learning on individuals' values is examined, holding constant other East–West differences at the individual level.

Beginning with parliamentarians, I constructed three separate measures for MPs' democratic values, namely: (1) a measure for MPs' liberal-democratic rights (described above); (2) a measure of MPs' egalitarian ideals which is a summary indicator of the number of egalitarian components mentioned by MPs; and (3) an additive indicator of the number of direct-democratic procedures presented in Table 5.5.

An East–West indicator measures the direct effect of institutional learning on elites' democratic values. If this variable is a significant predictor of MPs' conceptions of democracy, it would signify the importance of institutional learning independent of other individual-level East–West differences. Communist party membership is also used to measure the influence of institutional learning. As argued above, communist party members were exposed more intensely to the institutional norms of the socialist system than other MPs (Dalton 1994).[7] Further, the fact that PDS-MPs are exclusively from the East requires that I include this indicator in the analyses in order to remove its effect from the East–West indicator.

It is well-documented that individuals' religiosity tends to generate centre-conservative political orientations, such as conservative economic or cultural issue positions (Lipset and Rokkan 1967). Since religious values are considerably more important in western than eastern Germany, one must also include this characteristic in the model. Further, MPs' postmaterial value priorities are included because postmaterialists are more likely than materialists to favour broad citizen participation in politics and, to a lesser extent, sympathize with an egalitarian distribution of economic goods (Inglehart 1990). Since eastern Germans are less postmaterialist than western Germans, one must control for these value orientations in examining the influence of institutional learning on democratic values. Further, postmaterial values represent a proxy for the effect of socio-economic modernization on eastern Germans' democratic values (Inglehart and Abramson 1994). If postmaterial values are related to eastern MPs' democratic values, it would suggest that the socio-economic processes that transformed western Germany throughout the post-war decades are also influencing eastern Germany (Baker, Dalton, and Hildebrandt 1981).

In addition to MPs' cohort membership, MPs' education must be included because education, like generation, reflects elites' regime experience (Weil 1985). The acquisition of an advanced degree in a socialist state required individuals to receive thorough political education. Further, eastern Germans may support an egalitarian democracy because of their economic difficulties, but not necessarily because of their regime experience. This prompted me to include MPs' monthly income as a predictor of democratic ideals. Finally, I analyse the potential impact of respondents' gender on their ideological predispositions, because the eastern German state facilitated womens' efforts to join the workforce by providing, for example, access to day-care centres (Rüschemeyer and Lemke 1989). Therefore, female MPs from East Germany may endorse egalitarian-democratic principles because of the perceived difficulties in pursuing a career path under the West German system, but not because of their institutional learning.

The analyses proceed in three steps. I first examine the influence of these variables on democratic rights, and social-egalitarian and plebiscitarian ideals. This analysis is then repeated within the East and the West in order to examine whether predictor variables relate differently to MPs' democratic values. Finally, I estimate the model within the pre-war and post-war cohorts, paying particular attention to East–West differences within the pre-war and post-war cohort. This cohort analysis assesses how far apart younger eastern and western Germans have moved throughout their forty-year separation.

The most important conclusion to be drawn from these analyses is that the interpretations advanced thus far are sustained (Table B1 in Appendix B). Clearly, western MPs are more democratic than eastern MPs (beta = .17), independent of other East–West variations. In addition, when the same analysis is repeated for the post-war cohort only, East–West differences over democratic rights are minimal, as is indicated by a weak East–West coefficient (beta = .05). Post-war MPs differ little over democratic rights, because younger eastern MPs are substantially more democratic than is predicted by the institutional learning axioms. In contrast, East–West differences over social-egalitarian ideals are especially pronounced within the post-war cohort, as a large East–West coefficient indicates (beta = –.35)—especially younger eastern MPs strongly support egalitarian ideals. In terms of plebiscitarian procedures, East–West differences are about equally pronounced across age cohorts. The message is clear: liberal-democratic rights evidently diffused, but egalitarian and plebiscitarian ideals are predominately learned.

Similar patterns emerge at the mass level. In terms of publics' democratic rights, Russell Dalton has analysed eastern and western Germans' views about democratic rights, using the 1990 German identity survey. He reports that East–West differences are small because the eastern public strongly endorses democratic rights. The central reason for this finding is that 'there is a strong independent generational (age) difference in the democratic attitudes of Easterners, reflecting a gradual shift toward these norms among successive cohorts in the East. In the stable democracy of the West, age differences are insignificant when holding the effects of the other predictors constant' (Dalton 1994: 488–9). Just as on the elite level then, his analyses support the diffusion model with regard to publics' views toward democratic rights. However, in terms of publics' evaluations of socialism as an ideal, East–West differences are substantial (Table B2). For example, using the 1994 Allbus survey to predict publics' evaluations of the 'socialism-is-a-good-idea' statement, the East–West coefficient reaches substantial magnitude (beta = .34) which suggests that the eastern public values socialism-as-an-idea independent of several other East–West variations.[8] Unexpectedly, however, few age-related differences emerge at the mass level with respect to the socialism-is-a-good-idea statement. In the East, the correlation between the two variables is almost zero in 1991 ($r = .01$) and 1992 ($r = .01$), and weak in 1994 ($r = -.13$), which suggests that younger and older eastern Germans support this statement. Apparently, the term 'socialism'—if separated from how it was practised in the GDR—conjures up positive associations, such as humanitarianism, among all eastern Germans. Even citizens who were not exposed to the institutional learning of the GDR during their formative years may endorse this statement because the humanitarian component of socialist ideals represents a positive value. This (tentative) explanation would also explain the relatively large proportion of the western public which endorses the statement, although it is clearly below that in the East. Still, this exception notwithstanding, most of the findings fit the logic of the institutional learning and diffusion axioms (for a similar conclusion, see Arzheimer and Klein 1997).

DEMOCRATIC IDEALS IN EAST-CENTRAL EUROPE

Eastern Germans' democratic ideals are evidently influenced by their institutional learning. However, one may argue that eastern Germany was unusually efficient in its attempt to create a socialist personality. For underlying much of the literature about the GDR was the assumption that the 'Red Prussians' were much more effective than other socialist states in applying socialism to eastern Germany (Kopstein 1997). If this were true, the empirical results based upon eastern Germany would not be generalizable to other countries.

While it goes beyond the scope of this book to present a systematic analysis of democratic ideals in East-Central Europe, available evidence suggests that eastern Germans are by no means unique (Table 5.6). Shortly after the iron curtain fell, East-Central Europeans were asked what democratic components they associate with the term democracy (Fuchs and Roller 1994). Consider first the evidence as it pertains to the diffusion of general democratic rights. In terms of basic political liberties, such as free speech or the freedom of association, an absolute majority in all countries surveyed indicate that they associate these freedoms with the term democracy. Although the proportion of eastern Germans falls into the lower half, almost 60 per cent mention civil liberties. Similarly, eastern Germans are as likely as other European publics to mention 'equality before the law'.

Other analysts using different data sets also document the widespread support for general democratic rights. For example, James Gibson, Raymond Duch, and Kent Tedin (1992) find that 89.3 per cent of Moscow residents endorse the statement that 'It is necessary that everyone, regardless of their views, can express themselves freely' (p. 344). On the whole, there is little doubt that East-Central Europeans, like eastern Germans, strongly support general democratic rights—the diffusion of civil liberties evidently reached most areas of the former eastern bloc.

TABLE 5.6. *Democratic ideals among East-Central European publics* (%)

Democratic component	Eastern Germany	Bulgaria	Czecho-slovakia	Estonia	Hungary	Lithuania	Poland	Romania	Slovenia	Ukraine
Political liberties (e.g. freedom of speech and association)	59.6	75.8	79.6	76.5	75.3	63.6	70.3	55.6	51.7	73.7
Equality before the law	72.2	89.0	63.0	82.8	77.6	77.5	62.4	48.9	44.6	85.1
Governments should control banks and large private enterprises	48.4	69.0	61.7	60.7	53.8	44.4	53.6	37.3	60.7	55.6
N	1,011	883	924	811	1,067	714	765	1,045	532	1,345

Note: Respondents were asked: 'People associate democracy with diverse meanings such as those on this card. For each of them, please tell me whether, for you, democracy has: (1) a lot; (2) something; (3) not much; or (4) nothing to do with it.' Percentages are respondents who associate an element a lot or somewhat with the term 'democracy'.

Source: Post-Communist Survey, 1990–2.

At the same time, the socialist ideals of publics in East-Central Europe parallel the pattern found in eastern Germany. When asked whether they associate government control of banks and large enterprises with a democracy, a significant proportion of East-Central European publics indicated that they associate this dimensions with a democracy. Indeed eastern Germans are somewhat less likely to mention this component—48.4 per cent of the eastern German public links the control of large banks and enterprises with a democracy, which is the third lowest proportion in East-Central Europe. If the 'Red Prussian' thesis adequately described the formation of democratic values, eastern Germans would be among the strongest supporters of socialist ideals. However, the comparative patterns suggest that substantial parts of publics in East-Central Europe also endorse a socialist democracy.

In a similar vein, Finifter and Mickiewicz (1992; 1996) find that the better-educated in Russia are slightly more supportive of an interventionist state which helps the poor to improve their economic and social situation. They also conclude that 'there has not been a wholesale abandonment of socialist principles' (1992: 861). These patterns provide evidence that the institutional learning argument can, indeed, be generalized to other post-socialist publics.

Few analysts compare the views of mass and political elites in East-Central Europe. One exception concerns a study of mass publics and political elites in Russia, Ukraine, and Lithuania (Miller, Hesli, and Reisinger 1997). The mass–elite contrasts reported by these analysts are similar to those found in eastern Germany. On the one hand, political elites and mass publics embrace a political system that secures civil liberties. On the other hand, elites and mass publics also prefer a system that produces socialist outcomes (Miller and Checcio 1996). When asked 'Should there be a mechanism to regulate income so no one earns much more than others?' 45.1 per cent of the Russian elite and 53.4 per cent of the Russian mass public agreed with the proposition. Comparable percentages emerge in the Ukraine (29.9 and 47.9 per cent for elites and the public, respectively), and Lithuania (42.9 and 56.4 per cent, respectively). The authors conclude that their findings 'contradict the . . . hypothesis that an ideology of inequality has gained wide acceptance in these post-Soviet societies' (Miller and Checcio 1996: 5; see also Miller, Hesli, and Reisinger 1997).

Overall, available evidence suggests that political elites in East-Central Europe are, like eastern German MPs, more committed to democratic rights and ideals than post-socialist publics. At the same time, political elites' views are ambivalent when one considers the *absolute* levels of support for ideological values representing a liberal democracy. For a substantial proportion links the idea of a democracy to social-egalitarian outcomes.

CONCLUSION

This chapter has examined several hypotheses concerning democratic ideals which were derived from the institutional learning and diffusion axioms. The overwhelming message is that, no matter how one examines citizens' democratic values, the institutional learning axiom is supported in the context of egalitarian and plebiscitarian ideals, whereas the diffusion axiom is supported in the context of liberal-democratic rights. If one examines support for liberal-democratic rights, differences between eastern and western Germans are relatively minor, particularly among younger citizens. The near-universal East–West consensus among citizens born after the Second World War over liberal-democratic rights provides strong support for the diffusion axiom. Evidently, eastern Germans prefer a democratic system over an authoritarian one and they associate basic democratic procedures with a western-style democracy. While the selective recruitment of democratic elites contributes to eastern MPs' surprisingly democratic profile, the selection of elites alone cannot explain the convergence especially of post-war cohorts. This finding is better accounted for by the diffusion model. Insofar as democratic rights are concerned, then, this chapter's thrust parallels analyses of the German mass public which also find strong support for democratic rights in eastern Germany (Weil 1993; Dalton 1994; Veen 1997).

Although individuals may express support for liberal-democratic principles *and* still harbour intolerant views in specific contexts at the same time (Chapter 6), the acceptance of liberal-democratic rights in contemporary Germany sets the situation apart from western Germany in the 1950s and 1960s. During the founding years of the western German democracy, public-opinion surveys document the resistance among western Germans to such democratic principles as multi-party competition, the right to oppose a government, or the right to demonstrate, both at the level of mass publics (Merritt and

Merritt 1970; Kaase 1971; Boynton and Loewenberg 1973) and political elites (Roth 1976). The substantial support found at the mass and
elite level in eastern Germany after the 1989 revolution thus represents a significant departure from Germany's authoritarian legacy.

But the analysis of other democratic ideals clearly demarcates the
limits of the diffusion argument. For in the context of social egalitarianism and plebiscitarian ideals, the institutional learning axiom
receives strong support. Indeed, the gulf between the East and the
West remains wide, attesting to the persistence of two ideological
cultures. Equally important, East–West differences are particularly
pronounced among post-war MPs. And the majority of eastern MPs
interviewed in 1992 did not change their democratic ideals between
1992 and 1995. All of this evidence indicates that basic democratic
ideals, once acquired, tend to be robust over longer time-periods.
Clearly, the time series at the elite level is fairly short when measured
against the life-expectancy of individuals; MPs may convert toward
liberal-democratic ideals in later years. Some undoubtedly will. But
the evidence amassed here is clearly more consistent with the generational model underlying cultural studies than the conversion model
advocated by institutionalists.

In fact, in terms of MPs' democratic ideals, socialist ideals were
reinforced, not weakened, between 1992 and 1995; a result that is
clearly not accountable from the conversion perspective. How can this
'conversion' be explained? The most likely explanation is that eastern
MPs in 1995 felt freer to express their 'true' beliefs than in 1992. To be
sure, there is no indication at all that eastern MPs did not provide
honest and sincere responses during the first interviews.[9] However,
during the first interview period (10/91–6/92), there was a general
consensus about the desirability and inevitability of Germany's
unification, although the enthusiasm over Germany's unification had
already began to fade. By 1995, however, the problems created by
Germany's unification dominated the public debate. Politicians
openly discussed the difficult nature of the unification process and
frequently emphasized the different interests and preferences of
eastern and western Germans. In this atmosphere, it was evidently
easier for eastern MPs to criticize some aspect of how the process of
unification proceeded (e.g. to lament the way eastern German
property was privatized). Eastern Germans may therefore have felt
less compelled than in 1992 to add a liberal-democratic spin to their
responses in the second interview. Indeed, if this is true, the East–West

differences emerging in 1992 are even more remarkable: despite the enthusiasm over unification and the tendency of eastern MPs to downplay their egalitarian preferences, substantial differences emerge in the analyses, attesting to the difficulty of developing a consensus over democratic ideals in the unified Germany.

6

Political Tolerance

That's where the "Eastie" in me surfaces: What I don't like will be forbidden.

(An eastern Berlin parliamentarian explains why civil rights of disliked political groups should be curtailed: R135)

This chapter continues the exploration of eastern and western Germans' commitment to the democratic creed by posing several challenging questions about citizens' commitment to the democratic process: Are German citizens willing to extend democratic rights to disliked ideological groups—what has been termed political tolerance (Sniderman 1975; Sullivan *et al.* 1982)? Should communists, for example, be allowed to demonstrate after they withheld this right from eastern Germans for forty years? Or should communists enjoy the same liberties extended to anyone in the community? Likewise, should fascists be allowed to demonstrate or to run for public office? These are emotionally charged issues in Germany, where the memory of socialist authoritarianism is vivid and where the persistence of right-wing extremism is exemplified by skinheads chasing foreigners or burning Turkish homes. Given Germany's authoritarian legacy, how willing are eastern and western Germans to grant democratic rights to ideologically extreme or other disliked political groups?

This chapter not only analyses citizens' tolerance of disliked ideological groups, but it also examines the reasoning that underlies MPs' decision to tolerate or curtail the activities of disliked groups. By examining MPs' rationale for their treatment of the subject, one may obtain insight into how they weigh conflicting goals, such as preventing the emergence of a viable fascist movement and the need to protect individuals' democratic rights. These analyses will generate important evidence needed accurately to assess the depth of democratic restraint in eastern and western Germany.

This chapter is structured as follows. I first discuss the rationale of why it is important to examine citizens' political tolerance. This discussion leads to four hypotheses which are then evaluated empirically. These findings reveal that Germany's experience with right and left-wing ideological extremism shaped eastern and western Germans' views on political tolerance in many ways. The third section provides direct evidence of how MPs' reasoning about political tolerance reflects Germany's authoritarian legacy as well as the democratic experience of western Germany. The fourth and final section compares political tolerance in the USA and Russia.

THE DEPTH OF DEMOCRATIC COMMITMENT

The strong support for democratic rights among western and eastern Germans suggests that the rudiments for a democratic citizenry exist among eastern Germans. Yet, while encouraging, this result represents only the first step in a comprehensive assessment of the democratic reservoir in eastern Germany. For the true test of one's commitment to the democratic process occurs when citizens are asked to extend democratic rights to disliked political groups. Citizens who are willing 'to "put up with" things that one rejects' (Sullivan, Piereson, and Markus 1982: 4) are more committed to the democratic creed than citizens whose overt commitment to democratic procedures falters when challenged by an ideological opponent. The central idea of political tolerance, then, is that one not only professes obeisant support for democratic principles (e.g. free press, the right to demonstrate), but is also willing to extend them to citizens whose ideological values fundamentally challenge one's own. Thus, a tolerant regime, like a tolerant individual, exercises democratic restraint by allowing a diversity of views, no matter how disagreeable such views may be.

Given that a tolerant response demands a considerable amount of democratic restraint, it is no surprise that support for democratic rights is typically considerably stronger than for political tolerance (Prothro and Grigg 1960; Sniderman 1975; Sullivan, Piereson, and Markus 1982; Duch and Gibson 1992). This gap sometimes takes on substantial proportions, both in mature democracies (Sullivan *et al.* 1989; Peffley and Sigelman 1990; Duch and Gibson 1992) and democratizing nations in East-Central Europe (Gibson, Duch, and Tedin 1992). One seminal study of political tolerance, for example, found that 94 per cent of US citizens agree that 'No matter what a person's political beliefs are, he is entitled to the same legal rights and protection as anyone else'. But 36 per cent also agree that: 'When the country is in great danger we may have to force people to testify against themselves even if it violates their rights' (McClosky 1964). Furthermore, although mass publics are typically less tolerant than elites, the latter are at times surprisingly intolerant as well, both in the USA and elsewhere (Gibson 1988; Shamir 1991). Given the low levels of intolerance found even in western democracies both at the level of mass publics and elites, one must certainly further scrutinize the depth of eastern and western Germans' professed support for democratic principles.

Despite the recognition that support for abstract democratic principles may coexist with intolerant orientations, analysts of democratic transitions in East-Central Europe, with few exceptions (e.g. Duch and Gibson 1993), do not distinguish between the two value-levels. These analysts typically use some variant of the democratic rights indicator discussed in the previous chapter, inferring from the results that the democratic reservoir is surprisingly well developed in East-Central Europe (Weil 1993; Fuchs and Roller 1994; see also Chapter 2 above). Consequently, proponents of the diffusion perspective do not examine the depth of citizens' democratic commitment in these nations. The institutional learning axiom, however, is less sanguine about the depth of such verbal support because it predicts that eastern Germans' lack of opportunity to develop democratic restraint ought to be reflected in intolerant responses:

- Hypothesis 1: *Eastern Germans are less tolerant than western Germans.*

The logic of the diffusion and institutional learning axioms also suggests a stronger relationship between general democratic rights and political tolerance in the West than in the East. Western citizens were exposed to a political process that encourages—with exceptions —the extension of democratic rights to a range of ideological groups. Eastern Germans, in contrast, lack this experience, which likely weakens the link between democratic rights and tolerance. Although eastern Germans support general democratic rights, it is easier to understand why, for example, one should have the right to vote than to accept that one's ideological enemy should enjoy the same liberty. Consequently, I expect that eastern Germans are less willing than western Germans to extend systematically democratic rights to political opponents, because the former lacked the opportunity to develop democratic restraint. This expectation is also consistent with Dahl's observation (1971: 36–41) that democratic transitions in the second half of the twentieth century typically involve, first, the evolution of 'majoritarian' rights (e.g. free elections or the right to demonstrate), and then the evolution of rules for minority protection. Therefore, a second hypothesis expresses the following expectation:

• Hypothesis 2: *Democratic rights are related to political tolerance in the West, but not in the East.*

The Historical Group Context as an Influence on Intolerance

While the discussion thus far has emphasized the contrasting operating norms of the eastern and western German system, one must also recognize that Germany's twin experience with a communist and a fascist regime led to a partial curtailment of fascists' and communists' civil liberties in western Germany. The failure of the Weimar democracy to fend off challenges from ideological extremists subsequently led the framers of the Basic Law to include a stipulation in Germany's constitution (e.g. article 18) which permits the curtailment of civil liberties of ideological extremists, provided that these extremists reject the democratic order. This clause is commonly referred to as *defendable democracy*. For example, the constitutional court outlawed the right-wing Sozialistische Reichspartei in 1952 and the communist KPD in 1956. Likewise, throughout the 1970s, left- and right-wing extremists were at times barred from entering the civil service. While I neither condone nor criticize these decisions, these restrictions convey to western German citizens the message that it is acceptable to relax the rule of democratic restraint with respect to ideological extremists. Therefore, the institutional learning axiom combined with the historical record of fascists and communists predicts that western Germans accept the curtailment of these groups' civil liberties under specific circumstances. Thus, the third hypothesis is:

• Hypothesis 3: *When respondents evaluate extremist groups (i.e. communists or fascists), levels of tolerance are lower than when respondents evaluate non-extremist organizations, both in the East and the West.*

Theoretically, the distinction between extremist and non-extremist groups is important because most tolerance studies typically assume that a group stimulus is equivalent across respondents if they are given the choice to select a disliked group. However, the discussion of civil liberties in Germany suggests that the historical record of a group (and its subsequent treatment by governments) must be accounted for in explaining why MPs may be unwilling to extend civil liberties to such groups. In essence, respondents who select a group which evokes violent images are expected to be less tolerant of disliked groups than respondents who, for whatever reason, select a group that does not evoke associations about political repression.

Given the historical legacy of fascism and communism in Germany, I also expect that the relationship between general democratic rights and tolerance is contingent upon the group that is being evaluated in the West. That is, citizens in the West may be as reluctant to extend democratic rights to ideological extremists as eastern MPs. For a magnified sense of danger attributed to unpopular minority groups may override any concern with democratic principles, thus reducing their impact on tolerance (Sullivan *et al.* 1985). Given that communists and fascists in Germany have proven beyond doubt their motivation and ability to abandon the democratic process, they may present such a strong stimulus in Germany that it is difficult to extend democratic rights to these groups even after a 'sober second thought'. This discussion suggests a fourth hypothesis:

• Hypothesis 4: *The linkage between general democratic rights and tolerance should be stronger for non-extremist groups than for extremist groups.*

In sum, the four hypotheses summarize the empirical expectations, by type of group stimulus, of the institutional learning axiom for political tolerance. I expect levels of tolerance to be higher among western MPs than eastern Germans, independent of the group stimulus, and that toleration of non-extremist groups is higher than tolerance of extremist groups, both in the East and the West. I also expect the linkage between democratic rights and tolerance to be stronger in the West than the East, although this relationship depends on the group evaluated. Before I discuss the reasoning of Germany's political elite about political tolerance, I will first examine the validity of these hypotheses.

DEMOCRATIC RESTRAINT AND MINORITY GROUPS

In order to analyse whether MPs are willing to extend democratic values to minority groups, I asked MPs to identify two groups they dislike and then evaluate their political activities. This approach assumes that respondents have an opportunity to be tolerant only if they must extend civil liberties to groups they find objectionable (Sullivan *et al.* 1982). Unlike democratic rights discussed in the previous chapter, where MPs may express support for democratic principles without reference to threatening circumstances, this approach probes the depth of MPs' commitment to the democratic creed.

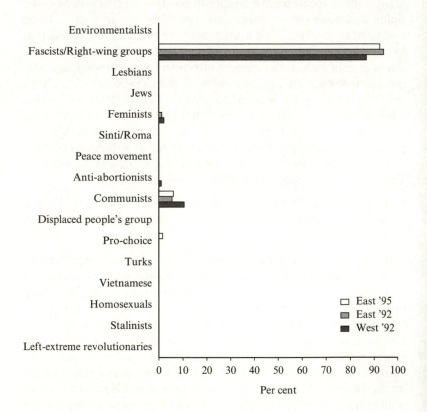

FIG. 6.1. MPs' least-liked groups
(*Note*: no entries indicates that a group has not been selected.)

From a list of groups I assembled and which could be supplemented by MPs, the vast majority of MPs selects fascists in 1992 (Fig. 6.1), both in the East (93.6 per cent) and the West (86.5 per cent). This tendency remains unchanged by 1995 (92.3 per cent). There is more variation across the ideological spectrum in MPs' selection of the second least-liked group (Fig. 6.2). Not surprisingly, communists are unpopular in 1992 with both eastern (37.7 per cent) and western MPs (47.2 per cent). By 1995 eastern MPs are more likely to choose communists as the second group (53.9 per cent) than in 1992. The focus on left and right extreme groups clearly reflects the concern many MPs have about the threat posed by these groups for a liberal democracy, especially in light of Germany's pre- and post-war history.

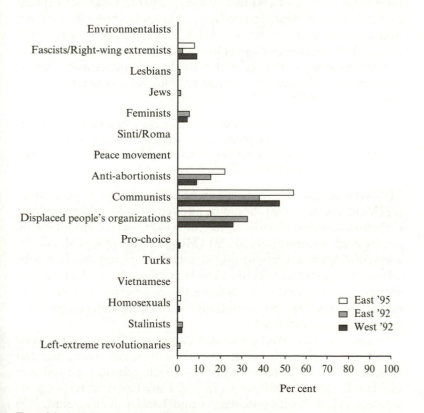

FIG. 6.2. MPs' second least-liked groups

(*Note*: no entries indicates that a group has not been selected.)

The expansionist policy of the Third Reich is also present in MPs' choice of the second group. About one-third of MPs select 'displaced people' organizations in 1992, both in the East (32.5 per cent) and the West (25.8 per cent). These groups represent individuals who were expelled after the Second World War from the former German, now primarily Polish, territory, and they advocate Germany's unification within the borders of 1937. But this proportion is reduced by 1995 (15.4 per cent) because several eastern MPs shifted their resentment from these organizations to communists. Finally, women's groups also constitute an important basis in MPs' perception of political enemies. If the pro-feminist groups (feminists, lesbians, pro-choice) and anti-abortionist groups are combined in 1992, then a significant proportion of MPs selects one of these groups (22.1 and 14.6 per cent in the East and West, respectively). The polarizing effect of the womens' movement continues to be felt in 1995, when 21.5 per cent of eastern MPs select anti-abortionists as the second group.

The crucial test of the depth of MPs' democratic restraint consists of examining whether MPs extend civil liberties to these groups. I therefore asked MPs:

I would like to know your personal opinion on the following statements regarding the activities of each group. Let us begin with (LEAST-LIKED GROUP). Independent of the existing legal framework, would you tell me how strongly you agree or disagree with the following statements?

MPs were then shown a card containing the following four statements: (1) (Members of group) should be allowed to hold demonstrations; (2) Political parties primarily representing (Members of group) should be declared unconstitutional; (3) (Members of group) should be allowed to teach in schools; (4) (Members of group) should not be allowed to appear on television and state their views. The card also displays a seven-point scale, defining the polar ends of 'Agree completely' (7) and 'Disagree completely' (1), with a middle category (4) reserved for undecided MPs.

Despite the East–West consensus on viewing fascists as the most objectionable group, the substantial East–West differences manifest eastern MPs' lack of opportunities to develop democratic restraint (Table 6.1). The percentages in Table 6.1 are based on respondents who agree (7, 6, 5) with statements 1 and 3 and who disagree (1, 2, 3) with items 2 and 4. The percentages thus reflect tolerant responses. In 1992 about one-third of eastern MPs would allow members of the

TABLE 6.1. *Political tolerance among East and West parliamentarians* (%)

Activity	Least-liked group			Second least-liked group			Second least-liked non-extremist group			Second least-liked, extremist group		
	1995 East	1992 East	1992 West	1995 East	1992 East	1992 West	1995 East	1992 East	1992 West	1995 East	1992 East	1992 West
Allow demonstrations	12.3	30.4	67.4	36.9	60.3	78.7	48.0	75.1	91.9	30.0	41.0	69.2
Against outlawing party	13.9	39.7	60.7	43.1	62.8	75.3	68.0	72.7	86.5	27.5	50.0	67.3
Allow to teach in schools	1.5	3.8	13.5	10.8	15.4	24.2	24.0	25.0	48.6	2.5	2.9	7.7
Against banning group from TV	12.3	27.8	53.9	35.4	50.0	68.5	44.0	59.1	86.5	30.0	38.2	55.8
Four tolerant responses	1.5	2.5	0.0	10.8	2.5	0.0	20.0	25.0	48.6	5.0	0.0	0.0
(N of cases)	(65)	(79)	(87)	(65)	(78)	(87)	(25)	(43)	(37)	(40)	(34)	(52)

Note: Entries are percentages of tolerant responses. The second least-liked, non-extremist category represents non-communist and non-fascist groups.

first group (predominately fascists) to demonstrate (30.4 per cent), to engage in party activities (39.7 per cent), or to state their views on television (27.8 per cent). This proportion is substantially larger in the West, where one-half to two-thirds of respondents would grant these rights to fascists. The difference is smaller (and levels of tolerance are considerably lower) for the 'teach-in-school' indicator, although here too western MPs are somewhat more willing to extend this right to unpopular groups. The same tendency holds for the second least-liked group. Yet, although western MPs tend to be more tolerant of disliked groups than eastern MPs, one must also note that western MPs do not extend civil liberties to fascists and communists unequivocally. As MPs' explanations indicate (see below), their reasons for these responses are related to the political repression that fascism produced in Germany's modern history and the attempts by the Federal Republic to prevent the evolution of a viable right-authoritarian movement.

In order to investigate whether the nature of the group stimulus influences MPs' responses (H3), I divided the second least-liked groups into extremist (fascists and communists) and non-extremist groups (any other group). These groups presumably represent equivalent stimuli across respondents because all of the groups were chosen as the second group. However, MPs are considerably more likely to extend civil liberties to non-extremist than to extremist groups. For instance, the proportion of MPs which would allow non-extremist groups to demonstrate is substantially higher than those willing to grant this liberty to extremist groups, both within the East and the West (H3). Simultaneously, East–West differences persist across all groups (H1). Surprisingly, only one-fourth of eastern MPs would allow members of non-extremist groups (e.g. feminists) to teach in schools, whereas about half of western MPs would not curtail this right. In short, East–West differences exist across the entire group spectrum, but the aggregate level of tolerance partially hinges upon the groups evaluated.

These findings attest to the important distinction between extremist and non-extremist groups. Evidently, the historical record of a group (and its subsequent treatment by governments) must be accounted for in explaining why one may be unwilling to extend civil liberties to such a group. Respondents who focus on groups that evoke violent images are less tolerant of disliked groups than respondents who, for whatever reason, select a group that does not evoke associations about political repression.

How does the mass public fare in comparison with political elites? The available data allow one to conduct a rough East–West and mass–elite comparison, but one must exercise caution in interpreting it. The question wording and response categories are not always identical, and some of the data were collected in different surveys, which further reduces the comparability of findings across levels and time. Although these shortcomings necessitate caution in interpreting the ensuing results, they nevertheless provide initial evidence about: (1) whether the western mass public is more tolerant than the eastern public as the institutional learning axiom predicts; and (2) whether elites are more tolerant than mass publics.

Let me begin with the results presented in the top half of Figure 6.3. In a *Times/Mirror* survey conducted in 1991, eastern and western Germans were asked to evaluate the following statements by means of a four-point agree–disagree scale: (1) freedom of speech should not be granted to fascists; (2) books that contain ideas dangerous to society should be banned from public school libraries; and (3) homosexuals should not be permitted to teach in school. Both publics were also asked to indicate whether they would (4) permit the existence of parties irrespective of their democratic orientations. The results, with one exception, reflect the East–West differences found at the level of political elites. The eastern public is less likely than the western public to allow fascists to demonstrate. Likewise, the eastern public is more likely than the western public to ban books from the public domain that contain ideas dangerous to society, and to outlaw undemocratic parties. However, the eastern public is more likely than the western public to tolerate homosexuals as schoolteachers, albeit by a small margin (11 per cent). Generally, the greater tolerance of publics toward homosexuals in the East and the West parallels the greater tolerance of elites toward non-extremist groups. As on the level of elites, it is evidently easier for the German public to extend civil liberties to groups that have not terrorized Europe in the past. At the same time, one must also note that levels of tolerance never represent the majority for any of the four indicators: intolerance prevails in the East and the West.

The bottom half of the panel provides further evidence about mass intolerance in Germany. The 1995–7 World Values survey asks respondents three questions about their willingness to extend civil liberties to a least-liked group. Respondents first selected a group from a list comparable to the one that I showed MPs. They then indicated

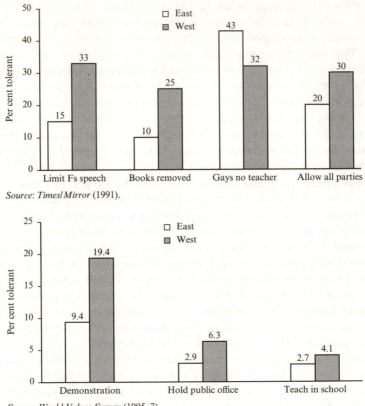

Source: *Times/Mirror* (1991).

Source: *World Values Survey* (1995–7).

FIG. 6.3. Tolerance: the view from the public
(*Note*: In the second graph respondents selected a disliked group. Entries are percentages who would permit an activity to a disliked group.)

whether members of the disliked group should be allowed: (1) to demonstrate; (2) to hold a public office; and (3) to teach in schools.

As on the elite level, right-wing extremist groups (fascists, neo-Nazis, skinheads) are the front-runners among the eastern (76.4 per cent) and western (74.9 per cent) public (Fig. 6.3). This focus on right-wing groups is undoubtedly related to the Third Reich and the subsequent policies of western Germany to prevent fascists from becoming a viable political force. Similarly, the historical legacy is also reflected in the small minority willing to extend to a disliked group (primarily fascists) the right to demonstrate, to hold an office, and to teach in schools in the East and the West. Regarding the right to demonstrate, levels of tolerance are somewhat higher in the West, where about 20 per cent of respondents would permit this political activity. In contrast, only 9.4 per cent of eastern Germans would grant this liberty to the least-liked group. Overall, these patterns indicate a widespread unwillingness to tolerate ideological extremism.

The East–West differences are minor, although the western public is somewhat more tolerant than the eastern public. Nonetheless, the East–West difference parallels those revealed in the *Times/Mirror* survey, which uses a different set of questions. Evidently, the western public is slightly more tolerant than the eastern public, but the widespread reluctance of both publics to tolerate a least-liked group (primarily fascists) is the dominant pattern.

The major difference in tolerance emerges when one compares the views of mass publics and political elites, especially in the West. Although the response format used in the Berlin and public-opinion surveys is not identical, it probably did not produce the substantial mass–elite difference. For example, 19.4 per cent of the western public would allow the least-liked group to demonstrate, whereas 67.4 per cent of western MPs would tolerate this activity (Table 6.1). The comparable percentages are 9.4 and 30.4 for the public and MPs, respectively. The differences are less pronounced in terms of teaching in schools. On the whole, however, western elites especially are more willing to allow political activities by ideological extremists than the mass public. A comparable pattern also emerges in the East in 1992, although the reduction in tolerance between 1992 and 1995 in the East reduces the mass–elite gap.

Overall, the eastern public appears to be even more intolerant than the western public, although differences at the mass level are moderate because of the high levels of intolerance in the East and the West. At the same time, the mass and elite contrasts within the East and West occasionally take on dramatic proportions. Within the West, the mass–elite contrast corroborates the logic outlined in Figure 2.2: elites' higher education and their parliamentary involvement increase their democratic restraint and thus their support for tolerance. Within the East, the mass–elite comparison suggests that political elites' education may partially counterbalance their disproportionately intense exposure to the authoritarian system. Evidently, elites' higher education does produces a kernel of restraint even within a socialist context.

But one must also recognize that eastern elites are relatively intolerant when compared to western elites. The limited effect of education on tolerance in Germany also emerges at the mass level.[1] The appropriate conclusion, then, appears to be that elites' higher education engenders the beginnings of democratic restraint, although the lack of opportunity to practise restraint inhibits the full development of this citizenship-quality among eastern MPs.

Conversion toward Tolerance? Eastern MPs' evaluations of disliked groups in 1995 also reveals the difficulty in developing democratic restraint. After three years in the Berlin parliament, eastern MPs tended to be *less*, not more, tolerant in 1995. The reduction in tolerance sometimes reaches substantial levels when, for example, the proportion of MPs who would extend to the first disliked group the right to demonstrate is reduced from 30.4 per cent in 1992 to 12.3 per cent in 1995. The reduction of tolerance occurs across the entire group spectrum, and thus cannot be interpreted as a reaction to fascists' recent attacks against foreigners.

Because the aggregate pattern may mask fluctuations at the individual level, I also examine the rate at which eastern MPs changed their views over the three years. The conversion perspective predicts that some conversion toward tolerance took place, even though the aggregate development is toward intolerance. That is, while eastern MPs have become less tolerant at the aggregate level, this finding may mask substantial changes at the individual level. The generational model, in contrast, would lead us to expect that relatively little change occurred at the aggregate *and* individual level.

To compare MPs' tolerance over time at the individual level, the responses to the four statements for each group were combined into two additive indicators, one for each group. Each indicator ranges from 4 to 28. I then recoded each indicator into three groups, representing intolerant, ambivalent, and tolerant views (see Appendix A for further details). The two indicators summarize MPs' overall tolerance toward each group, and facilitate the presentation of the dynamic aspects of the development of tolerance between 1992 and 1995.

There is little evidence that MPs became more tolerant over time (Fig. 6.4). In terms of the first group (primarily fascists), the vast majority of those who were intolerant in 1992 continue to be intolerant in 1995 (84.6 per cent). In fact, conversion primarily occurs because MPs become less tolerant. Not a single eastern MP remained

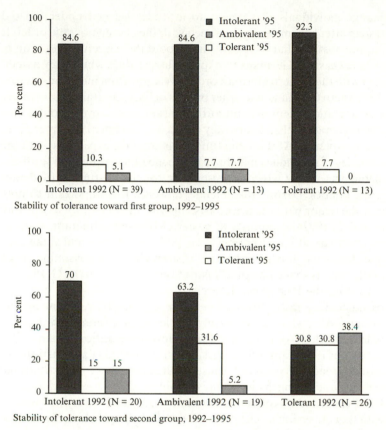

FIG. 6.4. Stability of tolerance among MPs, 1992–1995

tolerant over the three-year span with respect to the first group. Further, only 15.4 per cent of eastern MPs moved out of the intolerant category over the three-year span. The dynamic in the context of the second group generally parallels that of the first one—if conversion takes place it is toward intolerance. The views of eastern MPs toward the second group are somewhat more stable (38.4 per cent), although here too a majority became less tolerant over time (61.6 per cent).

One might argue that the decline of tolerance among eastern MPs between 1992 and 1995 is inconsistent with the institutional learning model. As the previous chapter suggested, however, following a regime change individuals may revert to attitudes learned under the old system after becoming disillusioned with the new democratic order. It is quite possible that the enthusiasm about the peaceful revolution in 1989 led eastern Germans to express those values which they associated with the western German order. We know from numerous studies that eastern Germans, like other publics in East-Central Europe, prefer a democratic system over an authoritarian model, even though they also prefer a socialist democracy over a liberal system (Chapter 5; see also Chapter 8). At the same time, their concrete experience with the activities of extremists may have dampened the enthusiasm for those ideological values which represent the rough-and-tumble of democratic politics. Despite this decline, however, it is important to note that the major patterns are consistent with the institutional learning model. In 1992 the majority of eastern MPs were intolerant. And the majority stayed intolerant between 1992 and 1995. Finally, the analyses below will further show that eastern Germans' reasoning about intolerance is shaped by their institutional learning in the GDR.

In sum, the East–West differences in 1992 attest to the power of parliamentary institutions to generate democratic restraint among western MPs, while the relatively low levels of tolerance in the East reflect a lack of opportunity to develop democratic restraint. This pattern in 1992 is broadly consistent with culturalist and institutionalist approaches, because it attests to the importance of institutional learning underlying institutionalist analyses of democratic transitions. But the decline of tolerance between 1992 and 1995 is inconsistent with the conversion model. Instead, the slow pace at which democratic restraint evidently evolves is more consistent with the generational model which is favoured by cultural approaches.

Tolerance and Party Groups. The institutional learning axiom emphasizes that all members of a society are provided with similar opportunities to develop democratic restraint. But the logic of this axiom also raises the possibility that tolerance levels vary across party groups. For example, members of the opposition groups in eastern Germany faced a powerful adversary. They thus had to balance their own political preferences with those of the socialist order, which may influence their appreciation for political diversity. Closely related to this 'attitudinal pluralism' is the fact that those who opposed the socialist state also experienced directly what the lack of restraint entails for a political minority. They may thus be more sensitized to the need for protecting minority rights. In contrast, MPs affiliated with the socialist system did not have to muster this restraint because they controlled the means to stifle any opposition by non-democratic methods. Thus, within the GDR, MPs who were affiliated with opposition groups may be more tolerant than MPs who were affiliated with the socialist state. At the same time, East–West differences should persist across all party groups, because the institutional learning process affects all members of a society.

As a proximate indicator for MPs' relationship to the socialist state, I use MPs' party membership. After all, most (though not all) parties had a fairly unambiguous relationship to the socialist state. The PDS, CDU, and the predecessor of the FDP (the LDPD) were united under the National Front, and these organizations represented important pillars of the socialist system. In contrast, members of the Bündnis '90/Greens tended to be recruited from the opposition spectrum of eastern German society. The latter should therefore be more tolerant than the former, although all of them should be less tolerant than their western German counterparts.

These expectations are borne out with surprising clarity (Fig. 6.5). In the East, the PDS and the CDU are the least tolerant with respect to the first and second group in 1992. In stark contrast, the Bündnis '90/Green MPs are among the most tolerant MPs, irrespective of the group that is being evaluated. The difference between the PDS and the Bündnis '90/Greens is particularly instructive in the context of fascists. Since both party groups are located at the left end of the ideological spectrum, the lack of practise among PDS-MPs, not their leftist ideology, appears to be a central reason for their intolerance. For if ideological proximity were the main determinant of intolerance, as one might contend, both PDS and Bündnis '90/Green MPs should be about equally intolerant of fascists. The SPD falls between these two poles, perhaps reflecting its status as a new party which recruited a mix of former system supporters and opponents. The relative ordering of parties from most to least tolerant does not change much over the three-year period, with the exception of FDP-MPs, who move from being the most tolerant in 1992 to being the least tolerant party. However, given the small number of cases within the East-FDP (N = 6 in 1992; N = 5 in 1995), I am reluctant to interpret the observed changes within the FDP in substantive terms.

The results for western party groups in 1992 generally parallel those in the East—Green MPs are somewhat more tolerant than other MPs.

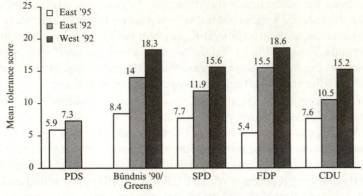

MPs' tolerance toward least-liked groups, by party

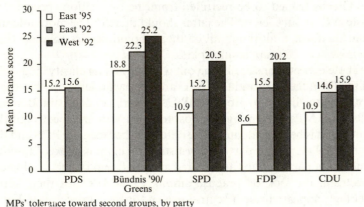

MPs' tolerance toward second groups, by party

FIG. 6.5. MPs' tolerance toward least-liked groups

However, it would be implausible to suggest that the western German political system provided more opportunities for the Greens than, say, the CDU/CSU, to develop democratic restraint. Instead, the greater tolerance among western Greens undoubtedly reflects western Germany's post-war democratic transformation. For the Greens represent the younger, better-educated voters who epitomize western Germany's success in creating a democratic political culture (Inglehart 1977, 1990; Baker, Dalton, and Hildebrandt 1981). In contrast, members of the eastern German Bündnis '90/Greens developed democratic restraint through their opposition to an omnipotent authoritarian state. Consistent with this interpretation, when tolerance is regressed on Green party membership and postmaterialism, the party indicator is significant in the East, while it is insignificant in the West. Thus, Bündnis '90/Green party membership explains MPs' tolerance in addition to eastern Greens' postmaterialist values, but not in the West where Green party membership is largely synonymous with postmaterialism.

Overall, it is important to recognize that the main differences emerge across the East–West divide, not across parties. The central source of tolerance is the basic institutional learning engendered by the institutional framework. This effect, in turn, is accentuated by citizens' position within the GDR society relative to the socialist state, but it does not outweigh the basic East–West effect.

Tolerance and Democratic Rights: A Causal Analysis. The analyses thus far reveal that eastern Germans are less tolerant than western, *and* that their commitment to democratic rights is somewhat weaker than that of western citizens (Chapter 5). An important question raised by these results is: what is the specific process by which institutional learning affects MPs' support for democratic rights and their tolerance? Previous studies suggest that general democratic rights are systematically linked to tolerance; individuals who support democratic rights also tend to be more tolerant (Sniderman 1975; Sullivan *et al.* 1982). The third hypothesis, however, partly conflicts with this prediction, because it anticipates Germany's historical context to render this linkage conditional in terms of the group that is evaluated. Further, research shows that individuals who prefer a hierarchical political system or favour order and discipline tend to be less tolerant (Sniderman 1975). Since the lack of liberal institutional learning in eastern Germany may have contributed to the evolution of authoritarian predispositions, I will examine the relationship between institutional learning, tolerance, and democratic and authoritarian predispositions.

There are several other sources of tolerance, but MPs' authoritarian and democratic values are especially relevant in uncovering the specific process by which institutional learning affects (in)tolerant views. A predominately direct process—independent of democratic and authoritarian predispositions—would point toward a reflex-like predisposition among eastern MPs to deny civil liberties to disliked groups. More likely, however, is the process whereby MPs' institutional learning influences both democratic and authoritarian views, and these factors, in turn, jointly affect MPs' willingness to tolerate disliked groups. The presence of direct and indirect effects would attest to the power of institutional learning to shape levels of tolerance as well as its sources.

To examine the nature of this process, I analyse the impact of authoritarianism, democratic rights, and regime experience on MPs' tolerance, holding constant several other variables (Appendix B contains the complete analyses). The influence of institutional learning on democratic rights was determined in Chapter 5. The influence of institutional learning on authoritarianism is obtained when I regress the authoritarianism indicator (see Appendix A for indicators) on the same predictors as the democratic rights index.

Importantly, eastern MPs' lack of democratic institutional learning directly and indirectly reduces their tolerance toward both groups (Fig. 6.6). First, eastern MPs are substantially more authoritarian and less democratic than western MPs (beta = –.21 and beta = .17, respectively). Authoritarianism, in turn, reduces MPs' tolerance (beta = –.34 and beta = –.24, respectively). Furthermore, eastern MPs are significantly less tolerant toward both groups than western MPs, even holding constant several other variables (beta = .17; beta = .14, respectively). One important result is, then, that eastern MPs tend to be less democratic and more authoritarian than western MPs, which reduces their willingness to tolerate disliked groups.

But the relationship between democratic rights and tolerance also reflects the complex trajectory of Germany's democratic experience. In the context of the most disliked groups, most MPs in the East *and* in the West do not apply their professed support for democratic principles to these groups (H4). Therefore, the relationship between democratic rights and tolerance is weak in the pooled analysis (beta = .10) and in the separate analyses in the East and West (see Table B3 in Appendix B). MPs' views toward the second group are similar with respect to extremist groups; the correlation between democratic rights and tolerance approaches zero (r = .05) and is fairly weak in the West as well (r = .18). However, in the context of non-extremist groups, western MPs do systematically extend democratic rights to disliked groups (r = .67), whereas eastern MPs are still unwilling to grant these liberties to such groups (r = .20). Evidently, as the group stimulus becomes less threatening, it becomes easier for

First disliked group

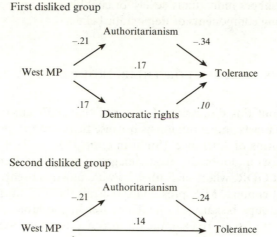

Second disliked group

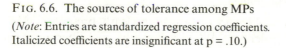

FIG. 6.6. The sources of tolerance among MPs

(*Note*: Entries are standardized regression coefficients.
Italicized coefficients are insignificant at p = .10.)

MPs to grant democratic rights to disliked groups (cf. Shamir 1991; Gibson 1992). And one central East–West difference is that the threshold beyond which democratic rights are extended to disliked groups is lower in the West than in the East. Furthermore, this relationship does not become stronger over time among eastern MPs. In fact, in 1995 those who claim to be more democratic are slightly *less* tolerant toward non-extremist groups (r = –.12)—clearly not a sign of democratic value conversion.

Overall, this causal analysis reveals the intricate process by which institutional learning shapes MPs' views toward civil liberties (see also Rohrschneider 1996*b*). The lack of opportunities to develop democratic restraint among eastern MPs increases their authoritarian predisposition, reduces their support for general democratic rights, and lowers their support for civil liberties. The lack of democratic restraint also entails that eastern MPs do *not* systematically apply democratic rights to disliked groups, unlike western MPs, who systematically apply democratic rights to non-extremist groups. Evidently, institutional learning shapes individuals' levels for civil liberties and the relationship among components of democratic beliefs.

MPS' REASONS FOR THEIR GROUP EVALUATIONS

Throughout this discussion, I assumed that MPs are unwilling to tolerate fascists and communists because these groups 'pose a threat to the norms of tolerance' (Sullivan *et al.* 1982: 167). Fascists and communists undoubtedly evoke images of the Third Reich and the collapsed GDR, where civil liberties were mostly absent. Given this historical context, MPs presumably curtail the civil liberties of extremist groups because of the Third Reich, the Holocaust, or the communist system. To examine this premiss directly, I asked MPs to explain their response:[2]

Could you give me the reasons behind your response? I am particularly interested in why you (support/oppose) limiting the political activities of (members of groups).

The historical legacy of fascism is clearly present in MPs' reasoning about (in)tolerance. When asked why civil liberties of fascists and communists' should be curtailed, one respondent, for example, argued that the historical record of these groups:

makes it impossible to conclude differently. In terms of communists, take the years between 1918 and 1933 and, even worse, the so-called communist regime between 1945 and 1989. In terms of fascists, just think of the late 1920s or Adolf Hitler. (R8)

Another respondent agrees with this assessment when she argues that:

there are plenty of reasons to outlaw activities of fascists . . . this is related to the history and contemporary events. (R31)

Some MPs mention the Holocaust as justifications for the curtailment of fascists' civil liberties:

I think that a survivor of Auschwitz, who lives in Berlin, should not have to endure the sight of fascists marching through Berlin. (R102)

Others, in turn, mentioned their personal family involvement in the Third Reich:

My father was a Nazi, and I never understood why. I wanted to be different. (R118)

Some respondents refer to the collapse of the Weimar Republic in justifying the curtailment of fascists' civil liberties. One MP, for example, argues that the collapse of the Weimar Republic shows that Germany's democracy must defend itself against ideological extremists:

The Weimar Republic didn't use the full authority of the government to defend itself against the threat from the extreme right and left. (R66)

Theoretically, I expect few East–West differences to emerge in terms of MPs' reasoning about intolerance, because fascists and communists represent similar and unambiguous historical referents in eastern and western Germany:

- Hypothesis 5: *Historical reasons predominate eastern and western MPs' rationale for curtailing democratic rights of extremist groups.*

The historical legacy and the notion of a defendable democracy are clearly on the minds of most MPs (Table 6.2). I first present the responses to the fascist stimulus, excluding the small proportion of MPs who selected communists as the first group, in order to relate MPs' reasoning unambiguously to fascists. I then present the responses when communists were chosen as the second group, and contrast these with the reasoning behind MPs' evaluations of non-extremist

TABLE 6.2. *MPs' reasons for extending or denying civil liberties to disliked groups* (%)

Reasons for:	Fascists (first Group)		Communists (second Group)		Non-extremists (second Group)	
	East	West	East	West	East	West
Explaining intolerance						
Historical reasons	59.5	38.2	50.0	25.6	2.2	—
Defendable democracy	46.0	57.9	12.5	34.9	2.2	2.7
Explaining tolerance						
Principled tolerance	21.6	35.5	18.7	13.9	2.2	18.9
Public control	35.1	19.7	31.3	7.0	8.9	2.7
Groups is harmless	1.4	2.6	3.1	4.7	28.9	32.4
(N)	(74)	(76)	(32)	(43)	(45)	(37)

Note: Entries are percentages; multiple responses were permitted. Appendix A presents the code categories. (a) variable not included in the analyses.

organizations. The focus is on the relative importance of reasons given within the East and within the West because the absolute frequency partially depends on MPs' initial level of tolerance.[3]

MPs both in the East and West explicitly mention the Holocaust or the Third Reich as reasons why they would curtail civil liberties of fascist groups. Not surprisingly, eastern MPs in particular mention the socialist GDR as the main reason for restricting civil liberties of communists. In the West, several MPs justify intolerance by arguing that a democracy must defend itself against its undemocratic foes (57.9 per cent). As expected, historical events exert a weaker influence on MPs' justifications in the context of non-extremist groups, partly because there are fewer clear historical referents that could be referred to by MPs. Overall, these responses indicate that Germany's twin experience with fascist and communist systems shape MPs' perceptions of political activities of extremist organizations.

In addition to explaining intolerance, however, I also examine the reasons *for* a tolerant response. Initially this may be surprising, because it seems as though it matters little why a group is tolerated. However, it is 'not enough that citizens have done the right thing; it is important to learn if they have done it for the right reason' (Sniderman *et al*. 1989: 36). I do not suggest that certain reasons for a tolerant response are actually harmful for civil liberties. But I submit —and will provide initial evidence—that some reasons for a tolerant response reflect a firmer commitment to civil liberties than others.

A first reason for a tolerant response is an explicit commitment to democratic principles. In this scenario, MPs believe that *any* ideological group ought to be tolerated in a democratic system. MPs focus on what they believe is essential to a democracy, and less on the attributes of a disliked group. As one respondent from the Bündnis '90/ Greens put it when asked why she would extend civil liberties to fascists:

These groups too must have an opportunity to present their views to the public. A genuine democracy must be able to display such liberalism. (R3)

Another respondent echoes this sentiment because he believes in the educational influence of public debates on extremists:

Civil liberties should be extended to everybody . . . These groups can only participate in public discussions when they enjoy these liberties. And I expect that their participation will integrate them a little bit and perhaps change their views. (R30)

One respondent emphasizes the power of persuasion when she refers to the failure of the right-wing *Republikaner* to garner enough votes to re-enter the Berlin parliament in the 1990 election:

Every individual ought to enjoy civil liberties. It is necessary that one argues out these ideological differences; that's why I support extending civil liberties to these groups, even though they are violent. Berlin's experience shows that it is possible successfully to fight right-wing extremists. (R121)

One respondent also refers to the Third Reich in explaining her response, but this time the actions of the Third Reich are used to justify a tolerant, not intolerant, response:

If you curtail civil liberties of extremist groups, you do the same thing that Communists and Nazis did. These groups are dangerous for a democracy, but it must endure them. (R135)

Another respondent is concerned that outlawing a group might initiate a chain-reaction of further restrictions on public debates:

If you start to suppress one group, then it may entail that groups, which are ideologically close to the suppressed one, become the next target for restrictions. This dynamic is quite strong. One must attack extremist groups in public, but one shouldn't suppress them. . . . (R153)

Finally, one MP presents a balanced assessment of the necessity to discuss controversies openly in a democracy:

Every political viewpoint must have an opportunity to participate and compete in public debates. That is the only way to fight extremism. And this is a fundamental principle of a democracy. This also has practical implications. Everybody who tries to attract a majority quickly learns that it is one thing to express extreme viewpoints in a pub over a beer, but it is a different story to attract a majority for one's positions. This cold-water test for extremists is very useful for a democracy. (R12)

This *principle-based* toleration reflects a firm commitment to civil liberties and occupies a central position in MPs' democratic belief system.

In contrast, a second motivation for a tolerant response is of a strategic nature, namely, to maintain public control over a disliked political group. A frequent line of reasoning in this category emphasizes that a group, if outlawed, would be forced to go underground, which would make it difficult for state authorities to maintain control over group activities. For example, when explaining why fascist parties should not be outlawed, one MP argued that

Outlawing a party does not accomplish anything. To the contrary, these parties would be forced to operate underground and resort to illegal activities to oppose the state. This makes it even more difficult to fight them. . . . (R27)

This *control-based* motive therefore indicates a weaker commitment to the democratic creed than principle-based tolerance because it focuses on being able to observe a group.

A final reason for extending civil liberties to members of a disliked group characterizes groups as politically harmless. In this case, groups are tolerated because they do not have a record of violating civil liberties or because they do not threaten the existing democratic order in Germany (e.g. anti-abortionists; homosexuals).

The institutional learning axiom predicts that western MPs are more likely than eastern MPs to mention a principle-based commitment to civil liberties. For principle-based toleration reflects the essence of democratic restraint: one extends democratic rights to disliked groups independent of competing considerations. In contrast, a control-based motive predominately reflects tactical motives which may reduce MPs' willingness to tolerate groups as societal circumstances change. Thus:

- Hypothesis 6: *Western MPs are more likely than eastern MPs to mention principle-based reasons for extending democratic rights to a disliked group.*

This expectation is generally borne out. Within the West, the major reason for extending civil liberties to disliked groups is a principle-based commitment to tolerance (35.5 per cent), while control-based toleration constitutes a significant minority (19.7 per cent). Although a significant minority in the East also mentions a principle-based reason (21.6 per cent), the most frequently given reason reflects a control-based motive (35.1 per cent). Although the difference is not dramatic, it does suggest that the control motive represents the primary reason for tolerance among eastern MPs, while a tolerant response among western MPs is primarily driven by a principle-based motive.

Does it matter why MPs tolerate a group? I believe so. A control-based toleration of disliked groups depends on political expediency while a principle-based commitment to civil liberties does not. If, for example, public-opinion sentiments become more negative about a particular minority group, MPs who are driven by a control-based toleration of groups may then support curtailing groups' civil liberties. In contrast, if civil liberties are extended to extremist groups out of a commitment to democratic principles, political circumstances by definition should be less likely to lower one's willingness to tolerate a disliked group. Consistent with this reasoning, MPs who express a principle-based commitment for tolerating the first group are also more tolerant toward the second group (r = .29 between mentioning principles as a reason to tolerate the first group and MPs' tolerance score for the second group). Likewise, if MPs tolerate the second group because of a commitment to democratic principles, they are more likely to tolerate the first groups (r = .44).[4] In contrast, there is virtually no relationship between the control motive when the first group is tolerated and MPs' tolerance toward the second group (r = .05); neither is a control-based toleration of the second group related to MPs' tolerance toward the first group (r = .04).[5] The control motive thus represents a shallower commitment to civil liberties than principle-based toleration. In sum, eastern MPs are less tolerant than western MPs, and eastern MPs' tolerance is less firmly rooted in democratic principles than western MPs' tolerance.

POLITICAL TOLERANCE IN COMPARISON

Are the intra-Germany differences unique to this country? Two surveys—one conducted in the European part of Russia in 1990 and a second conducted in the USA in 1987—contain several identical questions gauging respondents' tolerance. Since the USA is among the oldest democracies, while Russia had just begun to establish a democratic system, this comparison provides another test of the institutional learning argument. Both publics were first asked which groups they like the least, and then to evaluate whether they would extend a variety of civil liberties to members of groups. The identical question-wording and response format in the two surveys as well as their comparability to the Berlin surveys permit one to situate the Germany-based findings in a comparative context.

In the Russian survey the majority of respondents selected neo-Nazis as the least-liked groups (35 per cent), but several other groups also made it on to the list, including Stalinists (16.9 per cent), homosexuals (16.1 per cent) and nationalists (9.7 per cent). The list of second least-liked groups also contains several groups, including neo-Nazis (22.4 per cent), nationalists (19.8 per cent), and Stalinists

(15.2 per cent).The responses of the US public reflect a similar pattern in its focus on extremist organizations. The Ku Klux Klan is chosen by 42 per cent of the US public as the first least-liked group, followed by the US communist party (19.3 per cent), people against churches and religions (10 per cent), and US Nazis (8.1 per cent). These groups also top the list of second-least liked groups, with Nazis leading it (26.8 per cent), followed by the US communist party (16.2 per cent), and the KKK (19 per cent). Compared to Germany, there are more least-liked groups selected by a substantial proportion of the Russian and the US public. But the basic pattern is comparable to that in Germany insofar as Russian and US citizens clearly focus on extremist organizations at the left and right.

How tolerant are Russian and US publics? The basic pattern is comparable to the intra-Germany results—Russians are considerably less tolerant than their US counterparts (Table 6.3). For example, 14.9 per cent of the Russian public would permit a least-liked group to hold a public rally. This percentage is twice that in the USA (29.4 per cent). The same pattern emerges concerning the second group (15.7 and 31.3 per cent in Russia and the USA respectively). Both publics are more willing to extend the right to free speech to least-liked groups. But the Russia–US differences remain basically stable, sometimes exceeding the 20 per cent mark. Consistent with the institutional learning model, the US public is consistently more tolerant than the Russian public.

TABLE 6.3. *Political tolerance in Russia and the USA* (%)

Activity	European Russia		USA	
	First group	Second group	First group	Second group
Allow public rally	14.9	15.7	29.4	31.3
Against outlawing group	11.4	12.3	29.4	33.8
Allow to teach	n/a	n/a	13.6	19.7
Allowed to give speech	22.9	21.8	46.4	45.6
Against banning group from office	8.9	9.8	24.5	28.6

Note: Entries are percentages of tolerant responses.

Sources: Russia: *Survey of Soviet Values* (1990); USA: *Freedom and Tolerance in the United States* (1987).

However, the responses of the American public also document the difficulty of developing restraint. In each and every instance, a majority of citizens does not select the tolerant response. At the same time the US public is the most tolerant by international standards. And if one considers that a significant minority selects the neutral middle category in the USA—and thus neither qualifies as tolerant or intolerant—then the patterns do not appear overly bleak. Again, the point here is not to provide a fully fledged comparative study of tolerance. But the data are consistent with the central argument of this book, namely, that the development of restraint requires extensive exposure to institutions providing opportunities to practise democratic restraint.

In terms of the mass–elite contrast, Sullivan *et al.* (1989) report that in a 1978 survey of members of the US Congress, 93 per cent would allow a disliked group to organize a public rally; 74 per cent would oppose outlawing a group, 47 per cent would allow a disliked group to teach in schools, and 93 per cent would allow a speech. These percentages are substantially higher than those at the mass level. As in western and (though to a lesser degree) in eastern Germany, members of Congress are substantially more tolerant than the US public.

In sum, available evidence corroborates the Germany-based findings in numerous ways. The US public is considerably more tolerant than the Russian public, while members of Congress are more tolerant than the US public. The mass–elite differences in the USA are comparable to those in Germany, reflecting the widely accepted tenet that elites' cognitive sophistication and intense exposure to democratic rules enhances their toleration of ideological dissent.

CONCLUSION

This chapter invokes complex moral and political issues: Does the restriction of democratic rights of ideological extremists represent a legitimate act on behalf of Germany's democracy in order to avoid the re-emergence of some viable authoritarian movements? Or should such restrictions be deemed as undemocratic and unacceptable as it is for other disliked groups?

This dilemma shapes the views of German citizens toward civil liberties in many ways. Both eastern and western citizens are reluctant to extend democratic rights to members of ideological extremists. MPs' reasons for their views reveal the strong presence of Germany's authoritarian legacy, because MPs frequently refer to Germany's double experience with fascism and communism when justifying the restriction of ideological extremists' democratic rights. But while Germany's experience with authoritarian political systems explains the reluctance to tolerate extremist groups, the collective memory alone cannot explain why eastern Germans are substantially less tolerant than western Germans. Instead, the differences in institutional learning across the East–West divide reflect different opportunities to develop democratic restraint. Because the socialist state did not encourage toleration of political opposition, eastern Germans lacked the opportunities to develop this crucial citizenship-quality and, consequently, they are less tolerant than their western counterparts. Yet within the East the greater tolerance among MPs compared to the eastern public indicates that higher education may partially compensate for the lack of opportunities to practice restraint. Higher education augments the capacity of individuals for abstract analytical thinking, and it increases the odds that individuals are exposed to information about western political systems (Chapter 2). At the same time, one must recognize that eastern elites' higher education provides incomplete compensation for the lack of practising restraint: the majority of eastern MPs are intolerant, both in absolute percentages and when compared to western MPs. Furthermore, even when eastern MPs tolerate a group, they are frequently motivated by a desire to control a group efficiently. In contrast, western MPs predominately mention a principle-based commitment to the democratic creed. Eastern MPs thus have developed the seeds for democratic restraint, but this beginning must be developed through democratic practice. The fact that eastern MPs have not become more tolerant over the three-year period suggests that the development of restraint is a long-term process indeed.

At the same time, Germany's experience with extremism also left its traces among western Germans. In terms of the mass–elite contrasts over tolerance in the West, the differences in levels of tolerance corroborate the logic outlined in Chapter 2. Western elites' are comparatively tolerant because of their cognitive skills and their greater involvement in parliamentary practices. Western elites are therefore more likely to overcome Germany's authoritarian legacy than the western German public.

At the same time, western Germans, including MPs, are also equivocal at times in extending civil liberties to communists and fascists. It is indeed difficult to draw the appropriate lesson from Germany's history: should one follow the logic of those quoted earlier who wish to prevent the emergence of a viable fascist movement by curtailing its civil liberties? Or should one accept the logic of those who pursue the same goal by putting faith in the power of democratic persuasion by tolerating ideological extremists? This study cannot speak directly to the proper course of action, but it highlights one important consequence of the various alternatives. If a political system restricts civil liberties, citizens' opportunities to develop democratic restraint are reduced which, in turn, lowers their tolerance toward extremist *and* non-extremist groups. Consistent with this argument, when fascists are chosen as the first disliked group, the relationship between tolerance toward fascists and tolerance toward a second, non-extremist group is substantial (r = .46 and r = .37 in the East and West respectively). Therefore, it would appear illusory to assume that restrictions of fascists' civil liberties do not affect citizens' tolerance toward other groups. Certainly, one may still arrive at the conclusion that the restriction of specific organizational activities of ideological extremists is inevitable. But one must also consider that such restrictions may have grave consequences for the development of democratic restraint irrespective of the well-meaning intentions of democracy's defenders.

Finally, this chapter clearly reveals the limits of the diffusion perspective. While eastern Germans are generally supportive of democratic rights, political tolerance is evidently more difficult to develop in authoritarian systems than is support for democratic rights. Civil liberties that are based upon democratic restraint are not easily diffused across systemic boundaries, as the diffusion axiom suggests. In fact, since eastern MPs did not become more tolerant over the three-year period, it would be implausible to suggest that a large majority of MPs and, especially, the mass public developed tolerant views through value diffusion. The lesson of this chapter is as simple as it is persuasive: tolerant orientations are developed by practising, not watching, democracy.

Pluralism

> Conflicts of interests in the public ought to be limited. People just don't understand the partisan bickering.
>
> (An eastern SPD-MP discusses why pluralist conflicts reduce Berlin's governability: R159)

This chapter continues to examine the validity of the and diffusion axioms by analysing eastern and western Germans' views about pluralist competition. Pluralist conflicts of interests constitute a cornerstone of liberal democracies (Dahl 1989). Any society that values liberties and democratic rights must permit its citizens and groups to compete peacefully for their share of influence in the policy-making process. However, observers of German society, such as Ralf Dahrendorf (1967), attribute the failure of the Weimar Republic to Germans' reluctance to view conflicts of interests over political, social, and economic issues as a desirable element in a well-functioning polity (see also Edinger 1960; Loewenberg and Boynton 1973). While this assessment applies primarily to pre-war Germany, eastern Germans' lack of opportunities to practise democratic restraint and self-reliance once again raises the following question: how supportive are eastern Germans of rules which assume that non-violent contests over conflicting interests—pluralist competition—are necessary elements in a well-established polity?

To address this question, I first discuss the importance of pluralist competition in liberal democracies and, using Dahrendorf's analysis as a guide, describe how pluralism has been viewed in Germany. (In the interest of brevity and clarity, the term conflicts of interests, without further specification, hitherto connotes the democratic variant of conflicts).[1] I then apply the institutional learning axiom to the context of eastern and western Germany, which produces three hypotheses about expected East–West differences. This discussion suggests, in short, that while eastern MPs likely hold anti-pluralist views, western

MPs are anticipated to hold pluralist orientations. The chapter then presents the views of eastern and western Germans about pluralist competition.

PLURALISM AND INSTITUTIONAL LEARNING IN GERMANY

Political conflicts and political competition occupy a central role in liberal democracies. Since, as Dahrendorf (1967: 138) puts it, wherever 'there is human life, there is conflict', liberal democracies are based on the premiss that conflicts of interest provide useful instruments to identify and reconcile diverging policy preferences among groups and individuals. In contrast to extreme left- and right-wing ideologies, liberal democracies assume that peaceful conflicts of interest constitute productive components in the political process. A liberal democracy must balance two important dimensions. On one hand, some conflict is necessary in shaping public policies so that a wide range of preferences are reflected in these policies. Simultaneously, however, a citizenry ought to be willing to settle conflicts of interest peacefully—citizens must be willing to compromise. If citizens are unwilling to compromise, conflicts may become serious obstacles in the policy process.

Societies that do not achieve this delicate balance frequently exhibit too much conflict and too little motivation to compromise. However, Germany exemplifies a political tradition which emphasizes non-conflictual, harmonious relations among social and political groups (Boynton and Loewenberg 1974; Merritt 1995). Consider Dahrendorf's seminal analysis of German society where he diagnoses a

> perverted attitude to social conflict that permeates German society and prevents the spread of the democratic principle in it . . . The suppression of conflict has seen many forms in history . . . In Imperial Germany, for example, suppression was mixed with benevolence and a modicum of rationality . . . The suspicious liaisons of freedom and necessity, or freedom and authority, in German political philosophy have often been remarked upon . . . In all of them we will find the same nostalgia for ultimate solutions (Dahrendorf 1967: 133–41)

This aversion to conflict, according to Dahrendorf, has permeated significant parts of German society. Dahrendorf and others (e.g. Edinger 1960; Bracher 1971) partly attribute the slow development of liberal democracy in Germany during the nineteenth and twentieth centuries to the underdevelopment of norms that legitimize pluralist conflicts of interests. The ambivalence with which German society has confronted conflicts of interests is, according to Dahrendorf, partly rooted in how the relationship between the 'state' and 'civil society' has been viewed by dominant social groups (Dahrendorf 1967: 188–203; Dyson 1980). According to this *statist view*, civil society is divided by diverging interests which, if they encroach upon the state, prevent it from developing and attaining morally superior policies. Since the state allegedly represents justice and morality, while civil society with its diverging interests is supposedly incapable of elevating a nation to higher moral grounds, citizens ought not to interfere in state activities, such as formulating public policies. Consequently, groups and individuals trying to influence public policies were frequently viewed as obstacles to reaching the (allegedly) moral public policy.

Although one may disagree with specific aspects of Dahrendorf's characterization of German political thought, most analysts agree that German society evidenced considerable reluctance in accepting pluralist conflicts of interests during the first half of the twentieth century. For example, the characterization of the Weimar parliament as a 'chatterbox' or the half-hearted endorsement of party competition among the mass public immediately after the Second World War is frequently attributed to the equivocal acceptance of pluralist practices even during the founding years of the Federal Republic (Conradt 1974; Roth 1976).

Institutional Learning and Pluralism in Eastern and Western Germany

Individuals' institutional learning is likely to exert a major influence on their evaluations of pluralist principles. Most important, the acceptance of pluralist rules requires citizens to become accustomed to having their preferences challenged, because a liberal democracy requires 'both open conflict among organizations and a capacity for inventing and accepting compromise solutions' (Dahl 1971: 142). This means that citizens accept a range of interests as legitimate which, in turn, implies that conflicts over the most desirable policy may result in political defeat of one's preferences. Therefore, individuals must be ready to accept short-term defeat so that society as a whole may reap the long-term benefits of pluralist competition. Losers of the political process must refrain from using non-pluralist means (e.g. violence) to avert the consequences of defeat. And winners of pluralist competition must not use their winning position to preclude losers from participating again in pluralist competition. Even if there are no clear winners and losers, participants must design a compromise which, by definition, involves making concessions to the opponent. In short, restraint is central to the pluralist process. This restraint is difficult to develop because, as in the context of political tolerance, the societal and individual benefits of pluralist competition appear remote and abstract, particularly when one is unable to realize one's personal interests.

Restraint alone, however, does not suffice to make the pluralist process work. What is also asked of individuals is a considerable amount of self-reliance. One crucial requirement of citizens in pluralist competition is that they must make decisions, muster resources to pursue their interests, and sometimes face a competitor of overwhelming strength when individuals try to ascertain their interests in the public arena. To be sure, under certain conditions, citizens may appeal for help to government institutions when, for example, a competitor engages in unfair practices. By and large, however, the pluralist process assumes that citizens rely on their own resourcefulness to advance their interests in the political (and economic) context (see Chapter 8 on the importance of self-reliance for economic competition). It may seem unnecessary for somebody with a western perspective to point out the importance of self-reliance in pluralist competitions. As I will discuss in a moment, however, the socialist system prevented the development of restraint and self-reliance, which lowers the likelihood that citizens would develop these qualities needed for the operation of the pluralist process.

The fact that pluralist norms may be developed—albeit slowly—when citizens are exposed to the pluralist process is illustrated by the gradual emergence of pluralist norms in western Germany after the Second World War. Initially a large number of western Germans were reluctant to accept such pluralist elements as multi-party elections or interest-group competition, both at the level of mass publics (Merritt and Merritt 1970; Kaase 1971; Boynton and Loewenberg 1973) and political elites (Roth 1976; Hoffmann-Lange 1992). However, during the 1960s and 1970s pluralist competition became increasingly accepted by western Germans. In particular, the generations born after the Second World War—having been exposed only to the political process of the Federal Republic—exhibit the strongest support for democratic ideals and practices. It is evident from the development in western Germany that citizens' institutional learning in a parliamentary democracy has a strong effect on the development of restraint and self-reliance over the long haul, thus shaping citizens' willingness and ability to endorse pluralist competition.

However, the institutional learning axiom also raises questions about eastern Germans' views on pluralism because: (1) the socialist state did not practice liberal pluralism; and (2) because of the partisan view of socialist ideology on societal conflicts.

The State-centred Practices of Socialist Politics. The socialist state in the East emphasized the need for harmony among social groups, thereby de-legitimizing conflicts of interests over basic economic and social issues. The popular saying that the socialist system provided citizens with the basic needs from the cradle to the grave symbolizes the control that the socialist state exercised over eastern Germans. Consequently, the socialist state did not expose eastern MPs to the intricate logic of pluralist competition which prevented eastern Germans from developing democratic restraint and self-reliance. Further, the socialist-authoritarian operating norms reinforced the traditional respect for the state. For example, despite an attempt to create the appearance of diversity by allowing the existence of parties with non-socialist labels (e.g. the East-CDU), the National Front was closely supervised by the socialist party (Krisch 1985; Glässner 1989). Thus, the GDR reinforces Prussian traditions that 'are being cultivated by the present leadership. The main tradition is the respect for the state' (McCauley 1983: 1–2). To be sure, the socialist system allowed for controlled discussions to take place, for example, at the workplace or within expert circles of, say, the technical intelligentsia (Ludz 1972). However, such discussion cannot be compared to the free and relatively unconstrained expression of interests that occurs in a liberal democracy. Based on the institutional learning axiom, then, the continuity of East Germany's state-centred political process raises the following expectations regarding eastern and western MPs' views on pluralism:

• Hypothesis 1: *Eastern Germans are more likely to view conflicts of interests negatively than western Germans.*

The generational model, in turn, predicts that in the East citizens born after the Second World War are less supportive of pluralist principles than older citizens. The post-war generation in the East was almost exclusively exposed to non-pluralist practices of the GDR, whereas the pre-war cohort experienced some limited exposure to conflicts of interest, especially cohorts which experienced the pluralist competition during the Weimar Republic. In the West, in contrast, one would not expect distinct cohort differences to exist. The western German post-war cohort experienced the democratic system of the Federal Republic, while older Germans may also have experienced the pluralism of the Weimar Republic. The differing East–West and pre-war–post-war experiences lead to a second hypothesis:

• Hypothesis 2: *Post-war citizens are less likely to be supportive of pluralism than pre-war citizens in the East, but not in the West.*

Socialist Ideology and Societal Conflicts. A second component of socialist ideology that may have shaped citizens' views on pluralist conflicts is socialism's partisan view of societal conflicts. While democratic ideology views the expression of any interest as equally legitimate, independent of the socio-economic source of societal conflicts, socialist ideology favours the expression of the interests of the working class—especially in a capitalist environment (Held 1987: ch. 4). At the same time, socialist ideology de-emphasizes the legitimacy of employers' interests ('big business'). Within the context of a capitalist society, then, socialism views class relations as highly divisive, and it prefers an activist state which helps the working class in its political struggles with the owners of the means of production. Consequently, socialist ideology rejects the notion of neutral political institutions and instead favours a state that takes the side of the working class and the socially weak.

In addition to buttressing the rationale of the first and second hypotheses, the partisan premiss of socialist ideology regarding societal conflicts is important because the analyses in Chapter 5 revealed that a substantial proportion of eastern MPs define an ideal-typical democracy in social-egalitarian terms. Moreover, nearly half of post-war eastern MPs hold egalitarian-democratic ideals, whereas fewer than 7 per cent of western Germans hold social-egalitarian ideals. Thus, a significant proportion of eastern Germans explicitly subscribe to democratic ideals which are partly incompatible with the pluralist notion that a state ought to be neutral toward societal conflicts. Given the partisan premiss of socialism, I hypothesize:

• Hypothesis 3: *Eastern Germans' egalitarian conceptions of democracies are related to anti-pluralist views.*

EVALUATIONS OF PLURALIST COMPETITION

I begin by discussing MPs and publics' evaluations of two closed-ended statements which gauge whether they believe that interest-group clashes reduce a nation's welfare (Kaase 1971).[2] The first statement in Table 7.1 expresses the view, based on the statist tradition in German political thought, that clashes between interest groups endanger the overall public welfare of Germany. The premiss of this measure is that those who agree with it also assume that conflictual relationships between contending interests reduce the quality of the democratic process, thus reflecting a less democratic view than is expressed by disagreeing with this measure. Among MPs, in 1992, a vast majority disagrees with this statement in the West (87.4 per cent) and the East (94.9 per cent); there is hardly any MP who endorses this viewpoint.

A second indicator poses a conflict between national interests and group interests. Typically, when respondents disagree with the statement, it is interpreted as the democratic response. In turn, when respondents agree with it, analysts interpret such a response as undemocratic because it presumes that national policies may be formulated without the expression of different views. Although the interpretation of this indicator remains somewhat controversial (e.g. Dalton 1994), most analysts assume that agreement with the statement represents an undemocratic view (Fuchs 1997).[3] East–West differences among MPs emerge more sharply for the second indicator. Almost one-third of eastern MPs espouse anti-pluralist views—and this proportion remains essentially unchanged by 1995—while this proportion is substantially smaller among western MPs (17.3 per cent).

Surprisingly, East–West differences at the mass level shortly after unification seem to suggest that the eastern, not western, public is more apt to endorse pluralist competition. In the East there is strong disagreement with this proposition in April 1990 which seemingly suggests that eastern Germans view conflicts of interests favourably. However, the survey upon which this percentage is based took place while the GDR still existed as a separate state. It is highly likely that eastern Germans disagreed with the statement because they took as their reference-point the existing GDR, where pluralist conflicts of interests were only beginning to form after the communist party lost its hegemonic grip on eastern German society. Against this backdrop

TABLE 7.1. *Publics and elites' views on pluralist conflicts* (%)

Pluralist component		Political elites			Mass publics							
		East		West	East				West			
		1995	1992	1992	1990	1991	1992	1993	1990	1991	1992	1993
Per cent disagree												
A. The general welfare and interests of the Federal Republic are seriously endangered by the continual clash of and demands posed by interest groups		90.8	94.9	87.4	51	50	46	32	47	56	49	36
	Pre-war	88.6	93.3	84.1								
	Post-war	93.3	97.1	90.7								
Per cent agree												
B. A country's general welfare should always override the special interests of groups and organization		30.8	30.4	17.3	92	93	93	90	89	92	92	85
	Pre-war	37.2	31.1	18.1								
	Post-war	23.4	29.4	16.3								

Note: See appendix A for details on response categories.

Source: See Table 5.2.

where no or little conflicts existed, the initial opposition to the statement is not surprising. After Germany became unified in October
1990, the proportion of the eastern public disagreeing with this statement is reduced first to 51 per cent by December 1990 and it declines
further to 32 per cent by 1993. A few years into unification, then, the
eastern German public is roughly as reluctant as the western German
public to endorse the pluralist component of this indicator.

In terms of mass–elite differences, political elites are substantially
more supportive of the pluralist position than mass publics. As in the
context of democratic rights and political tolerance, western *and* eastern elites are more democratic than the western and eastern public.
For example, 90 per cent of the eastern public agree with the second
statement (Table 7.1) in 1993 but only 30.4 per cent of eastern elites
support this proposition—an astounding difference of 58.6 per cent.
The mass–elite difference is even larger in the West for this time-point
(67.7 per cent). Since better-educated citizens at the mass level are also
more inclined than the less educated to endorse pluralist conflicts,[4]
these mass–elite contrasts are consistent with the notion that elites'
higher education, along with the disproportionate recruitment of the
democratic elite in the East, partially offsets elites' lack of opportunities to practise restraint and self-reliance.[5] At the same time, this
initial analysis also reveals East–West differences over pluralist principles among MPs, especially with regard to the second statement.

Pluralist Principles Applied. One might be tempted to conclude, on the
basis of the initial evidence, that there exists considerable support
among western and eastern MPs for conflicts of interests as a
legitimate means to regulate societal differences. However, as in the
context of civil liberties, it is relatively easy to endorse pluralist principles if they are not applied to a specific context. In the daily policy-
making process MPs frequently must consider goals which sometimes
conflict, such as formulating policies speedily while considering the
diverse interests of their constituencies. In order to probe the depth of
MPs' commitment to conflicts of interests when faced with such pressures, I invited them to discuss the influence of conflicts of interests
on the policy process in Berlin within an issue context MPs deemed
important. At the beginning of the interview MPs were asked to name
the two most important problems in Berlin. After discussing a variety
of other topics, I asked:

You mentioned earlier —— as an important problem in Berlin. There are a number of conflicts of interests involved in solving this problem since different groups and people have different conceptions of how to solve the problem. Do these conflicts of interests have a positive or negative effect on the governability of Berlin?

This question has two advantages over the closed-ended indicators. First, since MPs express their views in their own words, the responses offer an opportunity to investigate in detail MPs' evaluation of conflicts of interests. Secondly, the question is positioned within an issue context that relates directly to MPs' work as parliamentarians. Consequently, MPs could draw on their daily experience in responding to the question, which increases the odds that their evaluations of conflicts reflect their true values.

This question, not surprisingly, elicited a wide range of responses, but the basic results can be summarized as in Table 7.2. Less than half (46.8 per cent) of eastern MPs but 72.4 per cent of western in 1992 mention at least one basic fundamental advantage of conflicts of interests. Essentially, these respondents argue that conflicts of interests are central to the democratic process and that a democracy cannot exist if such conflicts are suppressed. Consider the following verbatim responses which reflect a fundamental commitment to pluralist principles. One western MP from the CDU is clearly positive about the opportunities created by conflicts of interests when he argues:

Certainly, one has to adhere to the rules of the game. But within these parameters, open fire. (R118)

A western MP from the Greens agrees with this assessment:

Governability shouldn't be understood just in a technocratic sense where one wants to make life easy for the government. Governability also means that one makes decisions correctly, that is, one has to debate issues. (R102)

A parliamentarian from the Bündnis '90/Greens concurs:

A government must principally be exposed to conflicts of interests . . . A democracy needs such conflicts. (R104)

And an eastern MP from the SPD emphasizes that conflicts of interests are positive if they are carried out within agreed-upon rules of conflict resolution:

If [conflicts of interests] are carried out properly, then it is helpful. Political discussion is always positive if one does not denigrate the political opponent. Conflicts of interests provide the basis for [political] solutions. Conflicts of interest are the salt and pepper of politics. (R169)

TABLE 7.2. *MPs' evaluations of the pluralist process* (%)

Pluralist component	East		West
	1995	1992	1992
Positive views on conflicts	65.6	46.8	72.4
Pre-war	71.4	57.8	70.5
Post-war	56.7	32.4	74.4
Statist aversion to conflicts	10.7	22.8	24.1
Pre-war	14.3	17.8	15.9
Post-war	6.7	29.4	32.2
Socialist aversion to conflicts	13.9	27.9	1.2
Pre-war	8.6	13.3	—
Post-war	20.3	47.1	2.3

Note: Entries are percentages of respondents who mention at least
one positive component, statist aversion, or socialist aversion.

In fact some MPs, such as the following western MP from the
Greens, argue that the *absence* of conflicts leads to ungovernability:

The existence of problems does not lead to ungovernability. Just the opposite
is the case: conflicts contribute to governability. (R161)

A similar viewpoint is advanced by an eastern MP from the opposition movement in 1995:

If conflicts of interest lead to durable compromises, then they don't hurt the
governability. To the contrary, they help to govern. (R5)

Another eastern SPD-MP also argues in 1995 that:

conflicts of interests are necessary ingredients of a democracy . . . because a
plural society is composed of a diverse range of interest groups . . . (R66)

One balanced positive view weighing the advantages against the
disadvantages is expressed by the following senior western MP who
plays a prominent political role in Berlin:

Conflicts of interests cannot hinder governability. While such conflicts slow
down arriving at a decision, they do not reduce governability. It is good that
conflicts exist; one may use them to assess one's own decisions. Conflicts of
interests have made me more secure in my decision-making. Clearly, conflicts
are uncomfortable, especially if one is yelled at, but they are necessary. (R144)

The overwhelmingly positive outlook toward conflicts of interests
especially among western MPs indicates that Dahrendorf's concerns

have been partly redressed by the forty-year experience with a pluralist political system. This evidence is especially encouraging in light of the fact that MPs discussed the merits of conflicts within an issue context that they are deeply involved in. They were engaged when discussing the governability of Berlin, and provided numerous examples from personal experiences illustrating larger points. Still, a large majority of western MPs view conflicts of interests and pressure groups as essential ingredients of the democratic process.

The evidence is more equivocal as far as eastern MPs' responses in 1992 are concerned. They are less likely to express positive views about the pluralist process, especially MPs from the post-war cohort. Only about one-third of post-war MPs express such positive sentiments about conflicts of interests, whereas pre- and post-war western MPs endorse the pluralist process—a result that is consistent with the logic of the institutional learning axioms (H1 and H2). However, the results from the 1995 interviews suggest that a significant group of eastern MPs developed positive evaluations about conflicts of interests between 1992 and 1995. By 1995 65.6 per cent of the re-interviewed eastern MPs express at least one positive element, up by almost 20 per cent since 1992.[6] Furthermore, while a little over half of eastern MPs did not change their evaluations—they remained positive or negative over the three-year period—almost one-third (31 per cent) developed a positive view about pluralist conflicts (Fig. 7.1). Still, even after the increase, barely half of post-war MPs expressed at least one positive

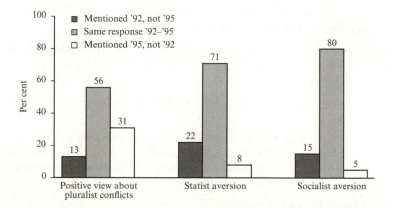

Fig. 7.1. The stability of MPs' views about pluralist competition, 1992–1995

pluralist element (56.7 per cent) in 1995. Despite the development of pluralist views among several eastern MPs, Dahrendorf's assessment continues to be particularly relevant for the post-war political elite in the East in the years after unification.

Statist Aversion to Conflicts. Despite these positive evaluations of pluralist principles, especially in the West, a significant minority of MPs in the West and a substantial proportion of eastern MPs also express considerable reservations about the utility of conflicts, especially in 1992. Germany's state-centred tradition fostered respect for a state that viewed societal conflicts of interests as an undesirable component of the political process. And this statist aversion to conflicts of interests persists. While many MPs who view pluralism positively also recognize its shortcomings (e.g. the disproportionate influence of strong economic groups in pluralist competition), the statist aversion expresses largely negative sentiments about the *entire* process. A little over one-fifth of both eastern and western MPs expresses at least one statist aversion toward conflicts of interests in 1992. One eastern MP from the SPD, for example, views conflicts as the main reason why decisions are not made fast enough:

Unfortunately, conflicts of interests have only negative repercussions for the governability of Berlin. I don't have any understanding for that. People just try to blame each other, and everything is slowed down somewhat. The most important decisions are not made; only unimportant ones are. (R160)

This statist aversion to conflicts also exists among western MPs. One western MP from the CDU criticizes the extensive input that interest groups and citizens have in the political process:

Conflicts of interests lead to the ungovernability of the city. Opportunities for citizens and the bureaucracy [to influence] the policy process should be drastically limited. (R84)

One eastern MP from the CDU is strongly averse to conflicts of interests:

The diverse range of interest groups jeopardize the governability of the city. There are many problems which have to be solved. It is therefore impossible to keep on discussing [*man kann nicht ständing herumdiskutieren*]. In my view, democracy has gone too far. (R170)

And a member of the western CDU argues:

Long discussions have negative repercussions because good ideas frequently get talked to death. (R166).

The responses sometimes could have been copied directly from Dahrendorf's analysis, as in the case of the following members of the East-SPD:

Conflicts of interests influence the governability negatively. There are too many discussions and debates. The entire process doesn't work fast enough in my view. (R103)

And an eastern Berlin MP from the CDU concurs:

There are too many discussions. The right policy is not implemented. Problems are not solved if these discussions take place. (R79)

These responses indicate that aversions to conflicts persist because several MPs continue to view them as a hindrance in the policy-making process. Underlying these criticisms is frequently the premiss that there *are* certain policy ideas which deserve to be pursued and implemented by the government independent of the views of interest groups or ordinary citizens about these policies. These critiques do not reflect a dissatisfaction with the speed of finding a solution to a pressing problem or the fact that interest groups sometimes use more or less legitimate tactics in slowing down the policy process; such sentiment was coded in a different category when voiced alongside positive evaluations of conflicts of interests. Rather, these responses reflect a fundamental distrust with the way interest groups are able to influence the policy-making process. Consistent with the institutional learning axiom, post-war eastern MPs are more likely to share this aversion than pre-war eastern MPs.[7] There is a noticeable reduction in the proportion of eastern MPs who mention a statist aversion in 1995 (10.7 per cent) than in 1992 (22.8 per cent). This decline results from the conversion of 22 per cent of eastern MPs who mention a statist aversion in 1992 but do not express this shortcoming in 1995 (Fig. 7.1).

Socialist Aversion to Conflict. While the statist aversion to conflict is a relic of Germany's state-centred tradition, which was reinforced by the GDR, the socialist regime experience may have generated a second source of aversion to conflicts of interests (H3). In contrast to pluralists, who also frequently recognize the upper-status biases of liberal-pluralist competition in the western democracy, the socialist aversion arrives at the conclusion that these flaws are beyond remedy within the pluralist framework. In turn, in contrast to the statist aversion, which wishes to elevate the state above societal conflicts, the socialist aversion views conflicts of interests as legitimate within a capitalist context if they serve the cause of the working class or the socially weak. More pointedly, the state should become an advocate of the interests of the working class, and not hover above them.

Consider the following accounts. One PDS-MP argues that the existing rules of conflict resolution do not allow the expression of what he regards as the proper interests:

> Those contradictions that are really important are not being discussed. One has to change the entire system in order to be able to carry out those conflicts of interests that really matter. (R50)

The following PDS-MP also expresses this view when she argues that:

> Real diversity of opinion is positive if the entire range of opinions is equally represented. If this were the case and the public had an influence on policy decisions, then conflicts of interests would be positive for the governability of Berlin. This, however, is not the reality. Citizen movements are suppressed; only those groups close to the governing parties have an influence on politics. Even the freedom of the press is limited because minority opinions are not represented. (R171)

One clear aversion to existing rules is expressed by a PDS-MP:

> These problems cannot be solved by the present government because we live in a pseudo-democracy. The interest of big capital influences the government and therefore prevents the problems from being solved on the basis of a majority decision. (R138)

Another variant of the socialist aversion toward pluralist rules of conflict resolution maintains that the existing problems are so severe that the pluralist framework is incapable of handling the demands posed by the socially weak. For example, one eastern MP from the citizen movement argues that the problems of eastern Germany:

> may develop into an explosive potential [for conflicts of interests] . . . People are disappointed about the forty years of socialism. Now they are disappointed again because they thought everything would become better, although people should have seen that conditions would not improve for them. They are now doubly disappointed. (R11)

Clearly, this concern with the socially weak is concentrated within the PDS, but it is also expressed by members of other parties. Consistent with H3, 27.9 per cent of eastern MPs express this view, and this percentage increases to 47.1 per cent among the post-war MPs. If the

PDS is excluded from the frequency count in Table 7.2, about 13 per cent of eastern MPs express a socialist aversion to conflicts of interests in 1992, and this percentage for the post-war cohort is 19 per cent—a minority to be sure, but a significant one. In contrast, the socialist critique of pluralist principles is virtually absent in western MPs' responses. Furthermore, the intensity of commitment to pluralist competition is stronger in the West than the East (Table 7.3). Among western MPs, 42.5 per cent mention at least two advantages of the pluralist process, whereas this proportion is substantially lower among eastern MPs (16.4 per cent). This East–West contrast clearly corroborates the institutional learning axiom. By 1995 the proportion of eastern MPs mentioning a socialist aversion is also substantially reduced. The main shift between 1992 and 1995 concerns the proportion of eastern MPs who fall into the '0' or '1' category. Evidently, a number of eastern MPs became sufficiently convinced about the virtues of the pluralist process that they mention one positive aspect of pluralist competition. At the same time, the proportion mentioning two positive aspects remains almost identical—conversion toward pluralism occurs, but slowly and gradually. In the context of pluralist

TABLE 7.3. *MPs' views about the advantages and disadvantages of pluralism* (%)

Component	Score	East		West
		1995	1992	1992
Positive aspects	0	35.4	53.2	27.6
	1	44.6	30.4	29.9
	2	18.5	15.2	37.9
	3	1.5	1.2	4.6
Statist aversion	0	89.2	77.2	75.9
	1	9.2	15.2	14.9
	2	1.5	7.6	9.2
Socialist aversion	0	86.2	72.1	98.9
	1	12.3	16.5	1.1
	2	1.5	11.4	0.0

Note: Entries are percentages of respondents who mention the number of conflict components indicated by the score. For example, 53.2% in the East did not mention any positive component while 15.2% mention two positive components.

view, then, there is some support for institutionalists' assumptions about a value conversion after a new democratic system is established.

In order to examine the relationship between positive views about pluralism and their criticisms, I constructed a summary indicator which gauges the extent to which MPs view conflicts positively. The new indicator is composed of one closed ended indicator (indicator B from Table 7.1) and the 'positive-aspects' score from Table 7.3. (I did not include indicator A from Table 7.1, because of lack of variance.) First, I re-coded both indicators such that they range from 0 (indicating negative evaluations of conflicts) to 2 (indicating support for pluralism). Secondly, the two re-coded variables are summed, generating a five-point pluralism index ranging from 0 to 4.[8] The higher the value, the more positive MPs are about conflicts of interests.

The relationship between the summary index of pluralist views and the statist aversion is quite substantial, both in the East ($r = -.23$) and the West ($r = -.50$). Likewise, the link between a socialist aversion and the summary indicator in the East ($r = -.18$) suggests that those who are critical of the pluralist process also see fewer benefits in pluralist rules. (This coefficient could not be computed in the West for lack of variance.) These relationships indicate that aversion to pluralist practices represents a fundamental rejection of pluralist rules. Theoretically, it would have been conceivable that MPs should point to the flaws of the pluralist process and view it positively in principle. Indeed, that is the view many western MPs adopt. The fact that egalitarian ideals also correlated negatively with positive views about conflicts in the East ($r = -.19$) also suggests that eastern MPs' concerns are not easily addressed within the pluralist framework. Thus, one important reason why eastern MPs are less supportive of pluralist conceptions is that they have developed an egalitarian conception of democracy that emphasizes equality in outcomes, not opportunities—undoubtedly a result of their socialist institutional learning. This relationship cannot be examined meaningfully among western MPs, given that 92.1 per cent do not hold egalitarian-democratic ideals (see Chapter 5).

One final piece of evidence concerning the effects of conflicts of interests concerns the mix of positive and negative views within parties (Table 7.4). In the West, a statist aversion frequently coexists with positive views toward conflict. For example, within the West-CDU, where statist aversions are concentrated—32 per cent of western CDU-MPs express at least one statist aversion—a majority of CDU-MPs also evaluate pluralist competition positively (58 per cent). In

TABLE 7.4. *MPs' views about pluralism, by party*

Party	East				West			
	Positive aspects	Statist aversion	Socialist aversion	(N)	Positive aspects	Statist aversion	Socialist aversion	(N)
CDU	.45	.61	.06	(18)	.92	.45	0	(38)
	(.39)	(.44)	(.06)		(.58)	(.32)	(0)	
FDP	.83	0	.17	(6)	1.70	.45	0	(9)
	(.67)	(0)	(.17)		(.78)	(.33)	(0)	
SPD	.81	.42	.04	(26)	1.30	.13	(0)	(30)
	(.54)	(.31)	(.04)		(.83)	(.10)	(0)	
Bündnis '90/	.92	.08	.50	(12)	1.70	.10	.1	(10)
Greens	(.50)	(.08)	(.42)		(.90)	(.10)	(.1)	
PDS	.35	.06	1.30	(17)	n/a	n/a	n/a	
	(.35)	(.06)	(.83)					

Note: Entries are mean scores, by party, of the conflict component. The scores in parenthesis represent the proportion of MPs within each party who mention *at least* one conflict component. For example, in the West SPD, the mean score of mentioning positive elements is 1.3. The proportion of West SPD-MPS mentioning at least one positive conflict component equals .83.

contrast, in the East the statist aversion is frequently mentioned without acknowledging the positive features of pluralist principles. Thus, in the West most MPs agree that some pluralist competition is desirable, while differing over the precise extent that conflicts are required in formulating public policies. In the East some MPs still debate whether conflicts of interests are desirable at all. The most pluralist party in the West is the Green party, where almost every Green MP mentions at least one positive aspect (92 per cent) *and* hardly any MP mentions a statist or socialist aversion. In the East, MPs from the Bündnis '90 also hold the most positive views about pluralism, except that this coincides with a fairly high proportion of MPs who also mention a socialist aversion (42 per cent). Thus, even among eastern MPs who endorse conflicts of interests, their endorsement is frequently infused with a social-egalitarian notion about which interests are most legitimate. Not surprisingly, the PDS-MPs are the most likely to criticize the weak position of lower classes and the socially weak; 83 per cent of PDS-MPs mention a statist aversion. However, despite the concentration of socialist aversion within the socialist party, East–West differences exist within all parties. Likewise, negative aversions to conflicts are higher within the eastern party groups.

Overall, the East–West contrasts over pluralist conflicts of interests corroborate the institutional learning axiom. Especially within the context of the open-ended question, eastern elites turn out to be considerably less likely to discuss the benefits of pluralist competition, and instead emphasize its shortcomings. There is some conversion among elites toward the positive polar end of this spectrum, but the scale of conversion can best be described as a cautious move toward positive views. It occurs because several eastern MPs mention at least one advantage by 1995, while there remains little evidence for an unqualified 'thumbs-up' for pluralist competition—few MPs mention more than one positive aspect.

VIEWS ON PLURALISM: THE GENERAL PATTERN

In order to examine whether the East–West differences over pluralism persist as other variations are considered simultaneously, I conducted a multivariate analysis of MPs' views about pluralism, using the pluralism index developed earlier. The strongest support for the institutional learning axiom would emerge if: (1) East–West differences persist while other individual-level differences are being considered simultaneously; (2) egalitarian-democratic ideals are a significant predictor of anti-pluralist views among eastern MPs; and (3) the cohort variable within the East turns out to be a significant predictor of eastern MPs' views on pluralism.

As in the previous chapters, an East–West variable measures the direct effect of institutional learning on the pluralism indicator. I also included MPs' egalitarian ideals as a predictor, because these ideals are expected to reduce MPs' support for pluralist principles. Those who favour a representative democracy ought to be more likely to associate conflicts of interests with such a system, whereas MPs who favour a social-egalitarian system are expected to be less supportive of pluralist competition. To measure MPs' egalitarian ideals, I used the indicator developed in Chapter 5. For a similar reason, I included MPs' evaluations of basic democratic rights. Those who are sceptical about the value of party competition or free elections, for example, may be less inclined to endorse pluralism. For reasons discussed

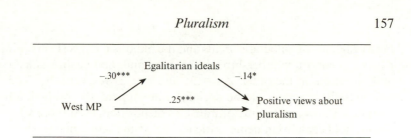

FIG. 7.2. Institutional learning and pluralist views: a causal model
(*Note*: Entries are standardized regression coefficients. The effect of the variable 'West MPs' on egalitarian ideals was determined in Chapter 5 (see also Table B1 in Appendix B). The full analysis of the sources of positive views about pluralism is presented in Table B4. An * and *** indicate that a coefficient is statistically significant at the .10 and .01 level, respectively.)

earlier, I hypothesize that post-war MPs in the East are less likely to hold pluralist values than post-war western MPs (H2). Furthermore, several studies document that postmaterialists are more likely than materialists to demand a participatory political process. I therefore expect postmaterialists to be more supportive of pluralism than materialists. Finally, as in the other chapters (and for the same reasons), I included a number of background variables in order to remove their potential effect.[9]

The overall results of these analyses confirm the power of institutional learning (Fig. 7.2). Note the strong effect of the East–West variable on pluralism (beta = .25), despite the fact that several other predictor variables are included which also reflect the different regimes that MPs' were exposed to (Table B4 in Appendix B). Eastern MPs are substantially less likely to view conflicts of interests positively even after the effects of several East–West differences are removed. The unstandardized coefficient (b = .63) indicates that eastern MPs are located more than half a point toward the anti-pluralist position, which represents a substantial difference on a five-point scale. MPs' egalitarian ideals also reduce the odds that they mention a positive aspect about pluralist competition (beta = .14), but this effect is subdued in the pooled sample because western MPs, by and large, do not hold these ideals. The egalitarian indicator is considerably stronger when this analysis is repeated separately for eastern and western MPs (beta = .22 in Table B4). This finding is especially noteworthy because I simultaneously included MPs' cohort membership, which is related to both egalitarian-democratic ideals and the pluralism index (Pearson's r between cohort membership on the one hand, and egalitarianism and pluralism on the other, is r = .35 and r = . 21 respectively). The non-pluralist practices of the socialist state apparently 'pushed' all eastern MPs toward an anti-pluralist predisposition, even those who do not hold egalitarian democratic ideals. At the same time, eastern MPs who endorse egalitarian ideals are even more opposed to pluralism than other eastern MPs (see also Rohrschneider 1996c).[10]

CONCLUSION

Pluralist rules are essential to the democratic process, for the reconciliation of diverging interests through public policies may enhance the well-being of individuals and nations in the long term. This prospect makes the idea of pluralism attractive. But to reap these benefits, pluralist rules impose considerable demands on citizens. For one, citizens must accept the possibility of defeat. As in the case of political tolerance, they must accept the eventuality that political rivals gain control of an office or win a referendum. Pluralism's rules thus require a considerable amount of restraint, because clashing interests must be resolved peacefully. Pluralist practices also require one to act on behalf of one's interests. Citizens have to muster the resources to compete against powerful rivals. They must form preferences, develop strategies to compete, and invest the resources it takes to pursue goals. These qualities perhaps appear self-evident to those who were exposed to pluralist rules at an early age. But to citizens who did not have an opportunity to practice self-reliance, the pluralist process may appear onerous.

The institutional learning axiom consequently predicts that eastern Germans are less willing to endorse pluralist practices than western Germans, because the paternalistic socialist state provided few opportunities to develop restraint and self-reliance. At the risk of being repetitious, the broader conclusions of this chapter parallel those of the previous two. Eastern Germans view conflicts of interests more negatively than their western German counterparts. Eastern MPs' criticisms often represent a basic aversion to pluralism, so that their concerns cannot be addressed within a pluralist framework.

In terms of the mass–elite contrasts, elites in the West and the East endorse pluralist rules more strongly than the mass publics. This evidence corroborates what emerges as one central finding of this research, namely, that the higher education of eastern elites partially offsets their lack of institutional learning in a democracy. Undoubtedly, one reason for the greater democratic outlook of eastern elites compared to the eastern public is the disproportionate recruitment of democratic citizens. However, the relationship between higher education and pluralist views at the mass level also provides evidence that elites' cognitive skills at least partially account for their stronger endorsement of pluralist practices.

At the same time, MPs' responses to the open-ended question about pluralist conflicts indicates the presence of substantial East–West differences. Eastern MPs, especially those born after the Second World War, exhibit relatively low levels of support for pluralism, and they are more likely to voice serious criticisms about pluralist assumptions to the point where pluralism is rejected. In terms of the first and second decision rules discussed in Chapter 4, this pattern indicates that one's views about pluralism are predominately influenced by the institutional learning process. Moreover, egalitarian-democratic ideals more strongly 'push' eastern MPs who hold these ideals toward the anti-pluralist position. In sum, in terms of MPs' pluralist views, it not only matters where one stands ideologically, but also where one develops one's ideological stance.

8

Economic Values

> The Social market economy is perverse right now. You can write
> it down like that.
>
> (An eastern SPD-MP describes how he views the new economic
> order: R160)

Eastern and western Germany's systemic differences were manifested
most visibly in the eastern and western Germany economies. In light
of socialism's diagnosis that the existence of private property is a
central cause of poverty and inequalities in capitalist economies, the
eastern German and Soviet authorities quickly moved to nationalize
key industries after 1945. In contrast, western Germany's authorities
re-established after the Second World War a social market system that
reflects both private market forces and Germany's welfare tradition.
Given the different foundations of a socialist and market economy, do
eastern and western Germans' economic values reflect these differences? Do eastern Germans, for example, endorse socialist-economic
values as the institutional-learning axiom predicts? Likewise, do western Germans support economic values that reflect the social market
economy? With respect to eastern MPs, these questions may initially
appear surprising, given the abysmal failure of the socialist economy
to satisfy the material aspirations of eastern German citizens. After
all, many eastern Germans joined the demonstrations against the
GDR regime precisely because they were dissatisfied with the economy (Küchler 1992). Nevertheless, while the collapse of the socialist
economy in eastern Germany unequivocally attests to the superior
performance-capacity of a market system, the institutional learning
axiom predicts that the western *and* eastern systems imbued citizens
with the ideological foundation of the economic framework. In fact,
given the poor performance of the eastern German economy, economic values represent an especially intriguing value domain in which
to test the institutional learning axiom. If eastern Germans hold

socialist ideals it would attest to the power of institutional learning, because these ideals persist despite the obvious failure of a socialist economy to satisfy the preferences of consumers.

In addition to the institutional learning axiom, this chapter also considers one other potential source of eastern and western Germans' views about economic principles, namely, the desolate economic situation in eastern Germany. It is evident even to the casual observer that there is ample occasion for eastern Germans to be concerned about their personal economic future. In the years following unification, unemployment rates by conservative estimates reached at least 15 per cent in the East, and this figure excludes those jobs that the government temporarily funded. Given the salience of economic difficulties, the conditions for linking personal economic problems to socialist values are favourable because socialist values champion the protection of individuals from the negative repercussions of rugged market competition. I will therefore consider the influence of eastern and western Germans' perceptions of the economy on their economic values.

Theoretically, the question about the sources of economic values in eastern and western Germany has broader relevance beyond Germany because the two principal sources considered—cultural transmission versus economic perceptions—represent diametrically opposing views on human nature. In the former view, individuals are perceived as largely shaped by their institutional context in developing basic economic preferences. In this view, individuals do not freely choose their basic economic values but develop them as a result of long-term institutional learning. Explanations moored in economic perceptions, in turn, view individuals' economic preferences as deliberately generated by cost–benefit calculations which are subject to revisions based on individuals' perceptions of economic conditions (Downs 1957). Individuals presumably engage in rational calculations as to which economic rules best match their interests. The results of this chapter thus have implications for Germany and, more generally, the acquisition of citizens' economic values.

This chapter first discusses the central socialist and market economic values. Then, based on the institutional learning and diffusion axiom, I will develop several predictions about economic values in eastern and western Germany in order to examine whether economic values reflect the different economic structures existing during Germany's division. That done, the following section examines these predictions in light of MPs' and mass publics' evaluations of several economic principles.

SOCIALIST AND MARKET ECONOMIC VALUES

As in the realm of political culture theory, there is no fixed set of economic values that defines exhaustively a free market culture and a socialist economic culture. Yet, based on the works of political theorists (e.g. Held 1987; Dahl 1989) and empirical studies of mass economic values (Chong, McClosky, and Zaller 1983; Verba *et al.* 1987; Gibson 1993; Heath, Evans, and Martin 1994; Roller 1997, 1994), one may identify several economic values that are mainly compatible either with a market or a socialist economy. As with the chapter on democratic ideals, the purpose of the discussion is not to provide a complete overview of economic theory. Instead, I will summarize the basic features of market and socialist economies and their underlying rationale. This discussion provides the foundation for analysing whether eastern and western Germans' evaluation of economic principles reflects the different economic orders.

A central argument advanced by advocates of a free market economy is that a liberal democracy is more compatible with a market-based economy than any other economic order (Ward 1979; Dahl 1989; Chapter 5 above). Defenders of market principles maintain that a market economy maximizes individuals' political liberties because citizens may pursue their material interests without being restricted by governments. Because of this emphasis on individuals' liberties, a free market economy relies heavily on citizens' initiative and resourcefulness in promoting economic well-being. In particular, citizens may own property and use it to advance their material well-being which, in the long run, presumably increases a nation's wealth (MacPherson 1977; Ward 1979). Underlying the market process is the premiss that the profit motive connotes a positive value because it stimulates economic activities by appealing to the self-interest of individuals. Consequently, an ideal-typical free market system not only accepts differential income levels, but highly values them. Thus, in contrast to socialist ideology, which views the incentives unleashed by private property relations as destructive for society, free market advocates view them as a productive force. Consequently, free market advocates favour limiting government interventions in the economy because individuals supposedly know better than governments what products to offer on the market and when to offer them.

In stark contrast to an ideal-typical free market culture, a socialist economic culture rejects these principles and the priorities assigned to conflicting values (Ward 1979; Chapter 5 above). A socialist economy is based on the assumption that private property leads to unacceptable social and political inequality, which reduces individuals' political liberties. Therefore, a socialist economy prioritizes social equality over political liberty, because the latter is presumably meaningless in light of the severe social inequality created by a capitalist economy. Consequently, economic activity ought to be initiated and managed by the state which, through its ownership of the means of production, is supposedly better able than market forces to satisfy the needs of citizens. In fact, because of the impossibility of achieving political liberty while social and economic inequalities persist, freedom and liberty are defined in social-economic terms. Citizens presumably do not enjoy political freedom unless social and economic equality is established.

This synopsis, along with the discussion in Chapter 5, highlights the basic structure and rationale of the two ideal-typical economies. At one polar end is the ideal-typical free market culture where a vast majority of citizens believe in: (1) the right to own private property; (2) the right to profit-maximization; (3) the premiss that the achievement principle should govern the distribution of income; (4) the superior efficiency of free markets; and (5) the premiss that income inequality provides incentives for economic activities. Two institutional corollaries of these premisses are: (6) the view that governments should stay out of private markets as much as possible; and (7) the belief that unions should be limited in their role as political actors. A set of ideal-typical socialist economic values defines the opposite pole. A socialist value system rejects the use of private property and income inequalities as economic motors, and governments with the extensive support of unions regulate the economy and attempt to reduce income inequalities, while they view profit motives as harmful.

Although listing the basic characteristics of an ideal-typical market and socialist economy is relatively straightforward, no existing economy in western Europe fully reflects these ideal types. In fact, the emergence of the welfare state in western Europe and, to a lesser degree, in the USA reflects a mix of free and interventionist elements, where government policies try to soften the worst repercussions of unfettered market competition. Western Germany's social market economy represents an economic system that falls between the socialist and free market models. In particular, the extensive welfare system, initiated by Bismarck's social policies during the nineteenth century, establishes a minimal level of social security based on citizens' needs independent of their achievements (Flora and Heidenheimer 1981). Given the emergence of the welfare state in western Europe over the past century, a vast majority of European citizens typically endorse state-sponsored measures that help those hit hardest by economic problems (Smith 1987; Mason 1995). However, it is important to emphasize that the acceptance of such measures occurs within the framework of a market-based economy. Unlike the socialist system, where private property is nationalized to remedy social ills, a social market economy continues to employ market forces as the economic engine. That is, the welfare system aims at providing a minimum level of social security but, unlike a socialist system, it does not strive to eradicate social inequalities. To put it more pointedly, the welfare components in the western German economy establish a social floor below which individuals should not fall, but, unlike the socialist system in eastern Germany, the social market economy does not establish an egalitarian ceiling beyond which one may not rise.

Economic Values and Institutional Learning

In its most basic version the institutional learning axiom suggests that citizens acquire those economic values they are permanently exposed to. In the East, the socialist authorities quickly began to nationalize core industries in 1945, and by the time of the collapse in 1989 over 90 per cent of private property was under the control of the state (Glässner 1989; Chapter 3 above). Paralleling the nationalization of private property, the GDR attempted to instil in its citizens a socialist value system (Krisch 1985). Thus, while eastern Germans rejected the existent socialist economy in 1989, the institutional learning axiom suggests that they continue to value socialism *as an ideal*.

In addition to this straightforward expectation about the support for socialist economic values, the generational perspective about value adjustments defines specific guidelines about the demographic manifestations of the socialist institutional learning axiom. Based on the premise that individuals' pre-existing values delay the acquisition of new values, the generational model predicts that the full impact of socialist learning should be felt primarily among those who only experienced the socialist economic system—those born after the Second World War, in the case of eastern Germany. Further, because post-war MPs in the West were not exposed to a socialist economy, generational differences should not emerge within the West. In contrast, the conversion model predicts that no cohort differences exist in the East because the eastern German system was established over forty years ago.

In addition to levels of support for economic values, the institutional learning axiom implies that eastern Germans' democratic and economic ideals are linked. Given the logic of the institutional learning axiom and the fact that a substantial proportion of eastern Germans conceptualize democratic ideals in social-egalitarian terms (Chapter 5), one would expect that these democratic ideals are linked to MPs' economic values. After all, the people's democracy in eastern Germany was first and foremost a *socialist* democracy. In contrast, the western German political order does not list specific social-egalitarian accomplishments which the political system ought to achieve. The principles of individual freedom, combined with the social responsibility of private property, are frequently taken as evidence that the western German constitution favours a social market economy (Dalton 1992). One would therefore expect that eastern MPs' economic values are linked to egalitarian conceptions of democracies, whereas one would not expect to find such a linkage in the West.

At the most basic level, then, eastern Germans, independent of their democratic ideals, are expected to be more supportive of socialist-economic ideals than western Germans. Additionally, eastern Germans who hold egalitarian democratic ideals ought to be more likely to endorse socialist economic values than eastern Germans who do not hold such ideals. Given this interrelationship, the strongest evidence for the institutional learning axiom emerges if eastern Germans, on the whole, are more supportive of socialist ideals than western Germans *and* if social-egalitarian ideals further push those eastern Germans, who hold such ideals, toward the socialist polar end of the capitalism–socialism continuum.

The empirical expectations based on the institutional learning axiom are summarized in three hypotheses:

- Hypothesis 1: *Independent of other East–West differences, eastern*

Germans are more supportive of socialist economic values than west-ern Germans.

The generational model predicts:

- Hypothesis 2: *Within the group of eastern MPs, post-war elites should be especially supportive of socialist economic values. Such generational differences are not expected to emerge in the West.*
- Hypothesis 3: *Independent of other factors, egalitarian-democratic ideals are related to socialist economic values among eastern Germans.*

The logic of the diffusion axiom supplies two related reasons why market values are likely to be in scarce supply in the East (Chapter 2). One reason concerns the impossibility of reconciling the pillars of a market and socialist economy. Unlike democratic rights, which may be merged with socialist principles without abandoning the central tenets of socialism, the basic elements of a market economy cannot be reconciled with those of a socialist ideology. Given the degree of belief-system revision required to adopt market principles, it is un-likely that a large proportion of eastern Germans internalized market ideals during a time-period when eastern citizens were exposed to socialist institutional learning. Another reason is that the principles of a market economy require a considerable amount of restraint and self-reliance, which further decreases the odds that eastern Germans developed market values when they were exposed to a paternalistic state. Restraint is required because the market economy assumes that one uses a specific set of rules to compete against others for scarce re-sources. If one loses on the market—by having to declare bankruptcy, for example—one may only use those market rules that led to one's ruin in the first place to improve one's material circumstances. The acceptance of market principles, then, requires considerable restraint, especially from those who do not benefit from market competition. In turn, self-reliance is required because the market requires personal initiative to succeed. Unlike in a socialist state, which provides clear guidelines for behaviour from the cradle to the grave, a market system places individual resourcefulness at the centre of economic activity. Therefore I placed market values in the cell of non-diffusible values (Chapter 2): market values require fundamental revisions of socialist beliefs *and* they demand a considerable degree of restraint and self-reliance. For these reasons, the institutional learning and diffusion axioms predict that eastern Germans are substantially less likely than western Germans to endorse core principles of a market economy.

Economic Values and Perceptions of Economic Conditions

The manifestations of the institutional learning process are based on the notion that economic values are instilled, not freely chosen. In contrast to this model, a second perspective assumes that individuals support those economic values that best serve their economic interests. One variant suggests that individuals' economic views are determined by their personal finances (the 'pocketbook' variant). Although the empirical evidence in the USA and western Europe has produced only mixed support for the self-interest model, both in the context of voting behaviour (Lewis-Beck 1986; MacKuen, Erickson, and Stimson 1992) and welfare attitudes (Pescosolido, Boer, and Tsui 1986), eastern Germans may feel equivocal about the market economy during this transitional period because they experience considerable economic hardship. Consequently, eastern Germans may support socialist values because they prefer a system that provides economic protection in an environment of fundamental economic changes. Likewise, citizens who are concerned about the national economic situation may endorse massive government intervention in the economy to support the reconstruction of the eastern German economy. At the same time, it is uncertain whether perceptions of national economic problems caused by the transition necessarily lead to greater support for socialist values. On the one hand, if MPs perceive national economic problems, they may endorse welfare measures in order to ease the transition for East Germans. However, one may not find a relationship between *socialist* economic values and negative evaluations of the national economy if citizens blame the socialist system for contemporary economic problems (Duch 1993). With respect to perceptions of the contemporary economy, then, my expectations must remain uncertain.

The predictions are clearer, however, in terms of citizens' future economic development. Citizens who believe that the economy will improve may be more supportive of market systems than individuals who believe that economic conditions will worsen. Consequently, a belief in the ability of the market economy to create employment opportunities in the East may generate support for the market system. In contrast, those who fear that the eastern economy will recover slowly may not support market values. Finally, while the logic of the impact of economic conditions is similar across the East–West divide, one would expect that market values are predominately rooted in a reservoir of trust in the West because western Germans have personally experienced the efficiency of a market economy (Easton 1965; Baker, Dalton, and Hildebrandt 1981). In contrast, eastern Germans lack this personal experience with a market system and must therefore base their support for market values more on economic hopes than do their western counterparts.

These arguments may be summarized in four hypotheses. Independent of the effect of institutional learning:

• Hypothesis 4: *An anticipated decline in one's personal economic situation increases support for socialist economic values.*

Although the impact of citizens' evaluations of the contemporary economy is uncertain, I test the following hypothesis:

• Hypothesis 5: *Negative perceptions of the present economy may lead to an increase in support for socialist economic values.*
• Hypothesis 6: *Positive expectations about future economic developments increase support for market values.*
• Hypothesis 7: *Economic factors exert a stronger influence on eastern than on western MPs' economic values.*

The seven hypotheses provide the guide for the ensuing empirical analyses.

ECONOMIC VALUES AMONG ELITES AND MASS PUBLICS

Beginning with political elites, I asked them to evaluate a series of statements that measure how legislators view basic economic principles (Table 8.1). These statements tap MPs' willingness to endorse a wide range of economic principles. In accordance with the discussion of free market and socialist economies, I included four items which measure elites' support or opposition to basic tenets of market and socialist economies (A, B, D, G). One indicator assesses the degree to which MPs favour workers' participation at the workplace (C), and two items concern the organizational principles of market economies (E, F).

TABLE 8.1. *MPs' evaluations of economic principles* (%)

Economic value	East		West
	1995	1992	1992
A. Social market economies generally lead to acceptable differences in income distribution	56.9	49.4	67.4
B. The profit motive often brings out the worst in human nature	66.2	73.4	51.7
C. Democracy is only possible if individuals not only participate in general elections, but can also participate in important management decisions at their workplace	73.9	81.0	68.5
D. The poor are poor because they often don't make use of available opportunities which the economic system provides	21.5	8.9	16.9
E. The national government should play a greater role in the management of the economy	53.9	40.5	27.0
F. Unions should have more power in our society	38.5	48.1	23.6
G. When private industry is allowed to make as much money as it can, everyone profits in the long run	13.9	13.9	31.5

Note: Entries are percentages of parliamentarians agreeing with the statement.

Consistent with the institutional learning axiom, eastern MPs are more supportive of egalitarian goals than western MPs. About half of eastern MPs believe that social market economies lead to acceptable income inequality (49.4 per cent), whereas over two-thirds of western MPs agree with this proposition (67.4 per cent). Similarly, almost three-quarters of eastern MPs view the profit motive as a negative element structuring social relations, whereas half of western MPs agree with this proposition (B). Not surprisingly, eastern MPs are also substantially more supportive of greater government involvement in the economy (E) than western MPs, and they favour an expanded role for unions in German society (F). Eastern MPs in particular are significantly more likely to endorse welfare policies—as measured by an additive summary indicator of MPs' responses to these statements—than pre-war MPs ($r = .29$), but not in the West ($r = -.01$). It is noteworthy that eastern MPs' views hardly change between 1992 and

1995. Although the western German government was able to temper the worst economic effects of unification for eastern Germans through a range of financial subsidies, eastern MPs evidently continue to prefer an economy that maintains a strong social safety net.

It would be premature, however, to interpret these findings as evidence for the persistence of socialist values in the East. After all, western elites are also critical of some basic tenets of free market principles. For example, a majority of eastern *and* western elites are critical of propositions which squarely blame individuals for their economic hardship (D). Furthermore, a majority among eastern and western elites criticize a 'trickle-down' notion (G) of the distribution of economic wealth. This result undoubtedly reflects the fact that the basic principles of the welfare state are widely accepted by all significant political groups in western Germany.

What these considerations call for is a direct analysis of how elites assess the comparative advantage of the market and socialist economies. In order to invite MPs to make this comparison unobtrusively, I asked them an open-ended question:

What do you personally feel are the major advantages and disadvantages of establishing a social market economy in eastern Germany? (Probe if needed) Some people argue that socialist economies, despite several limitations, offered certain advantages, such as social security, job security, or greater collegiality at the workplace. How would you evaluate this argument?

Since this question is positioned within the eastern German context, the implied reference-point is the socialist economy. And because the question invites MPs to focus on the systemic features of a market system, the responses allow one to examine their views on the relative advantages and disadvantages of a social market and a socialist economy.

This question generated a variety of lengthy responses, but the results can be summarized as shown in Table 8.2. Almost all western (94.4 per cent) and a substantial proportion of eastern MPs (75.1 per cent) began by discussing the systemic advantages of a market economy. Consider the following verbatim responses which exemplify what many MPs said about the structural advantages of a market economy. For example, an eastern CDU-MP focuses on the personal freedom that market activities offer:

We now have a greater freedom because everybody has an opportunity to pursue their interests. That's positive . . . because people have to be creative. I

TABLE 8.2. *MPs' evaluation of a social market economy* (%)

Economic component	East		West
	1995	1992	1992
Systemic advantages of market economy	83.1	75.1	94.4
Short-term disadvantages	75.4	73.4	89.9
Systemic disadvantages of market economy	61.5	59.5	16.9
Reform social market economy	10.8	17.7	6.7
Positive aspect of GDR economy	9.2	15.2	1.1

Note: Entries are percentages of respondents who mentioned at least one aspect in each category.

believe that this new societal order rewards diligent and creative people and rewards them properly, expressed in money, for which you can buy things now. (R4)

Another western CDU-MP argues that there aren't any disadvantages inherent in market systems:

Well, one really can't speak of disadvantages. Clearly, the economic transition is taking a little longer than was anticipated initially, but that's a result of the fact that the socialist system ran the economy into the ground and not a problem of the social market system. And the statistics show that new companies are founded at an ever growing rate . . . It is clearly an advantage of the market economy that enterprises which are responsible only to themselves can be established again . . . (R8)

One eastern SPD-MP who has severe reservations about the market system (see below), nevertheless admits grudgingly that a market system has advantages:

What is an advantage? Well, there is greater environmental protection. And the system is more productive and efficient. (R2).

Some MPs, such as the following western MP from the Bündnis '90/ Green party, evoke the theme of self-reliance when describing the advantages of a market system:

The advantage is that people now have more opportunities than before, they are also more responsible for their lives. I mean they now have an opportunity to shape their own life; they have to look for a job, and they have the opportunity to make decisions. That's good. (R3)

Others focus on the material payoffs that a market system generates. One western CDU-MP, for example, submits:

The principles of demand and supply represent a positive economic model for everybody, including the working class. Just compare the so-called worker and peasant state of the GDR with that of western Germany. The working class is clearly better off in the West. Now, when you call a worker a proletarian, he is insulted because he thinks it's a bad word. (R15)

One eastern CDU-MP concurs, but also believes that social hardship must be cushioned:

I see many opportunities for people because of the social market economy. The challenge is to establish it in a way that minimizes the social costs. So, the advantage is strong economic growth and reduction of unemployment. This has to happen with strong unions and a strong social democracy. (R40)

On the whole, these responses refer to several of the themes mentioned in the discussion of a socialist and market economy. Western MPs especially not only refer to the superior efficiency of a market economy—as do several eastern Germans—but also to the personal freedom that market-based activities entail for individuals. They frequently evoked the theme of self-reliance and personal responsibility and contrasted this with the authoritarian nature of a command economy. With respect to the efficiency of a market and socialist economy, the open-ended accounts reflect the virtual consensus that exists across the East–West divide. Detailed analyses of the separate code categories show that the bulk of these respondents (76 per cent in the West; 57 per cent in the East) either mention the general superiority of market economies, or they explicitly specify their efficiency (see Appendix A, categories 11 and 12 in Table A1).

Most elites in the East and the West also acknowledge that the economic transition created a number of serious short-term disadvantages in eastern Germany (73.4 per cent in the East; 89.9 per cent in the West). One leading western SPD-MP, for example, argues that the main problem concerns the speed with which market rules were established in the East:

The disadvantage is that the market economy had to be established so quickly in the East. I think it was unavoidable, but it was possible only by subsidizing eastern Germany. So, it's only the speed; otherwise I don't see any disadvantage. (R9)

Another western SPD-MP concurs:

Just to be clear: I want to have the social market economy established. The problem is that everything happened too fast and, consequently, the establishment of the market system caused severe hardships. I should also add that what is established in the former GDR is a free market economy, not a social market economy. There is a gold rush there ... That's the main problem. (R10)

Another MP from the western CDU even relativizes the difficult economic transition:

Over the medium and long term, I only see advantages. In the short term, there is the issue of unemployment, but that existed in the GDR as well, only in a different form. (R16)

In particular, the collapse of numerous eastern German companies is reflected in MPs' concern with unemployment, both among eastern (21.5 per cent) and western MPs (35.9 per cent). At the same time, responses that fall into this category clearly characterized these problems as unique to the transition and not as a structural disadvantage inherent in market economies.

But here the East–West similarities end. Differences across the East–West boundary emerge over the extent to which eastern and western elites perceive systemic flaws of the market economy. Indeed, with respect to the systemic disadvantages, almost 60 per cent of eastern elites mention at least one component under this rubric, whereas only 16.9 per cent in the West mention one systemic disadvantage. Consider the following verbatim accounts of eastern MPs which have no parallel in the West. Not surprisingly, some of the most vocal critics of the market economy are found among the members of the reformed communist party (PDS). For example, one PDS-MP views the social components of market systems as a ploy to fool workers into accepting market systems:

Humans are just instruments [in this economy] because everything focuses on maximizing profit. A market system is only social to the degree that social components are needed to get people to accept a market system. If the economy could get away with it, it would establish the same conditions as in Third World countries. (R154)

Another PDS-MP specifically evokes the Marxist distinction between subjective and objective economic circumstances when he discusses why opinion surveys in eastern Germany reveal that citizens believe they are reasonably well off economically:

A market economy needs homeless people, unemployment, and drug addicts in order to survive. The GDR assured that everybody had a job. Now, people are better off subjectively, but they forget the context and that's why they are not better off objectively. (R78)

The following **PDS-MP** basically agrees with these assessments, even though she is a little bit more subtle in her response:

Well, after I got to know the German version of a social market economy, I am confused as to what is really social about it . . . I am aware of the social safety net, but these aren't gifts from employers to the working class, but represent hard-fought achievements of the working class and labor unions . . . That's why people enjoy relative social security, and I emphasize, that it is a relative security. Now, there are two-thirds of a society who benefit from it, and another third does not. And in eastern Germany, things are especially bad because we don't have a social market economy but a Manchester capitalism. (R21)

And one **PDS-MP** recommends throughout the interview that other forms of socialism should be tried out, because he rejects a market economy and maintains that the collapsed system was not representative of socialism:

I can answer this in one sentence. The social market economy is not social. Just as the real existing socialism wasn't socialism . . . The market economy isn't a market system either. We see it all the time that competition isn't really the most decisive factor. Neither is it social, because social aspects don't matter much. Instead, the most important issue is 'Who makes the most profit', as in the ancient forms of capitalism . . . Advantages? Well, compared to socialism, the market system allows more creativity and is more achievement-based than the real existing socialism which wasn't socialism. (R32)

While such damning criticisms are concentrated in the PDS, they also occur with some frequency in all other eastern parliamentary groups. For example, an eastern German member of the opposition movement responded:

The worst thing are the new property relations. Today, we have the worst form of capitalism because people lose their property overnight [*Leuten wird jeder Stück Boden unter dem Hintern weggekauft*]. (R15)

And an eastern SPD-MP laments the loss of the eastern German system and is as critical about the market system as the SPD-MP quoted at the beginning of the chapter:

In the GDR there was no competition, which was pleasant. I liked the role money played in the GDR. One couldn't be rich. Now, weak people have no chance, even if the government tries to take care of them. That is horrible . . . I have little interest in successful people; one should take away their property and nationalize it. (R101)

One eastern SPD-MP discusses the close relationship between democracy and the economy:

Of course, democracy and socialism are closely related. Complete democratization means that the economy needs to be democratized. As somebody said recently: the Dresdener Bank is not run by elected people. There are people on the board of directors who got there only because they have a lot of dough [*Leute die viel Kohle haben*] and not because they were elected. (R13)

The theme of alienation and lack of human contacts even emerges among eastern CDU-MPs. One CDU-MP points to the advantages of the eastern German economy:

[E]verybody had enough to eat and a place to live. And people showed more solidarity because they had to co-operate. Today, people are much more secluded because money has become the sole yardstick of human behaviour. Activities that have no monetary values are discarded. That's a loss. (R31)

This MP almost verbatim voices the same uneasiness with a market system in 1995:

Are there advantages? That's no question. People have what they need . . . However, everything is regulated by money. Other values don't count any more . . . Such values as solidarity and civility are pushed aside. This even affects families. (R31)

Another eastern CDU-MP first enumerates the advantages, but also complaints about some important structural problems:

Central advantages are the efficiency which creates jobs . . . A problem is that workers become alienated from the machines that they work with. Also, human relationships suffer. (R1)

Some responses, such as the following one from an eastern SPD-MP, explicitly indicate that their understanding of freedom differs from that of western MPs:

One disadvantage is that humans and their productive energies become a product. Today, how people relate and identify with their work and similar issues are not as well solved as they were in the GDR. Let me say it this way: individuals were freer in a factory in the GDR. You are probably going to say that everybody was suppressed. But that's not how I see it. People didn't depend on their job. Nowadays, people are ultimately more dependent on their employers, who give them a job, than they were in the GDR. (R2)

Another eastern SPD-MP also focuses on personal freedom, but sternly pointed to the negative aspect of it in 1995:

In the GDR, everything was decided for you until you retired. That can be positive and negative. For example, criminals and boozers [*Kriminelle und Säufer*] were not permitted to enter Berlin . . . Now people see that freedom also has its negative aspects. In earlier days, freedom looked a little rosier from a distance. (R140)

In addition to these negative comments about market systems, over 15 per cent of eastern MPs mention at least one positive aspect of the socialist command economy. One eastern SPD-MP began this discussion with the advantages of socialism and communism:

I must first list the advantage which the collapsed system had, namely, that socialism or communism succeeded in providing people with a decent standard of living compared to the rest of the world. That was a success. Of course, everybody knows that this reduced the efficiency of the economy . . . But everybody had a job and nobody had to worry about their basic needs . . . People only had to think about how their lives could be a little more luxurious, a little more comfortable . . . And a complaint about the GDR— that individuals didn't count much—isn't true . . . I am inclined to use the term democracy in describing the situation in eastern German companies. There was much more of it than there is now in the free market economy . . . This, of course, does not include political freedoms, that's a different story . . . But as along as one didn't touch on political subjects, people could freely express their opinions. (R26)

And in 1995 one member of the PDS even evokes a biblical image to explain that socialism's failure is rooted in human nature:

Socialism didn't collapse because of rigid rules, but because people had too much freedom at the workplace. Compared to a market economy, workers' freedom was almost without limits. The lower one's qualification, the more influence one had . . . Socialism is great, but its limits begin with Adam and Eve. (R133)

On the whole, a substantial number of eastern MPs find fault with the structural characteristics of a market system in eastern Germany. Eastern MPs frequently criticize the loss of solidarity, the competitive nature of market systems, or the gross inequalities produced in a market; criticisms that clearly reflect the economic structures existing in eastern Germany during its division. It is evident that these reservations represent a fundamental critique of the pillars of market mechanisms and do not denote a transitory uneasiness with an unfamiliar economic order. Although most eastern MPs recognize the efficiency of a market economy, and although most are doing well personally, they continue to echo those economic principles they developed during the socialist institutional learning. The East–West gap attests to the power of institutional learning in the economic sphere: while 59.5 per cent of eastern MPs mention at least one element in this category, only about one-sixth (16.9 per cent) of western MPs do so.

The East–West differences become even more pronounced when one tallies the positive and negative remarks in terms of the structural advantages and disadvantages of the social market economy (Table 8.3). The first panel of the table lists the number of times MPs mention either a systemic advantage or disadvantage. For example, only 11.3 per cent of western MPs mention no structural advantage at all, whereas 26.6 per cent of eastern MPs mention no advantage. Given the fact that eastern Germans acknowledge the superior efficiency of market systems—which moves them out of the zero category—73.5 per cent fall into the bottom two categories in 1992. The percentage is

TABLE 8.3. *Systemic advantages and disadvantages of social market economies* (%)

Score	Systemic advantages			Systemic disadvantages			Score	Net systemic advantages of social market economies		
	East		West	East		West		East		West
	1995	1992	1992	1995	1992	1992		1995	1992	1992
0	16.9	26.6	11.3	38.5	40.5	84.1	−4	1.5	2.5	—
1	47.7	46.9	38.2	43.1	22.8	13.5	−3	3.1	2.5	1.1
2	30.8	20.3	43.8	15.4	25.3	1.2	−2	6.3	16.5	—
3	4.6	6.2	5.6	3.1	8.9	1.2	−1	23.1	16.5	4.5
4	—	—	1.1	—	2.5	—	0	24.6	19.0	12.4
							1	21.5	27.9	36.0
							2	18.5	10.1	39.3
							3	1.5	5.0	5.6
							4	—	—	1.1

Note: Scores of the second panel are computed by subtracting the disadvantage score from the advantage score.

reduced, however slightly, to 64.6 per cent by 1995, but this figure also indicates that about two-thirds of eastern MPs remain sceptical—to put it cautiously—about the market system. In contrast, less than half of western MPs (49.5 per cent) mention none or one structural advantage; the majority of western MPs mention at least two structural advantages.

East–West differences over economic ideals are especially large with respect to the disadvantage scores (i.e. how many systemic disadvantages MPs mention). In 1992 the vast majority of western MPs do not mention a single disadvantage (84.1 per cent), whereas only 40.5 per cent of eastern MPs fall into this category. If one creates a net-advantage score by subtracting the negative score from the positive, the resulting scores reflect the different economic preferences in the East and the West: the majority of eastern MPs (57 per cent) fall into the neutral (0) or negative categories, whereas only 18 per cent of western MPs have a comparable score. This is perhaps the most impressive confirmation of the institutional learning axiom: a large majority of western MPs hold positive views about market ideals, whereas eastern MPs, on balance, hold negative views about them *despite the widely acknowledged efficiency of a market economy*.

The overall stability of MPs' responses over the three-year period indicates that MPs' economic values adapt only slowly to the new economic order. By 1995 58.6 per cent of eastern MPs fall into the negative group, which is virtually unchanged when compared to the 1992 interviews (57 per cent). The individual-level stability confirms that most MPs basically did not change their views about the market system over the three years (Fig. 8.1). Among those MPs who had a negative score in 1992 (i.e. their net score was below zero), 80 per cent continue to hold critical views about the market system. Likewise, the stability bar dominates the other two groups. Evidently, deeply held economic values do not change over a short time-period, which is a clear indication that the conversion model—once again—is undermined. Finally, just as the institutional learning axiom predicts, post-war MPs in the East are substantially more likely than pre-war MPs to evaluate market principles critically (r = .31). Such cohort-related differences do not exist in the West (r = –.08).

On balance, MPs' responses to the open-ended question and the persistence of socialist ideals in the East reflect the differing nuances of the interview conversations. In the West MPs largely focus on itemizing the benefits of market economies for eastern Germans, while

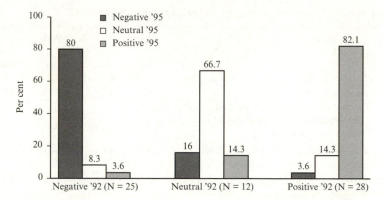

F IG. 8.1. The stability of economic values among MPs, 1992–1995

also acknowledging the significant short-term problems created by the transition. In the East MPs frequently acknowledge the superior capacity of market economies, and then enumerate the systemic flaws of market systems.

Economic Values and the Mass Public. Does the eastern German public share eastern elites' reservations about market principles? Public-opinion surveys conducted in eastern and western Germany after 1989 include several indicators that permit an examination of East–West differences at the mass level. Undoubtedly, it would have been ideal to have identical indicators at the elite and mass level, but such information is unfortunately not available. Nevertheless, several indicators in the public-opinion surveys measure citizens' views about market and welfare components (Table 8.4). For example, indicator A focuses on the incentives defined by income inequalities. East–West differences are surprisingly small in 1991, when 48.9 per cent in the East and 46.5 per cent in the West agree with the proposition that citizens' income should be determined by their accomplishments and needs. Likewise, there is virtually unanimous consensus among eastern and western Germans with respect to the proposition that the government should provide basic social security to the needy in a society (E). The strong endorsement of this proposition in both parts of Germany clearly reflects Germany's long welfare tradition, which assumes that a minimum level of social security is a basic right of all citizens. As on the elite level, eastern and western German publics by

T ABLE 8.4. *Economic principles and mass publics, 1991–1994*

Economic value	East		West	
	1991	1994	1991	1994
A. People's income should not only depend on their accomplishments. Instead, every person and his family should have enough for a decent living.	48.9	42.1	46.5	39.6
B. Income differences must be sufficiently large so that people work hard.	58.5	44.1	64.1	62.4
C. Status differences between people are acceptable because they essentially reflect individuals' accomplishments.	45.4	34.5	52.5	57.2
D. By and large, status differences in Germany are just.	15.2	11.2	47.8	45.2
E. The government should guarantee that everybody is provided for in case of illness, emergencies, unemployment, and old age.	98.8	96.7	90.4	86.9
F. In Germany, differences between property owners and the working class persist. One's personal situation determines whether one belongs to the upper or lower class.	n/a	91.0	n/a	62.6
G. In Germany, there are still large differences between social classes. One's social background largely determines what one will achieve in life.	n/a	74.3	n/a	56.8
H. Germany is an open society. What one accomplishes does not depend on one's social background, but on one's skills and education	n/a	53.9	n/a	74.5

Note: Entries are percentages of respondents who agree strongly or somewhat with a statement. Non-German nationals are excluded as are 'don't know' and no answers.

Source: Allbus (1991 and 1994).

and large agree that a government ought to provide a minimal safety net for the needy in a society. However, the limits of this consensus are also reflected with respect to the proposition that status differences in Germany are just (D). In the East only a small minority agrees with this proposition in 1991 (15.2 per cent) whereas almost half of western Germans agree with it (47.8 per cent). In general, however, East–West differences are fairly modest in 1991, a result which appears to be inconsistent with the institutional learning axiom.

By 1994, however, this pattern has changed substantially, mainly because eastern Germans' support for market principles weakened considerably between 1991 and 1994. For example, more eastern citizens agree with propositions B and C in 1991 than in 1994, which is a clear indication that eastern Germans' first-hand experience with the rugged world of economic competition lowered their support for market principles. For example, eastern Germans' views on income differences as incentives to work hard (B) drops from 58.5 per cent to 44.1 per cent. In contrast, the aggregate level remains virtually un-changed among the western public. Because of the reduction in the East and the stability in the West, East–West differences over eco-nomic principles are larger in the later survey. The most plausible explanation for these changes is that eastern Germans' views about the economy shortly after unification were biased in favour of eco-nomic principles that represent western Germany's market economy. By 1994, however, eastern Germans' exposure to the western German economic reality lowered their support for market principles, partly because the complex economic transition increases the need for welfare cushions. At the same time, these problems reinforced those messages eastern Germans were exposed to during the socialist in-stitutional learning period, namely, that a market economy neglects the needy and produces unjust inequality—a theme that frequently emerged in the conversations with MPs.

The growing disillusion with a market economy becomes even more apparent in the decline of eastern Germans' overall evaluations of a market economy between 1990 and 1998 (Noelle-Neumann 1998). When asked in the spring of 1990, before market rules were established on 1 July in the East: 'Do you have a positive or negative opinion about the economic system in Germany?' 77 per cent of the eastern German public responded that they had a positive opinion about it (Fig. 8.2). But this proportion declines dramatically to 19 per cent by the end of 1996 and recovers only slightly in the following two years. The steep decline in positive evaluations clearly indicates that eastern Germans have become much more sceptical about the blessings of the new economic order. Western Germans, in contrast, evaluate the economic system more favourably, even though economic problems

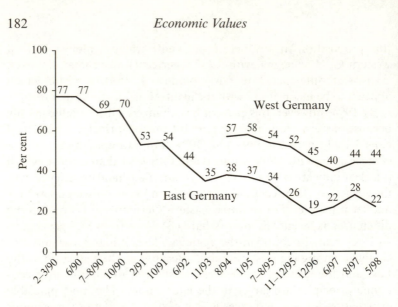

F IG. 8.2. 'Do you have a positive or negative opinion about Germany's economic order?'

(*Note*: Entries are percentages of respondents who have a positive opinion about the economy.)

Source: Allensbacher Institut für Demoskopie.

apparently reduce publics' favourable views by 1998. Overall, these developments suggest that both citizens' institutional learning and their present economic circumstances affect their evaluations of the market system.

In light of these dynamics at the mass level and the responses of parliamentarians, it would be premature to conclude that socialist institutional learning has not affected eastern Germans' economic values. One reason for the moderate East–West differences found shortly after Germany's unification is that eastern Germans were quite enthusiastic about the arrival of a more efficient economy. As we saw, however, this enthusiasm was reduced by the eastern public's exposure to economic difficulties and the rugged rules of market competition. Another reason why East–West differences appear to be surprisingly moderate after Germany's unification concerns the content of several closed-ended indicators. Typically, available economic indicators focus in broad terms on the *welfare* dimension of economies, but they tend not to measure *socialist* principles, such as establishing an income ceiling or on achieving social equality for everybody. The absence of indicators measuring typical socialist principles—as opposed to welfare principles—reduces the odds that significant East–West differences are found in empirical analyses. We already saw at the elite level that eastern elites are substantially more likely than western MPs to espouse socialist views when they evaluated the systemic properties of market and socialist economies, whereas East–West differences among MPs were fairly moderate with respect to the welfare indicators. Analogously, I suggest that analysts would find greater East–West differences over economic values if citizens' socialist values were analysed.

That this proposition is not pure speculation, but is grounded in empirical reality, can be documented by the following example. A comparisons of two indicators included in the International Social Justice Survey (1991) is instructive because they measure different degrees to which governments should intervene in the economy. A first indicator focuses on the welfare dimension by asking respondents to indicate their agreement with the following statement:

The government should guarantee everyone a minimum standard of living.

A second indicator, however, focuses on establishing an income ceiling—a socialist device to remedy social and political inequalities:

The government should place an upper limit on the amount of money any one person can make.

With regard to the first indicator, the familiar result emerges. Eastern (93.5 per cent) and western Germans (84.9 per cent) agree that individuals deserve a minimum level of support from their government irrespective of their achievements. However, the second indicator produces substantial East–West differences. Almost two-thirds of eastern Germans (60 per cent), but only 32.3 per cent of the western public agree with the establishment of income ceilings; those who prefer the establishment of a ceiling represent the majority in the East, but they constitute a minority in the West. The different responses of eastern and western Germans to these indicators clearly illustrate how cautious analysts must be in interpreting various economic indicators. Because of the consensus over welfare policies in the unified Germany, measures which tend to focus on the welfare dimension underestimate true East–West differences over socialist-economic ideals.

Overall, when one examines indicators that clearly distinguish between welfare and socialist components, East–West differences are considerably larger than one is led to conclude on the basis of measures that focus on citizens' views toward welfare activities alone. Cumulatively, these results suggest that publics' responses shortly after Germany's unification to welfare indicators frequently underestimate the true impact of socialist institutional learning on eastern and western Germans' economic values because: (1) eastern Germans were biased in favour of western economic principles; and (2) because of the frequent unavailability of indicators measuring core elements of socialist economies.[1] When one uses indicators that explicitly focus on socialist economic principles, East–West differences are substantially larger than when welfare indicators are used, and the empirical results reflect those patterns that are predicted by the institutional learning and diffusion axioms.

East–West differences exist within all parties (Figs. 8.3 and 8.4). For example, eastern CDU-MPs on balance hold positive views about the structural advantages of market economies, but western CDU-MPs are significantly more positive about a market system. Likewise, eastern SPD-MPs barely score above the neutral point whereas western SPD-MPs, on balance, view a market economy considerably more

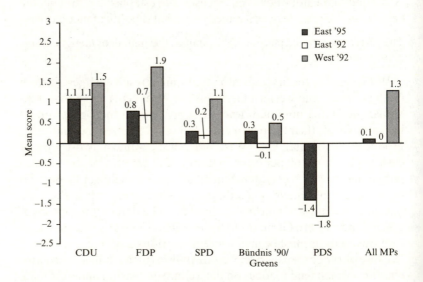

FIG. 8.3. Comparative market advantage, by party

(*Note*: Entries are mean scores of the net advantage indicator which ranges from a negative score of –4 to positive 4.)

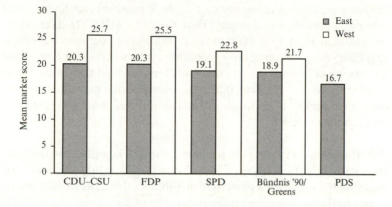

FIG. 8.4. Economic welfare values among mass publics, by party

(*Note*: Entries are mean scores of the market values index. The index is the summary score of publics' responses to the statements presented in Table 4.1. The index ranges from 8 (indicating little support for market values) to 40. N was too small to compute mean for western PDS supporters (N = 3).)
Source: Allbus (1994).

positively. It is important to note that eastern CDU-MPs come out in favour of a market system, both in 1992 and 1995, whereas most eastern MPs remain ambivalent (in case of SPD-MPs and MPs from the Bündnis '90/Green party) or clearly have negative views about the market system (PDS-MPs). One might be tempted to characterize these numerical differences as 'differences of degrees'. Yet, the persistence of East–West differences even within the CDU—recall some of the verbatim accounts by CDU-MPs presented earlier—attests to the difficulty of truly unifying Germany *within* party groups. These East–West differences over economic values concern basic pillars of a market-based economy and, in my view, cannot be qualified as marginal.

CULTURAL TRANSMISSION VERSUS PERCEPTIONS OF THE ECONOMY

The results thus far show that eastern citizens are considerably more equivocal in their support for market values than the western public. Is this difference a consequence of the desolate economic situation of the eastern German economy or the bleak prospect for the personal economic conditions of many East German MPs? Or does MPs' institutional learning dominate the formation of economic values so that East–West differences over economic values persist even when the perception of present economic conditions are held constant? These questions call for a multivariate analysis where one may assess the independent impact of institutional learning and economic perceptions on economic values.

The Measures. At the level of parliamentarians, I employ two dependent variables in the analyses. First, I constructed an additive indicator based on the statements presented in Table 8.1. For reasons of brevity, I refer to the closed-ended indicator as the welfare indicator, because agreement with most constituent measures does not automatically imply a rejection of market principles. Secondly, I employ the net advantage score of MPs' responses to the open-ended question in order to capture directly MPs' views on the systemic advantage of market economies compared to a socialist economy. I reversed the polarity of this systemic advantage indicator in order to have the same polarity for this and the welfare indicator. The relationship between these two indicators is substantial ($r = .51$), both in the East ($r = .53$) and the West ($r = .37$).

Three indicators measure the impact of institutional learning on economic values. First, a dichotomous indicator measures whether MPs are from eastern or western Berlin. According to H1, eastern elites are more supportive of welfare views and more critical of the market economy than western elites, independent of economic perceptions. Secondly, a dichotomous variable measures whether MPs are born before or after the Second World War. Consistent with H2, the initial analyses presented earlier indicate that eastern MPs born after that war are more supportive of welfare principles and more critical of market systems than pre-war elites in the East. Such cohort differences do not emerge within the West, because both pre-war and post-war elites were exposed to some form of market economy. A third indicator included under the rubric of institutional learning is MPs' egalitarian-democratic ideals (Chapter 5), because the third hypothesis links these ideals to critical evaluations of a market economy.

I included the communist party indicator, despite reservations, because communist party MPs are exclusively from the eastern part of the city. I therefore sought to control for this East–West difference in the multivariate analyses. The problem in using this variable as a predictor of economic values is that MPs' partisanship actually measures a significant portion of the dependent variable, namely, their economic values. The inclusion entails that the multivariate analyses represent a conservative test for the different manifestations of the institutional learning process.[2]

In accordance with hypotheses four through seven, four indicators measure the influence of economic conditions on economic values. First, MPs' expectations about their future personal finances assess whether the anticipated personal economic insecurity increases support for socialist values. Secondly, MPs' income measures their present economic conditions. Thirdly, an additive index based on an open-ended question about the most pressing economic problems in Germany and Berlin measures MPs' perceptions of contemporary economic problems. Fourthly, an additive indicator based on the open-ended economy question gauges whether MPs believe that the market economy will eventually generate higher income and better living standards within East Germany.[3] Together, these variables capture MPs' personal economic circumstances as well as an important part of MPs' evaluations of the national and regional economy. These analyses also included the control variables introduced in the previous chapters.[4]

At the level of mass publics, the dependent variable is the summary index based on citizens' response to the indicators presented in Table 8.4. The predictor variables are similar to those at the level of elites, but they are not identical. Still, with the necessary caution one may compare the structural origins of market and socialist values across the mass and elite level.

The Results. Table 8.5 presents the results of the multivariate analysis at the elite level. The main entry in each cell is the standardized regression coefficient from an ordinary least-square analysis. These coefficients allow one to determine: (1) whether a variable has a statistically significant effect on MPs' economic values holding constant the other variables; and (2) the relative strength of predictor variables compared to the other variables. Standardized coefficients, therefore, provide an opportunity to evaluate the relative importance of predictors in affecting individuals' economic values. The unstandardized coefficient appears in parentheses. These coefficients are used to assess the

TABLE 8.5. *Predicting MPs' economic values*

Predictors	Welfare economic values			Systemic disadvantages of market economies		
	East	West	Combined	East	West	Combined
Institutional learning						
West Berlin	—	—	-.10	—	—	-.23***
			(-1.90)			(-.69)
Post-war	.09	-.06	.03	.15	.02	.01
	(1.50)	(-1.10)	(.64)	(.46)	(.04)	(.03)
Egalitarian democratic conception	.17**	.13	.14**	.17*	.24**	.13*
	(1.50)	(4.50)	(1.90)	(.29)	(.89)	(.27)
Communist Party MP	.19*	n/a	.04	.41***	n/a	.36***
	(4.00)		(1.20)	(1.60)		(1.70)
Economic factors						
Better personal financial future	-.01	-.21**	-.16**	-.13	-.19	-.08
	(-.12)	(-3.20)	(-2.00)	(-.25)	(-.30)	(-.16)
Present income	-.26***	-.01	-.11	-.27***	-.03	-.11
	(-2.60)	(-.04)	(-.90)	(-.48)	(-.03)	(-.15)
Contemporary economic problems	.17*	.05	.04	.19**	.04	.08
	(2.00)	(.76)	(.72)	(.49)	(.06)	(.18)
Positive prospective national economy	-.30***	-.07	-.16**	-.34***	.29***	.01
	(-4.90)	(-1.00)	(-2.40)	(1.10)	(.44)	(.02)

Social values and demographics

Postmaterialism	.09	.24**	.22***	.07*	.09	.06*
	(.86)	(2.30)	(2.30)	(.12)	(.10)	(.09)
Religiosity	−.24***	−.28***	−.21***	−.08	.01	.03
	(−1.40)	(−1.80)	(−1.40)	(.09)	(.01)	(.03)
Gender (Female)	.01	.17*	.12*	.18*	.17	.05
	(.04)	(3.70)	(2.50)	(.61)	(.38)	(.17)
Education	−.25***	.09	.01	.06	.02	.03
	(−2.50)	(.69)	(.02)	(.10)	(.02)	(.05)
R-square	.63	.41	.48	.52	.25	.44
(N)	(77)	(84)	(161)	(77)	(84)	(161)

Note: Entries are standardized regression coefficients (unstandardized coefficients appear in parentheses). *, **, and *** denote significance on the .10, .05, and .01 level, respectively.

impact of the same variable in different groups. For instance, in order to compare the impact of MPs' present income on their welfare economic values among eastern and western MPs, I compare the unstandardized coefficients in the East (b = –2.5) with that in the West (b = –.02).

Beginning with eastern MPs, it turns out that economic factors strongly influence both welfare views and their evaluations of the systemic advantages of the market economy. MPs who believe that economic conditions will improve are less likely to view market values critically (beta = –.30) and are more likely to evaluate the systemic features of a market system positively (beta = –.34). Likewise, perceptions of contemporary economic problems increase eastern MPs' support for welfare measures (beta = .17) and generate critical evaluations of the systemic traits of a market economy (beta = .19). Finally, eastern MPs' economic values partially hinge upon their personal financial situation (the income coefficients are beta = –.26 and beta = –.27 for the two dependent variables). In short, among eastern MPs positive economic perceptions tend to increase their support for market values.

In contrast to eastern MPs, economic factors are considerably less important in shaping western MPs' views on the market economy (H7). Only if western MPs' believe that their personal financial situation will improve are they more likely to endorse welfare measures (beta = –.21). The different effect of economic conditions clearly reflects the Eastonian reservoir of trust in the market system among western MPs, whose confidence in a market order is less affected by short-term performance than in the East. In contrast to eastern MPs, the strongest influence on western MPs' welfare views are their basic value predispositions, such as religiosity (beta = –.28) and post-material values (beta = .24). Although positive prospective evaluations seemingly lead to negative, not positive, evaluations of the market economy (beta = .29), this surprising finding probably results from a methodological artefact.[5] Overall, these patterns clearly suggest that eastern MPs' economic values are substantially shaped by economic factors, but western MPs' economic views are less susceptible to the vagaries of variable economic conditions.

But economic perceptions are not the only source of economic values, because MPs' institutional learning equally affects their economic values. In particular, eastern MPs are substantially less likely than western MPs to view the market economy in favourable terms (beta = –.23). This result is noteworthy because the analysis controls for communist party membership and MPs' perceptions of the economy. Evidently, MPs' basic economic values, especially in terms of the systemic principles, are partially acquired through a process of institutional learning. Further, eastern MPs who hold egalitarian-democratic ideals are more likely to hold welfare orientations (beta = .17) and view a market economy critically (beta = .17). The moderate—though significant—magnitude of the egalitarian ideals coefficient is partly due to the strong influence of communist party membership on both egalitarian democratic ideals and economic ideals (Rohrschneider 1994: 934). Consequently, if the PDS-indicator is excluded from this analysis, the egalitarian ideals indicator is a highly significant predictor of MPs' net advantage score (beta = –.24, p = .01). This evidence corroborates the argument that MPs' demo-cratic conception influences their economic values (H3).[6] Finally, the cohort variable is insignificant, which initially conflicts with H2, although the zero-order relationship is quite substantial among East MPs (r = .29). The insignificance is undoubtedly due to the fact that the analysis includes variables, such as egalitarian conceptions, which are related to both economic values and cohort membership. In short, cohort membership indirectly, but not directly, shapes MPs' economic views.

Evidently, both economic factors *and* MPs' institutional learning affect their economic values. Given the inclusion of several control variables, the magnitude of the predictors measuring institutional learning is impressive. Especially with regard to the systemic advant-ages of market systems, the evidence points toward a long-term pro-cess shaping MPs' views about the preferred economic order.[7]

When a comparable model is estimated at the mass level, the results—to the extent that they are comparable—convey a similar message with the exception discussed below (Table 8.6). Most import-ant, the western German public is substantially more likely to endorse market values than the eastern German public (beta = .31). In fact, the East–West coefficient is unusually large, given the typical magni-tude of regression coefficients in analyses of public-opinion surveys. The East–West variable is by far the strongest predictor—none of the other variables comes even close in magnitude. In fact, the second-strongest predictor within the East is eastern publics' views on socialism-as-an-ideal (beta = –.20), which further corroborates the institutional learning axiom (Roller 1997). Eastern citizens who continue to hold socialist ideals are substantially less likely to endorse market values. The central message is unequivocal: welfare economic values at the mass level are to a large degree acquired through institutional learning independent of individuals' economic situation or their perceptions of the economy. In addition, as on the elite level, economic perceptions also affect citizens' welfare views. Indeed, with

TABLE 8.6. *Predicting market values of mass publics, 1994*

Predictors	East	West	Combined
Institutional learning			
West Germany	n/a	n/a	.31***
			(3.70)
Age	.01	.14*	.09***
	(.01)	(.05)	(.03)
Socialism is a good ideal	−.20***	−.14***	−.16***
	(−.79)	(−.51)	(−.60)
Communist party supporter	−.09**	−.04*	−.06***
	(−1.30)	(−4.70)	(−1.60)
Economic factors			
Better personal financial future	.10***	.02	.03
	(.71)	(.15)	(.17)
Present income	.10***	.19***	.16***
	(.14)	(.25)	(.22)
Contemporary economic problems	.14***	.12***	.11***
	(.97)	(.80)	(.84)
Positive prospective national economy	.14***	.12***	.11***
	(.87)	(.74)	(.78)
Social values and demographics			
Postmaterialism	.04	.04**	.02*
	(.23)	(.35)	(.08)
Religiosity	.01	.01	.02*
	(.07)	(.03)	(.08)
Gender (female)	.02	.02	.02
	(.21)	(.14)	(.25)
Education	.02	.04	.03
	(.09)	(.18)	(.16)
Adjusted R-square	.17	.12	.27
(N)	(756)	(1604)	(2360)

Note: Entries are standardized regression coefficients (unstandardized coefficients appear in parentheses). *, **, and *** denote significance on the .10, .05, and .01 level, respectively.

Source: Allbus (1994).

the exception of individuals' expectations about their future personal finances, all coefficients are statistically significant. At the same time, these coefficients are relatively modest, especially compared to the indicators measuring the impact of institutional learning (see also Rohrschneider 1996*a*).[8]

Generally, the structural origins of welfare economic values are comparable at the mass and elite level. However, there is one difference in the East which suggests a different process with respect to the formation of economic values at the mass and elite level in a new democracy. If one considers the overall contribution of institutional learning versus economic predictors, the former clearly has the stronger effect at the mass level compared to economic predictors. Among eastern MPs, however, the effects of economic perceptions and institutional learning variables are of comparable magnitude. Evidently, eastern MPs' economic perceptions are more likely to 'push' MPs toward market values if they evaluate economic conditions positively. Clearly, MPs' institutional learning has a substantial effect on MPs' economic values. This effect, however, may be offset to some degree by short-term calculations about which economic rules are more beneficial to eastern MPs in light of their assessment of various economic dimensions. The eastern public, in contrast, is less influenced by such short-term factors and predominately evaluates economic issues on the basis of their long-standing values acquired through their institutional learning. This structural difference suggests that MPs in a new democracy may be swayed more than a mass public by positive economic assessments. This is consistent with the attributes which are typically associated with mass publics and political elites: the former perceives the political world predominately in light of their long-standing predispositions, whereas political elites, who are cognitively more sophisticated and politically more skilled than mass publics, are guided by both long-term predispositions and shorter-term considerations.

In fact, this structural difference between mass publics and elites in the context of a new democracy initially supports institutionalists' focus on the power of new institutions to convert elites' values after regime transitions. At the same time, the results of the chapter also point to the limits of this argument. While economic perceptions may convert elites toward market values, their long-standing predispositions toward socialist-economic values puts a ceiling on the positive effects of economic perceptions. While eastern elites' economic values may be moved more toward market values in case of positive economic perceptions than the economic values of mass publics, eastern elites remain substantially less enthusiastic about market values when compared to political elites of the West. Further, the impact of economic perceptions on elites' economic values is a double-edged sword: if economic perceptions worsen, eastern MPs' views toward market principles become more negative. In sum, in the West market values are mainly shaped by individuals' institutional learning, both at the level of mass publics and political elites. In the context of a new economic system, eastern elites' economic views are more strongly shaped by short-term calculations than those of the eastern public, but economic values at both levels are substantially shaped by their institutional learning.

COMPARATIVE ECONOMIC VALUES

This chapter discussed at several junctures that western European publics endorse welfare programmes which provide citizens with the basic material needs. Therefore, one expects that western Europeans should endorse governmental programmes which provide citizens' basic needs. The same expectation emerges for East-Central European publics, given their socialist institutional learning. Greater East–West European differences are likely to appear when citizens evaluate socialist principles. Like eastern Germans, eastern Europeans may be more likely than western Europeans to endorse policies, for example, designed to establish income ceilings, given socialism's focus on social-egalitarianism.

Overall, these expectations are fulfilled (Table 8.7). The responses of mass publics to two indicators about individuals' income hint at socialism's persistent legacy. In terms of the provision of a minimal living standard, there is virtually unanimous support for welfare policies in the East and the West. With the exception of the USA, a large majority of publics endorses the idea that governments should supply citizens with essential goods. While it goes beyond the scope of this book to provide a full explanation for the cross-national differences, it is not surprising that the US public constitutes the exception. A bare majority of US citizens supports the notion that a government should provide a minimal living standard. This pattern reflects a

TABLE 8.7. *Welfare and socialist economic values in Europe* (%)

Country	Governments should provide minimal living standards	Governments should establish income ceilings
Bulgaria	92.5	42.3
Czech Republic	88.0	29.7
Eastern Germany	93.5	60.0
Hungary	91.0	57.8
Poland	87.0	47.4
Russia	88.0	34.2
Britain	82.8	38.6
Netherlands	74.9	30.9
Western Germany	93.5	32.3
USA	56.1	16.8

Note: Entries are percentages of respondents agreeing with the statements.

Source: *International Social Justice Surveys* (1991).

sentiment discussed in depth by McClosky and Zaller (1984), who document the pervasive support for free market competition in the largest capitalist economy. Indeed, given their research, it may appear surprising how many US citizens endorse the statement about minimal living standards.

More East–West variations emerge in the context of the socialist indicator. The strongest support in the West is displayed by the British public (38.6 per cent), followed by the western German public. As might be expected, only 16.8 per cent of the US public agree that government should establish an income ceiling, thus expressing the strongest rejection of this socialist principle among western publics. The corresponding percentages in post-socialist publics are, on average, significantly higher than in the West, indicating that eastern Germany does not represent an unusual case among East-Central European nations. Like eastern Germans, Hungarians (57.8 per cent) and to a lesser extent the Polish public endorse government programmes which would establish an income ceiling.

Surprisingly, however, only a third of Russian citizens support this socialist principle in 1991. Similarly, analysing the *Times/Mirror* surveys, Kaase (1994) also finds unexpectedly strong support for basic market principles such as accepting unemployment, or limited government intervention in the economy. In contrast to these results, a survey of the European part of the USSR in 1990 found that 68.1 per cent agreed that 'the government should try to equalize income levels', which prompted Duch (1993) to question the commitment of the Russian public to market reforms. These partially conflicting patterns undoubtedly reflect the turmoil which citizens in the former Soviet Union experienced. It is also possible that the responses in support of market principles in the International Social Justice and *Times/Mirror* surveys resulted in part from the time-point of the surveys (late 1991), when the full impact of economic reforms had not become clear yet. This conjecture is strengthened by the fact that East-Central European publics which support market reforms *also* favour a political system that generates social-egalitarian outcomes (Chapter 5). Although many citizens in post-socialist nations may prefer a more efficient economy—and the market system promises greater efficiency and affluence—they also prefer a political system that limits the extent to which market competition is implemented. Like eastern Germans, then, the Russian and other Central European publics may have endorsed market principles in the early 1990s because they represented a better economic future. Once they are confronted by the hardship of economic competition, especially during difficult transitions, individuals' support for market principles may falter.

Indeed, there is evidence paralleling the eroding support for a market economy found in eastern Germany. When asked in the early 1990s whether market reforms are right or wrong, there was considerable support for market reform in East-Central Europe (Table 8.8). The 'don't know' responses are included in the calculations of the baseline because these responses likely result from genuine confusion, given the economic and social havoc caused by economic transitions.

Most post-socialist European publics start out fairly optimistically. Almost two-thirds of the publics in Hungary and Poland favour market reforms in 1990. Support is still fairly high in 1991, even in the European part of Russia where almost half (46.7 per cent) of respondents think that market reforms are right. There is, however, a noticeable decline in most countries by 1996. The support for the Russian public for market reforms decreases substantially, at one time even dropping below 20 per cent. Support also decreases in Bulgaria, Hungary, and the Czech and Slovak republics. Only the Polish and Romanian publics maintain majority support for the idea of market reforms. There is a corresponding increase concerning the proportion of those who believe market reforms are wrong, although in some countries, like among the Czech public, the percentage of 'don't know' answers increases to the detriment of the support group. In this nation, market reforms may be viewed more sceptically than earlier, but they are not rejected entirely. Overall, with the exception of Romania and Poland, these data suggest a fairly significant drop in support for market systems.

As in eastern Germany, then, the developments in East-Central Europe indicate that market systems initially experienced a short 'honeymoon', where majorities of publics supported reforms and even appeared to accept the ideological values underlying a market system. The memories about the inefficiencies of state-run economies undoubtedly created a reservoir of support for market systems. However, as post-socialist publics experience the rough-and-tumble of economic competition, rising unemployment, and declining material security, publics' enthusiasm for market reforms is reduced substantially.

TABLE 8.8. *Are market reforms right or wrong in East-Central Europe?* (%)

Reforms are:	Bulgaria	Czech Republic	Slovakia	Hungary	Poland	Romania	Russia
Right							
1990	46.4	n/a	n/a	61.8	61.1	n/a	n/a
1991	61.8	n/a	n/a	65.1	56.0	35.3	46.7
1992	56.3	55.4	51.3	55.6	55.7	66.1	40.6
1993	52.1	51.8	42.1	46.2	57.3	66.1	30.7
1994	39.7	48.6	43.6	44.1	51.6	71.9	23.2
1995	40.3	43.7	39.8	40.3	64.2	71.5	19.9
1996	45.8	44.9	42.4	38.6	63.4	80.3	24.6
Wrong							
1990	24.4	n/a	n/a	12.6	13.8	n/a	n/a
1991	16.4	n/a	n/a	11.4	20.8	n/a	33.5
1992	20.4	32.8	38.3	17.9	24.3	24.5	41.6
1993	27.3	35.9	42.1	25.1	22.3	23.4	53.2
1994	42.7	36.3	42.0	23.5	23.3	20.9	62.7
1995	33.0	36.0	39.7	33.8	14.9	21.0	65.4
1996	32.1	14.5	40.6	30.8	20.7	13.9	58.4

Note: Don't-know responses were included in the computation of the baseline and constitute the third response category.

Source: Central Eurobarometers 1–7.

CONCLUSION

The overall message of this chapter parallels that of the previous chapters. Eastern and western Germans' economic values reflect the economic structures that existed during Germany's division. Western Germans are supportive of the basic structural parameters of a social market economy, but also value the economic and political advantages that a market-based economy presumably generates, such as greater efficiency, more national wealth, and greater personal liberties for citizens. Eastern Germans, in contrast, lament the loss of solidarity, the worsening climate in social and personal relations, and the loss of social security, while also recognizing the superior capacity of market economies. When given an opportunity directly to compare a market and a socialist system in their own words, eastern elites adhere to a surprising degree to socialist ideals, whereas western elites evince social market principles within all parties. And when publics' views about socialist principles are examined, East–West differences at the mass level parallel those at the elite level. This persistence of socialist economic values is especially impressive in light of the widespread acknowledgment that a market system is more efficient than a socialist economy. It seems reasonable to conclude that many eastern Germans prefer an efficient socialist economy over a social market system. Although comparable data do not exist for East-Central European countries, the declining support for market reforms in several post-socialist nations parallels the developments in eastern Germany. It therefore appears plausible to suggest that indicators measuring socialist economic values would produce significant differences between eastern and western European publics.

Importantly, East–West differences over economic values persist at the mass and elite level after individuals' perceptions of economic conditions are considered simultaneously. Undoubtedly, economic conditions are relevant, especially among eastern Germans. But predictors measuring institutional learning are at least as important as economic perceptions. The East–West variable, for example, is the strongest predictor at the mass level, and it is as strong as most economic factors in affecting economic values at the elite level. Additionally, among eastern MPs and the mass public, a relationship exists between their views toward socialist-egalitarian ideals and economic values. Eastern citizens who continue to value socialism as an ideal are considerably more reserved about market characteristics. And Chapter 5 documented the widespread persistence of these ideals among eastern MPs and the eastern mass public. As in the other chapters, these findings imply an intricate process by which East German MPs may come to accept market values unequivocally. Since eastern MPs' endorsement of market principles partially depends on the policy performance of the market economy, economic growth may offset East MPs' critical predispositions toward market economies. If, on the other hand, economic problems continue to plague the East German economic sector, economic problems are likely to reinforce eastern Germans' critical predispositions toward market principles, since market values are partly generated by economic expectations. I do not suggest that eastern MPs wish for a return of the collapsed socialist order. In fact, the widely acknowledged efficiency of market forces reflects the belief of a majority of eastern Germans that economic well-being cannot be accomplished within the socialist order. However, even under the best of circumstances (i.e. a booming economy), the institutional learning effect found in this study raises doubts about whether eastern Germans born and raised in the socialist state will ever fully endorse market principles. Strong economic performance may silence critics of market forces, but egalitarian ideals are likely to persist for a large proportion of post-war MPs even as economic conditions improve.

Theoretically, the persistence of socialist economic ideals once again confirms the institutional learning and diffusion axioms. The message is as brief as it is clear: market economic values did not diffuse into the East. The diffusion axiom provides the reasons why one would not expect such diffusion to occur in the first place. Even if market values are modified by welfare policies, market principles clearly conflict with a socialist belief system. Further, as I discussed earlier, market values are based on self-reliance and restraint—two citizenship-qualities that are difficult to develop in an environment that provides few opportunities for such development. As in the previous chapters, then, the results of this chapter again point toward the conclusion that Germany's unification is an ongoing process that may take several years, perhaps as long as a generation, to reach completion.

The Sources of Institutional Support

This chapter considers how individuals' ideological values affect their institutional support. How do citizens who favour an egalitarian democracy evaluate democratic institutions in unified Germany? How do individuals holding plebiscitarian preferences evaluate representative institutions? More generally, do ideological values that are presumably incompatible with democratic institutions lower individuals' support for them, as culturalists assume? Or are citizens' performance evaluations of institutions a better predictor of institutional support? Thus, while the previous chapters focus on the institutions-to-values process, this chapter examines the values-to-institutional support process at the micro-level.

In light of Germany's post-war history, the questions raised above are important in their own right, but their theoretical significance reaches well beyond Germany. The relationship between ideological values and institutional support is at the centre of cultural analyses which assume a link between the two phenomena (Chapter 2). Surprisingly, however, culturalists have conducted little research directly examining the relationship between ideological values and institutional support (more of which below). In turn, institutionalists dispute that ideological values influence citizens' institutional support, implying that the two phenomena are—if at all—only weakly related. Instead, they maintain that the distributional qualities of a system exert the strongest effect on institutional support. Therefore, directly examining these relationships at the micro-level, this chapter addresses an important controversy in the democratic transition literature. Germany's contemporary situation—a new democracy in the East and an established one in the West—offers an opportunity to examine how a nation's democratic experience affects levels and sources of support for democratic institutions.

The present chapter is structured broadly into two parts. The first part suggests that the original formulation of the congruence postulate in Almond and Verba's *The Civic Culture* actually contains two versions and that these variants subsequently complicate the dialogue between culturalists and institutionalists. Then, based on the ideological performance axiom, the discussion will suggest several hypotheses which are examined empirically in the second part.

WHY CITIZENS SUPPORT DEMOCRATIC INSTITUTIONS

Studies of democratic transitions which build on Almond and Verba's *The Civic Culture* assume that citizens' ideological values influence the stability of democratic institutions because, as Almond and Verba argue, a 'democratic form of participatory political system requires . . . a political culture consistent with it' (Almond and Verba 1963: 5). *The Civic Culture* adopts both an individual-level and national-level perspective in conceptualizing the congruence postulate. At the individual level, it maintains that individuals ought to hold those values that underlie a liberal democracy (p. 32). At the national level, *The Civic Culture* maintains that the overall distribution of orientations within a nation must be congruent with the institutional framework (pp. 31–2). The congruence argument, then, maintains that citizens must hold values that match democratic institutions. This presumably increases the stability of a democracy, provided that the national aggregate of democratic views is sufficiently large. Conversely, citizens who do not support democratic values should also be less likely to support a liberal democracy, which—if enough citizens share non-democratic orientations—reduces the stability of a democratic system. Although Almond and Verba note that other factors, such as the performance of institutions, affect the stability of a political system, they undoubtedly emphasize cultural values as the central sources of institutional support (Lijphart 1980).

However, *The Civic Culture* does not investigate the individual-level relationship between ideological values and institutional support empirically, despite the fact that the congruence postulate assumes the existence of this linkage. This reflects one central assumption of the research design of *The Civic Culture*. To illustrate this, consider Figure 9.1, which depicts the logic of the congruence postulate. Throughout *The Civic Culture* the study tests the congruence postulate by examining the value predispositions of citizens in five nations (e.g. social

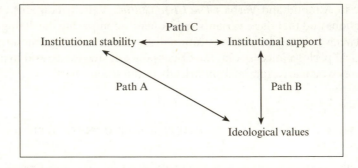

FIG. 9.1. The logic of the congruence postulate

tolerance, pluralism), and then correlates this value distribution, aggregated by nation, with institutional stability observed in the five nations (path A).

Importantly, *The Civic Culture* does not directly analyse the relationship between individuals' values and their institutional support (path B). However, the logic of the congruence postulate is that value predispositions shape citizens' institutional support (path B), which ultimately may influence the stability of existing institutions (path C). In those instances where *The Civic Culture* examines aspects of citizens' views on existing institutions, the analyses primarily focus on whether citizens are affected by institutions, laws, or regulations, or whether citizens believe they can influence the political process. Because the relationship represented by path B is, with few exceptions, not examined, the study assumes that a strong link exists between these two dimensions (a strong version of the congruence postulate). If this assumption is made, one may directly correlate ideological values, aggregated by nation, with the observed stability of institutions (path A) in order to examine the relationship between regime stability and individuals' ideological values.

Undoubtedly, the strong version of the congruence postulate is plausible for the historical period examined in *The Civic Culture*. Although one of the few direct analyses of path B in *The Civic Culture* actually finds only a modest correlation between citizens' support for existing institutions and their ideological values (pp. 248–9), it is plausible to attribute, for example, the instability of the Weimar Republic to the lack of democratic values among several elite sectors and significant parts of the mass public. However, the strong version downplays the necessity to examine empirically the linkage between institutional support and ideological values at the individual level. For if both dimensions are strongly correlated, there is no need to examine empirically its effect on institutional support. However, the relationship may be contingent upon time and place; a fact with which Almond and Verba actually agree. For example, they argue that the policy performance of a political system influences individuals' institutional support along with citizens' values (p. 35). In the same vein, Verba (1965a) suggests the contingent nature between ideological values and institutional support when he notes the surprising stability of democratic institutions in Germany's immediate post-war years, despite the persistence of anti-democratic views. Thus, if one moves beyond the historical context of *The Civic Culture*, the relationship between individuals' ideological values and institutional support may vary considerably—a soft version of the congruence postulate.

One unfortunate consequence of the strong version of the congruence postulate for subsequent research is an overemphasis on the differences between culturalists and institutionalists. Because the strong version suggests the predominance of values in shaping institutional support, regardless of a system's performance, institutionalists reject this 'deterministic' view (Barry 1970; Rogowski 1974). This critique prompted Almond to characterize it as a 'straw-man polemic' (1990: 144). Almond is correct in asserting that *The Civic Culture* frequently suggests a soft version of the congruence postulate. But the strong version implied by the study's research design leads culturalists and institutionalists to magnify their differences and to overlook their complementary contributions to this debate.[1]

Predicting Institutional Support: Ideological Values

Despite the sharp tones culturalists and institutionalists often use, they actually address the same question—what determines institutional support?—and their answers partially complement each other. The ideological performance axiom recognizes the complementary contributions of culturalists and institutionalists to this debate. Figure 9.2 presents a refined version of the axiom.

Let me begin by discussing a question that arises in the context of the congruence postulate: which ideological values are likely to affect citizens' institutional support (path 1)? Certainly, individuals' societal ideals define their expectations about the ultimate goals which a

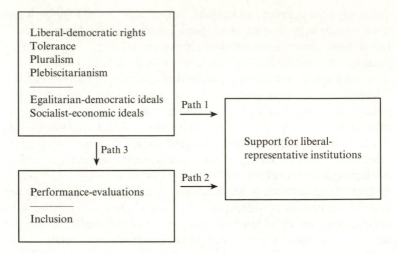

FIG. 9.2. An ideological performance model

political system ought to pursue. These ideals, for example, define the priority citizens attach to the conflicting goals of social and political equality. Therefore, if one disagrees with the ideals of a political system one should also be more likely to distrust these institutions. Based on the congruence postulate, then, the first three hypotheses are straightforward:

- Hypothesis 1: *Social-egalitarian democratic ideals reduce support for a liberal-representative democracy.*
- Hypothesis 2: *Socialist-economic ideals reduce support for a liberal-representative democracy.*
- Hypothesis 3: *Plebiscitarian ideals reduce support for a liberal-representative democracy.*

The connection between the remaining ideological values (i.e. democratic rights, tolerance, and pluralism) and institutional support is less clear. On the one hand, the congruence postulate would predict that those who are less tolerant, for example, are also less supportive of democratic institutions. On the other hand, historical precedents indicate the tentative character of the relationship between procedural values and institutional support. Western Germany's historical trajectory after the Second World War reminds us that democratic institutions may be accepted by a significant proportion of western

German citizens, even though a large proportion of the western German public and elites did not accept basic democratic principles (Gabriel 1987; Merritt 1995). More broadly, even if citizens are intolerant, they may support democratic institutions if they perform well. Therefore, I will test the following hypotheses derived from the congruence postulate, keeping in mind that these relationships are actually tenuous historically:

- Hypothesis 4: *Support for democratic rights increases support for a liberal-representative democracy.*
- Hypothesis 5: *Intolerant views reduce support for a liberal-representative democracy.*
- Hypothesis 6: *Anti-pluralist views reduce support for a liberal-representative democracy.*

Predicting Institutional Support: Distributional Qualities. In contrast to culturalists, institutional analyses emphasize the distributional qualities of institutions as the key to understand why citizens support a system (path 2). Specifically, institutionalists emphasize: (1) the perceived performance of a political system; and (2) the degree to which various elite sectors have access to the decision-making institutions in a political system.

A central contention of institutionalists is that a system's effectiveness influences the support it receives. As long as a new democracy functions well, the argument goes, most individuals are willing to accept these institutions even if they reject the ideological values a system embodies. In short, whether or not ideological values are incongruent with a democracy's premises is a secondary matter. The performance of a political system is not limited to the economic dimension, although this constitutes a central 'output' factor. Institutions must perform well across a range of policies, including administrative tasks, the implementation of laws, or satisfying the idiosyncratic preferences of citizens. Citizens' overall experience with governmental decisions across a range of dimensions shapes their summary evaluations of a system's performance. The perceived performance is especially important for newly established democracies, such as in eastern Germany, where citizens did not have the opportunity to benefit from of a well-functioning democracy (Easton 1965).

- Hypothesis 7: *Positive performance evaluations increase citizens' support for representative institutions.*

Undoubtedly, culturalists have few reservations about accepting this hypothesis—up to a point. The central difference between culturalists and institutionalists is that the former prioritize values as the main source, whereas the latter prioritize the performance of institutions. Indeed, this nuanced difference in emphasis suggests the need to synthesize their arguments. Both approaches essentially agree that citizens with congruent values may nevertheless reject institutions which perform poorly.

Given their importance, performance evaluations are frequently used to explain mass support—or lack thereof—for democratic systems in East-Central Europe (e.g. Kaase 1994; McDonough 1995). The second distributional quality, however, has received less attention in empirical analyses of democratic transitions, because most of them focus on mass publics and not on elites. In particular, institutionalists who examine the role of elites in democratic transitions argue that the openness of new institutions affects elites' willingness to accept a new system. As discussed in Chapter 2, elites who feel barred from important decision-making structures under a new system may reject the system. Conversely, elites with incongruent values may support new democratic institutions if they believe that these provide them with access to the political process. Indeed, although institutionalists focus on democratic transitions, the logic of this argument is not restricted to a newly established democracy. Social movements in western Germany, for instance, sought novel ways throughout the 1980s to influence established party systems and interest groups, because they were often under-represented in national parliaments (Kitschelt 1986; Dalton 1995). Because these movements were unsuccessful in influencing economically oriented policy-makers, they remained sceptical about the benefits of a representative system and often advocated a system with more plebiscitarian procedures. Thus, the openness of institutions may shape groups' evaluations of new and established systems. I refer to this process as the inclusion-argument, for reasons of brevity:

- Hypothesis 8: *Independent of their ideological values, citizens who are able to influence the decision-making process support an existing democracy more strongly than citizens who are excluded from the political process.*

The ideological performance model also considers that ideological values may have an indirect influence on institutional support, via citizens' assessment of a system's performance (path 3). The central notion is that one's societal ideals define the standards by which one assesses the performance of institutions. For example, a socialist evaluates the performance of liberal institutions according to the plight of economic losers and finds existing social problems outrageous. In contrast, a free-marketeer may view a certain level of unemployment as a sign of a smoothly running economy. Indeed, it appears that the central mechanism by which ideological values affect institutional support is predominately indirect. Citizens experience the performance of a political system in a myriad of tangible ways, through, for example, their income levels or their contacts with the government. Because a system's performance has an immediate effect on people's lives, it is likely to bear directly on one's support for a nation's institutional framework. In contrast, ideological values tend to operate in the background. They define the standards by which one judges the performance of a system and they are used to evaluate specific policies or arguments. In short, ideological values affect individuals' evaluations of the performance of a system which, in turns, affects one's institutional support:

• Hypothesis 9: *Ideological values influence citizens' evaluations of institutional performance.*

TRUST IN DEMOCRATIC INSTITUTIONS

MPs were first asked how much confidence they have in five institutions of the political system in Germany: 'Here is a list with important political institutions in our society. Would you tell me how much trust you have in each of these institutions?' MPs evaluated the court system, the constitution, the federal parliament, the bureaucracy, and the executive by means of the familiar seven-point indicator, where a '7' represents 'complete trust' and '1' indicates complete distrust. Widespread trust in institutions increases the stability of a system, because trust 'is the subjective probability of a citizen believing that the political system, or parts of it, will produce preferred outcomes' (Klingemann and Fuchs 1995: 22). This understanding of trust posits that if a system performs well over a longer time-period, it becomes partly insulated against short-term deficiencies—what Easton (1965) called diffuse support. Western Germans increasingly supported institutions regardless of short-term performance deficits because economic and democratic institutions functioned well (Baker, Dalton, and Hildebrandt 1981). However, eastern Germans did not have the opportunity to develop this reservoir of 'good will', which makes it more likely that their support for the new system is contingent on institutions' ability to deliver what eastern citizens expect. Because the sources (and consequences) of institutional trust ought to be measured separately, the indicator measuring MPs' trust in the system does not ask them to evaluate the performance of institutions.

In order to position the conceptual status of institutional trust relative to the legitimacy of a system, consider that distrust in institutions would not automatically indicate that institutions lack legitimacy. This also assumes that individuals value an alternative order more than the existing system (Linz 1978). It is conceivable that confidence in institutions is low but that no system offers itself as a plausible alternative to existing institutions. At the same time, I will provide evidence that MPs' trust in institutions does contain precisely such a comparative reference-point. Citizens' trust in existing institutions, then, reflects an important dimension of institutional support.

In evaluating five institutions in 1992, a majority of MPs in the East and the West strongly endorse the judicial system, the constitutional arrangements, and the parliament (Table 9.1). The support among eastern MPs for courts (71.8 per cent) and the constitution (79.5 per cent) probably reflects their experience with the socialist legal system, which did not limit the influence of the SED on the legal process (Schneider 1988). Eastern and western MPs' trust in the other institutions is noticeably lower, especially with respect to the bureaucracy, where less than one-third of eastern and fewer than half of western MPs trust these institutions. Trust in the executive hovers at the two-thirds mark in the West and falls slightly below the 50 per cent mark in the West.

Clearly, trust in these institutions is substantially weaker among eastern than western MPs, often by a considerable margin, as in the case of the federal parliament (51.3 per cent in the East compared to 77.1 per cent in the West). At the same time, eastern elites' trust passes the majority mark for three of the five institutions and almost half of eastern MPs trust the executive. Only the bureaucracy is distrusted by a clear majority. There is, in other words, equivocal support for several core institutions among eastern MPs.

TABLE 9.1. *Institutional trust of MPs and mass public* (%)

Institutions	East 1995	East 1992	West 1992
Political elites:			
Courts	66.2	71.8	81.6
Constitution	89.2	79.5	94.3
Parliament	53.9	51.3	77.1
Bureaucracy	29.2	23.0	42.5
Executive	49.7	44.9	64.4
		East	West
Mass Public (1994):			
Constitutional court		34.8	61.5
Parliament		14.9	28.4
Local administration		27.5	43.0
Justice system		26.7	47.8
Federal government		21.7	26.9

Note: Entries are percentages of respondents who trust institutions.

Source: (mass public): Allbus (1994).

Support for institutions is considerably weaker among the mass public. Citizens evaluated the constitutional court, the federal parliament, the local administration, the justice system, and the federal government by means of a seven-point scale identical to the one used by MPs. Although the labelling of each institution differs somewhat from the elite surveys—complicating the mass–elite comparison—it is evident that both the eastern and western publics have considerably less trust in Germany's institutions than elites. Only the constitutional court obtains a vote of confidence from a majority of the western public (i.e. a majority chooses response category 7, 6, or 5). But even this respected institution fails to pass the two-thirds mark (61.5 per cent). Levels of distrust at times reach dramatic proportions in both parts of Germany, when, for example, barely 15 per cent of the eastern public trust the parliament. Likewise, parliament receives the second-worst evaluations in the West (28.4 per cent). In light of this widespread distrust at the mass level, both western and eastern elites must be regarded as the pillars of Germany's institutions. In addition, the East–West differences are about as pronounced as those at the elite level, hovering at the 20 per cent mark.[2]

For Germany's democracy, it is a positive development that a significant proportion of eastern MPs supports core institutions. From the perspective of the conversion model advocated by institutionalists, however, it is less encouraging that eastern MPs' confidence in these institutions basically remains constant between 1992 and 1995 (Fig. 9.3). Neither the average trust-levels nor the individual-level conversion suggest that eastern MPs have developed substantially more trust in institutions despite three years of parliamentary work. As in the context of ideological values, this analysis reaches its limits given the relatively few cases in some subgroups. Still, the 'stability bar' dominates eastern MPs' trust. MPs, for example, who trusted the court system in 1992 also trust it in 1995 (81.8 per cent). The only major increase in trust between 1992 and 1995 occurs in the context of the constitution. However, because this was already the most trusted institution in 1992 (79.5 per cent), the development of trust occurred among a relatively small group of MPs. For all other institutions, the evolution of trust is limited to a maximum of about one-fifth of eastern MPs.

The limited development of trust among elites suggests that the situation among mass publics requires considerable time to improve. If elites' intense exposure to the operations of democratic institutions hardly increases their confidence in them over a three-year period, it seems even less likely that ordinary citizens will develop this trust over

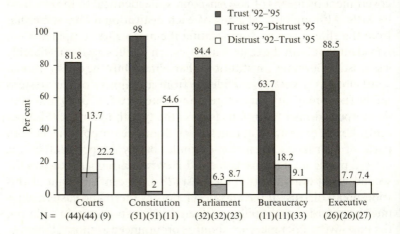

FIG. 9.3. The stability of institutional trust among Eastern MPs, 1992–1995

a comparable time-period. By all accounts, MPs are among the first to develop trust because they are more intensely exposed than mass publics to the operation of a political system (Chapter 2). Clearly, one needs comparable panel data to examine directly the development of institutional trust in the East and the West at the level of mass publics. In the absence of this data, the widespread distrust at the mass levels must be disconcerting.

WHAT DETERMINES INSTITUTIONAL TRUST?

How quickly eastern Germans develop trust in institutions depends partly on the determinants of trust. If institutional trust—or distrust —is primarily linked to ideological values, as culturalists maintain, the odds for short-term increases in institutional trust are low. MPs who hold egalitarian ideals or who favour a socialist economy are probably less inclined to support representative institutions than MPs who do not share these ideals. If, however, institutional trust is predominately determined by present-day performance evaluations, then institutional trust may increase in the short term if the eastern German economy improves. The differences between culturalists and institutionalists thus not only motivate academic debates, but have important ramifications for the viability of democratic institutions.

Institutional Trust and Ideological Values

I introduced various measures for MPs' ideological values throughout this research. With one exception, I will use them as they were developed in the individual chapters. To simplify the analysis, I combined MPs' tolerance score toward the first and second group into an overall measure of tolerance (see Appendix A for the construction of the separate indicators). All other measures for MPs' ideological values— democratic rights, egalitarian and plebiscitarian ideals, pluralism, and the comparative economic indicator (here called market ideals)— were developed in the previous chapters.

Most important, MPs' societal ideals have a significant influence on MPs' trust in institutions (Table 9.2). MPs who believe in the superiority of a market economy are also substantially more likely to trust

TABLE 9.2. *The relationship between ideological values and MPs' institutional trust*

Ideological value:	East 1995	East 1992	West 1992
Egalitarian ideals	−.38*	−.10	−.07
Plebiscitarian ideals	−.38*	−.37*	−.07
Market ideals	.55*	.52*	.30*
Democratic rights	−.43*	−.42*	−.21*
Tolerance	−.29*	.14	−.38*
Pluralism	.01	.01	.11

Note: Entries are correlation coefficients. A negative sign indicates that those who score high on an ideological value indicator disproportionately distrust institutions. * indicates significance at p = .05 level.

institutions, both in the East (r = .52 in 1992 and r = .55 in 1995) and the West (r = .30). The strong relationship between MPs' economic ideals and their institutional trust clearly reflects Germany's post-war history. In the West the strong performance of the market economy helped to bolster the growing acceptance of the liberal democracy in the post-war decades (Baker, Dalton, and Hildebrandt 1981). In the East the two dimensions are linked because the combination of western institutions—a representative system and a social market economy—was presented to eastern MPs as the major alternative to the socialist system.

Despite the moderate relationship in the East and the West, one must recall that western MPs' economic ideals predominately explain degrees of trust in institutions because virtually all western MPs trust them. Further, most western MPs favour a market system while eastern MPs have mixed sentiments about market ideals (Chapter 8). Therefore, eastern MPs' views toward market ideals represent a critical gap between institutional trust and distrust. In contrast, western MPs' market values influence their *degree* of trust, but a weaker commitment to market ideals among western MPs is weakly related to institutional *dis*trust.

Eastern MPs' plebiscitarian ideals are also substantially linked to their institutional trust. Put simply, those who prefer a direct democracy have considerably less confidence in Germany's representative system. Given the degree to which many eastern MPs support plebiscitarian procedures (Chapter 5), these preferences reduce their support for a representative system. If one prefers far-reaching plebiscitarian procedures, one also tends to reject those institutions which embody the idea of representation. In contrast, preferences for plebiscitarian procedures have virtually no influence on western MPs' institutional trust. The different relationships between plebiscitarian procedures and institutional trust in the East and the West parallel the discussion of democratic ideals (Chapter 5). Western MPs frequently want to supplement representative institutions with more citizen involvement, whereas eastern MPs frequently wish to replace representative institutions with a plebiscitarian system.

The relationship between egalitarian ideals and institutional trust initially does not corroborate the first hypothesis, because the coefficient is insignificant in the East in 1992 ($r = -.10$). However, eastern MPs who hold egalitarian ideals in 1995 are substantially less trusting of Germany's institutions than MPs who do not hold such ideals ($r = -.38$). I suspect that the tendency for eastern MPs to downplay their egalitarian preferences in 1992 also reduces the relationship between egalitarian ideals and institutional trust. Because eastern MPs shortly after unification felt compelled to support representative ideals (see Chapter 5), the true relationship between egalitarian ideals and institutional trust was probably underestimated in 1992. By 1995, however, the growing polarization in Germany has solidified the differences between MPs who hold egalitarian ideals and those who do not. Consequently, egalitarian ideals are now systematically related to how much trust eastern MPs have in (western) Germany's institutions. This interpretation is speculative, but it does parallel the 'conversion' toward socialist ideals discussed in previous chapters. Because hardly any MPs mention these ideals in the West, this relationship is virtually non-existent.

Overall, then, there is considerable evidence that eastern MPs' democratic and market ideals influence their institutional trust. The influence of societal ideals on institutional trust is substantially weaker in the West, although MPs' degree of trust is linked to how strongly western MPs endorse market ideals.

The evidence is less clear, however, for other ideological values. MPs' views on the pluralist process are not related to institutional trust in the East and the West. Further, the relationship between intolerance and institutional trust in the West actually indicates that those who are less tolerant have *more* confidence in institutions. Detailed analyses suggest that Germany's unique historical circumstances concerning ideological extremists generates this surprising link between intolerance and institutional support (data not shown). It is useful to recall that intolerance among western MPs is especially strong toward fascists and communists because the establishment of democratic institutions after 1945 was accompanied by the desire to keep ideological extremists out of the mainstream (Chapter 6). Consequently, western MPs who favour limiting the rights of communists and fascists are also those MPs who trust institutions the most. The conditions under which a democratic system was established after the Second World War thus created a situation where MPs who are the least likely to tolerate ideological extremists have the most confidence in Germany's institutions.[3] The historical context also helps to explain why MPs, who are the strongest supporters of abstract democratic rights, disproportionately distrust institutions.

Societal ideals also affect institutional trust among mass publics. For this analysis, I created an index summarizing the responses of eastern and western publics with respect to their trust in various institutions. This index ranges from a low of 5, indicating no trust in institutions, to a high of 35, representing complete trust in institutions. Citizens' views on socialism-as-an-ideal are used to gauge their democratic ideals. As on the elite level, the results support the congruence postulate. Citizens who believe that socialism is a good idea also distrust institutions the most ($r = -.13$ in the West; $r = -.17$ in the East). Although the relationship is not overwhelming, the moderate influence of socialist ideals on citizens' institutional trust is noticeable, both in the East and the West. However, this relationship is especially relevant in the East, where a large majority of citizens agree with this proposition (Chapter 5).

Given these associations, it is reasonable to conclude that both culturalists and institutionalists underestimate the complex relationships between ideological values and institutional trust. Culturalists seem unaware that ideological values reflecting the procedural dimensions of a liberal democracy affect institutional trust less forcefully than societal ideals. Those who are intolerant may actually trust institutions and those who are tolerant may distrust them. This does not imply that intolerant views are irrelevant for the actual performance of a political system; they may affect the behaviour of political elites and thus have important consequences for the operation of institutions (Chapter 10). But this issue is separate from the one raised by the results of this chapter, namely, that the link between institutional trust and MPs' civil liberties is more complicated than the congruence postulate suggests. Indeed, this pattern provides the strongest evidence yet for institutional analyses of democratic transitions, because it suggests the weak influence of procedural values on citizens' institutional trust. At the same time, the impact of societal ideals on institutional trust also corroborates the culturalist approach. The influence of societal ideals is particularly strong in the East, where MPs frequently do not accept the basic premises of a liberal democracy. In sum, the results tend to corroborate the congruence postulate with respect to MPs' societal ideals. And the results tend to corroborate institutionalists' arguments with respect to procedural values.

Institutional Trust and Performance Evaluations

Another influence on institutional trust might be the distributional qualities of a political system. Institutionalists and culturalists maintain that the performance of a political system shapes citizens' trust in institutions. In order to create an indicator of MPs' performance evaluations of institutions, I asked them in 1992 and 1995: 'On the whole, are you very satisfied, fairly satisfied, not very satisfied, or not at all satisfied with the way democracy works in Germany?' This question measures MPs' overall evaluations of the performance of the democratic system without specifying performance dimensions. While lacking specificity, the indicator allows MPs to weigh those performance dimensions they deem important.

Both western and—albeit to a lesser degree—eastern MPs are generally satisfied with the actual performance of democratic institutions. Indeed, almost all western MPs (94.2 per cent) believe in 1992 that democracy works very or reasonably well. The democratic system receives lower performance scores among eastern MPs in 1992 (60.7 per cent). This evaluation essentially remains unchanged by 1995, when 65.7 per cent of re-interviewed eastern MPs express satisfaction with the performance of democracy. It is encouraging from the standpoint of democratic institution-building that almost two-thirds of eastern MPs believe that democracy works very well or reasonably well.

Does the indicator which measures individuals' satisfaction with democracy also assess how MPs compare the performance of the present system to that of socialism? This comparative referent is central to most definitions of the legitimacy of institutions and it may correlate with institutional trust (Linz 1978; Weil 1989). I therefore asked MPs in 1995:

If you think of the time in the GDR before the fall of the Berlin Wall, do you think people in the former GDR are, all in all, better off now, worse off, or does it make no difference?

MPs' expressed their summary evaluation by means of a seven-point indicator. In addition to this overall evaluation, MPs also compared the conditions of eastern Germans before and after the Wall with respect to three sub-dimensions: (1) 'And when you just think of the personal freedom of people in the former GDR?'; (2) 'And when you think of the social conditions of people in the former GDR?'; and (3) 'And when you think of the economic conditions of people in the former GDR?'

Most eastern MPs believe that eastern Germans are, on the whole, better off now than they were in the GDR. Especially in terms of personal freedom, the present system receives positive marks—95.3 per cent selected categories 7, 6, or 5. The judgement is more equivocal in the social domain, where 55.4 per cent of eastern MPs say that the present system does more than the GDR to provide for the basic needs of eastern Germans. Still, even in terms of the social dimension, where the GDR prided itself as a paradigm for non-socialist nations, a majority of eastern MPs give the present system a higher performance score than the GDR. In terms of economic conditions, over two-thirds (69.2 per cent) believe that the present system performs better than the collapsed socialist system. Although eastern MPs perceive the greatest performance deficit in the social domain, it is evident that a majority evaluates the present system positively compared to the GDR: 83.8 per cent indicate that the overall performance is better in the new system.

These comparative performance evaluations are strongly related to eastern MPs' overall satisfaction with how democracy works in 1995 ($r = .69$). Although the detailed indicator is unavailable in the 1992 survey, this relationship in 1995 suggests that MPs partially use socialism's performance as a reference-point to evaluate the performance of liberal-democratic institutions.

How do mass publics evaluate the overall performance of democracy? Because eastern Germans were asked this question with reference to the entire system in Germany beginning in 1991,[4] I selected this time to begin the presentation of eastern Germans' views on the performance of institutions. For the West, I present data beginning in the mid-1980s. This time-point represents a benchmark of the positive performance evaluations which western Germany's institutions received before unification. Before the Wall fell, close to 80 per cent of the western public believe that the system performs very or pretty well (Fig. 9.4). Unification, however, created a number of serious problems—economic as well as social ones—which substantially reduced western citizens' performance evaluations. In fact, the decline in trust represents a European-wide phenomenon, because European publics evaluate democracy's performance more negatively after the fall of the Wall than before (Fuchs and Klingemann 1995; Newton and Kaase 1995). In the West, positive performance evaluations decrease from a high of over 80 per cent in 1990 to below 60 per cent during late 1992 and early 1993. Initially, this downward trend bottomed out by late 1994. However, a substantial decline occurred between spring 1995 and autumn 1997. The performance evaluations of the eastern

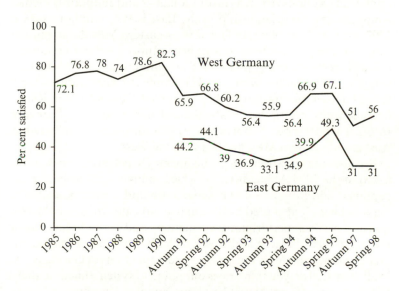

FIG. 9.4. Satisfaction with democracy, mass publics 1985–1998.

(*Note*: Entries are percentages of respondents who are very or pretty satisfied with how democracy works.)

Source: Cumulative Eurobarometer file for western Germany before 1991 representing the annual averages. From autumn 1991 onwards data are based on each Eurobarometer (36 through 49).

German public follow this pattern, except that they are substantially lower. They hover around the 40 per cent mark until spring 1995, when performance evaluations begin to decline to 31 per cent by the end of 1997. The trend after 1989 undoubtedly reflects the enormous economic and social costs created by Germany's unification.

It is noteworthy that western and eastern elites evaluate the performance of Germany's democracy more positively than the western and eastern publics, respectively. In the West, almost all MPs were satisfied in 1992 with how democracy works, and this proportion exceeds 60 per cent in the East. Indeed, at times eastern MPs' satisfaction is even higher than that of the western public. Undoubtedly, eastern elites are more cushioned from economic problems and have more opportunities to reconstruct their professional careers than the eastern public, which helps to explain their relatively positive performance evaluations.

Performance evaluations have a substantial impact on elite and publics' institutional trust, as institutionalists and culturalists predict. Among elites, the relationship in the East is very strong (r = .78 in 1992 and r = .79 in 1995). In fact, among eastern MPs the strength of this relationship indicates that trust in institutions is almost synonymous with performance evaluations. Compared to this strong relationship, the linkage in the West (r = .48)—while still substantial—partly reflects a reservoir of 'good will' because MPs' confidence in institutions depends less on their evaluations of institutional performance. In other words, poor performance evaluations substantially reduce trust among eastern MPs, but less so in the West.

Because the question about democracy's performance was not asked in the 1994 Allbus survey—which, unlike the Eurobarometer, contains indicators about the democratic and economic values of mass publics—I also used an alternative indicator to gauge the relationship between performance evaluations and institutional trust at the mass level.[5] Eastern and western German publics were asked to evaluate how well they thought the system functions in Germany: 'All in all, how well do you think does our political system function today? Which statements on this list best approximate your opinion?'

1. It functions well and needs no change.
2. Overall, it functions well, but it must be changed somewhat.
3. It doesn't function well and must be changed substantially.
4. It doesn't function well at all and must be completely changed.

The relationship between performance evaluations[6] and institutional trust (in 1994) is weaker at the mass level than at the level of elites ($r = .38$ in the West and $r = .44$ in the East). Still, given the magnitude of coefficients usually found in mass surveys, this is a strong relationship indeed. The similar magnitude of these coefficients suggests that trust in institutions is about equally performance-dependent at the mass level in eastern and western Germany (more of which below).

Institutional Trust and Party Affiliation

Students of regime transitions suggest that the openness of institutions influences how political elites and their supporters evaluate a new political system (the inclusion argument). According to this perspective, excluded elites and their supporters are less enthusiastic about new institutions than those who have the opportunity to influence political decisions under new institutional rules (Przeworski 1991; Higley and Gunther 1992). Independent of their ideological values and performance evaluations, then, individuals' proximity to the centre of political power may affect their trust in these institutions.

As a proxy of elites and publics' opportunities to shape political decisions, consider MPs' party membership or, at the mass level, the party preferences of publics (Anderson and Guillory 1997). In the context of the unified Germany, one's party membership broadly measures the degree to which various social groups may influence political decisions. Members of the CDU, which governed Germany and Berlin as the dominant partner in a coalition at the time of the survey, have considerable influence in the political process. They often personally shape public policies through, for example, holding important governmental office. Even if CDU-MPs do not personally occupy a government office, they may influence the political process in other ways, such as party meetings or through their status in the federal and Berlin parliament. At the level of mass publics, supporters of the CDU may believe that their preferences are better accounted for in the political process than, say, those of PDS-supporters. Consequently, if access to institutions affects one's trust in them, CDU-supporters are expected to trust institutions more than members of the PDS, for example. The SPD, in turn, formed a grand coalition with the CDU in Berlin after the 1990 election, thus providing SPD- and CDU-MPs with comparable opportunities in the political process. Likewise, although the SPD was in the opposition in the federal parliament at the time the surveys were conducted, the post-war history of western Germany indicates that her institutions do not permanently exclude this party from occupying government office. In short, the inclusion argument predicts that CDU- and SPD-MPs and their sympathizers should trust the institutional framework in Germany, both in the East and the West. For similar reasons, the FDP and its supporters fall into this category because the FDP has been included in most federal governments since 1949.

As the party representative of the alternative movement, the Bündnis '90/Green party has obtained more access to the decision-making process than the PDS by the time the surveys were conducted, but less than the established parties. On the one hand, the Bündnis '90/Greens have not participated in a federal government until 1998. On the other hand, the party participated in governments at the state level, including a Berlin government. This political experience signalled to them that the representative system provides them with access to decision-making institutions, given adequate electoral success. Finally, members of the PDS have comparatively little access to federal institutions. Therefore, in addition to their ideological view, the relative weak position of the PDS in the institutional hierarchy may reduce the support of PDS elites and their supporters for existing institutions.

Despite the relatively small number of cases for some parties at the

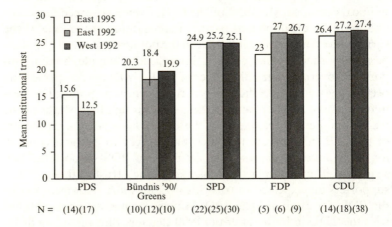

FIG. 9.5. MPs' institutional trust, by party

(*Note*: Entries are mean values of the institutional trust indicator which ranges from 5 (indicating distrust) to 35 (indicating trust).)

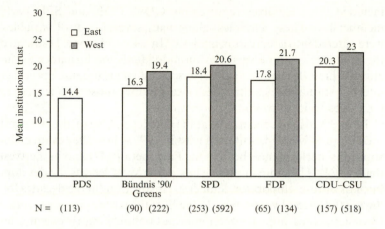

F IG. 9.6. Institutional trust of mass publics, by party, 1994

(*Note*: Entries are mean values of institutional trust. The indicator ranges from 5 (indicating distrust) to 35 (indicating trust). For the West, the number of cases endorsing the PDS was too small to compute the mean value (N = 4).)
Source: Allbus (1994).

elite level, the general pattern is surprisingly consistent with the logic of the inclusion argument (Figs. 9.5 and 9.6). CDU-, FDP-, and SPD-MPs have the most confidence in these institutions, both in the West and the East. In contrast, the PDS has the least confidence in them (mean = 12.5), with the Bündnis '90/Greens falling in between these groups. The same pattern emerges at the mass level. Citizens with CDU-CSU, FDP, and SPD party preferences have the strongest trust in institutions, while PDS supporters have the least confidence in them, with the Bündnis '90/Greens again falling in between these groups.

THE SOURCES OF TRUST: THE GENERAL PATTERN

What are the net effects of ideological values and distributional qualities on institutional trust? To answer this question I conducted several multivariate analyses. In a first step, the analyses examine the influence of MPs' egalitarian, market, and plebiscitarian ideals on institutional trust. The model also includes individuals' views on how well the system functions in Germany. In order to gauge the degree to which social groups have access to key institutions in Germany, I included three variables representing CDU, FDP, and SPD party membership. These variables, along with several control variables, were entered into a regression analysis.[7] In a second model I estimated the influence of these variables on individuals' performance evaluations. I limit this causal analysis to societal ideals because my earlier interpretation suggests that these ideals matter most with respect to the values-to-institutional support process.[8]

Table 9.3 displays the results at the elite level. One of the strongest predictors of MPs' institutional trust in 1992 is how they evaluate institutions' performance, both in the East (beta = .42) and in the West (beta = .24). The more moderate link in the West reflects the development of diffuse support for democratic institutions in the decades following the Second World War. In the East the strong link is generated by eastern elites' hope for economic and political improvement after the collapse of socialism. Not surprisingly, the performance of a system strongly affects individuals' institutional trust in a new democracy. When MPs' prospective assessments of the economy are included, this variable also strongly predicts MPs' trust in institutions in 1995 (beta = .30; p = .006). Although this variable is unavailable in 1992, the magnitude of the other predictors are hardly affected by the inclusion of the prospective indicator in 1995. On the whole, these results provide considerable support for institutionalists, who emphasize performance evaluations as a central source of institutional trust.

If MPs belong to one of the three parties that have governed Germany throughout the post-war period, they are also substantially more likely to trust institutions than members of the PDS and Bündnis '90/Greens (the reference group in the analyses). In particular, CDU-MPs trust institutions more than the Bündnis '90/Greens and the PDS in the East (beta = .28). Likewise, western CDU-MPs have considerably more confidence in institutions than the western Greens (beta = .59). Since the analyses control for MPs' performance evaluations, several ideological values, and a range of other factors, the strength of these predictors is most plausibly explained by the fact that MPs of these parties have considerably more access to the centres of decision-making under Germany's institutions than other MPs.[9]

MPs' ideological values also influence institutional trust, but in more subtle ways than their performance evaluations. On the one hand, eastern MPs' economic ideals are statistically insignificant predictors in the East and the West in 1992. On the other hand, if the analysis in 1992 is limited to MPs born after 1945, younger MPs' market values

TABLE 9.3. *Predicting MPs' trust in institutions, 1992*

Predictors:	East	West	Combined
West Berlin	a	a	.01
			(.13)
Egalitarian ideals	−.04	−.09	−.05
	(.32)	(1.60)	(−.40)
Market ideals	.07	.12	.13***
	(.32)	(.12)	(.55)
Plebiscitarian ideals	−.08	−.11	−.01
	(−.20)	(−.20)	(−.01)
CDU	.28***	.59***	.38***
	(4.70)	(5.50)	(5.10)
FDP	.16**	.27*	.21***
	(4.30)	(4.00)	(4.50)
SPD	.24***	.34***	.30***
	(3.60)	(3.20)	(3.90)
Democracy performs well	.42***	.24**	.35***
	(3.40)	(2.00)	(2.70)
Post-war cohort	−.16**	−.13	−.12**
	(−2.40)	(−1.20)	(−1.50)
Negative future personal finances	−.01	.17*	.03
	(−.03)	(1.20)	(.20)
Postmaterialism	−.09	−.14	.03
	(−.74)	(−.67)	(.46)
Gender	.01	.04	−.03)
	(.01)	(.37)	(−.15)
Income	−.07	−.03)	−.03
	(−.59)	(−.15)	(.46)
Education	−.10	−.08	−.06
	(−.83)	(−.26)	(−.35)
Adjusted R-square	.70	.30	.65
(N)	(76)	(84)	(160)

Note: The dependent variable is an additive index combining MPs' trust in each institution. Entries are standardized regression coefficients with unstandardized coefficients appearing in parentheses. *, **, and *** indicate significance of coefficients at the .10, .05, and .01 level respectively. An 'a' denotes the exclusion of a variable from the analysis.

strongly influence their institutional trust (beta = .32, p = .02); this coefficient remains insignificant in the West (beta = .10; p = .31). Furthermore, the relationship is quite strong in 1995, when I estimate the same model with the data from MPs interviewed a second time (beta = .23; p = .03). Among eastern MPs, then, there is considerable evidence that market ideals directly lower institutional trust. The importance of societal ideals is further documented by the impact of plebiscitarian values on institutional trust. Although the plebiscitarian indicator is insignificant when eastern MPs' party membership is included, the overlap between plebiscitarian ideals and membership in the opposition movement reduces this coefficient to statistical insignificance. When I exclude MPs' party membership, the plebiscitarian indicator is significant in the East (beta = −.14; p = .02) but remains insignificant in the West (beta = .04; p = .7). These findings match the discussion of MPs' democratic ideals in Chapter 5, where western MPs—unlike their eastern counterparts—indicate that they value plebiscitarian procedures within the framework of representative institutions. In contrast to market and plebiscitarian ideals, however, eastern MPs' egalitarian ideals do not directly reduce trust, both in 1992 and 1995, when other variables are considered simultaneously. Given the strong bi-variate relationship between egalitarian ideals and institutional trust in 1995 among eastern MPs (Table 9.2), the appropriate conclusion is that egalitarian-democratic ideals affect eastern MPs' institutional trust indirectly. In contrast, in the West, the net *and* total influence of egalitarian and plebiscitarian ideals approaches zero because of the broad consensus over representative ideals.

Ideological values also influence individuals' institutional trust indirectly via their performance evaluations (see Appendix B, Table B5). MPs who endorse market ideals also evaluate the performance of Germany's democracy more positively in the East (beta = .24) and the West (beta = .32). In terms of egalitarian ideals, there is growing evidence that the influence of these ideals on institutional trust is predominately indirect because these ideals are related to negative performance evaluations in the East (beta = −.14). Recall that egalitarian ideals also reduce eastern MPs' support for market ideals (Chapter 8). In short, egalitarian ideals generate socialist market ideals and lower citizens' performance evaluations of institutions, which curtails eastern MPs' institutional trust.

A similar pattern emerges at the mass level. With respect to citizens' institutional support (Table B6), democratic performance evaluations have the strongest effect. In fact, these coefficients are unusually strong in the East (beta = .29) and the West (beta = .25). Likewise, positive economic perceptions are significantly related to institutional trust. With the exception of future economic evaluations, which are related to trust in the East but not in the West, the impact of these variables is fairly similar in both parts of Germany. As on the elite level, then, performance evaluations strongly influence publics' institutional trust. At the same time, publics' views about socialism-as-an ideal also moderately influence their institutional trust (beta = –.06). To be sure, this coefficient is not very large, but it *is* significant— several other variables are insignificant despite the large sample size. Just as the ideological performance axiom indicates, trust in democratic institutions is reduced when citizens hold societal ideals that are incongruent with existing institutions. In addition, positive views toward socialism reduce publics' performance evaluations of democracy (beta = –.07) in the East, but not in the West (Table B7). Likewise, market ideals affect publics' performance evaluations, especially in the East (beta = .20). Given the large proportion of eastern Germans who endorse egalitarian ideals, the direct and indirect effect of these ideals on institutional trust suggests that ideological values put a ceiling on the development of institutional trust in the East.

Overall, these analyses indicate that: (1) eastern and, especially, western MPs have considerable trust in existing institutions; (2) confidence of mass publics in institutions is moderate in the West and weak in the East; (3) eastern MPs' trust in institutions did not increase between 1992 and 1995; (4) elites in the West and the East have substantially more trust in institutions than mass publics; (5) performance evaluations substantially influence citizens' trust in institutions; and (6) socialist ideals lessen institutional trust.

INSTITUTIONAL SUPPORT IN EASTERN EUROPE

The preceding analyses provide several reasons why East-Central Europeans are expected to show ambivalent support for new democratic institutions. Egalitarian ideals, held by a substantial proportion of East-Central Europeans (Chapter 5), presumably dampen their support for representative systems and market institutions. In addition, poor economic performance adds downward pressure on the approval ratings for new democracies, because citizens in East-Central Europe frequently do not distinguish between incumbents and the new system (Mishler and Rose 1996). Finally, like eastern Germans, publics in East-Central Europe probably base their satisfaction with democratic systems on their performance because citizens lack the experience that even well-functioning democracies must weather difficult economic times.

At the same time, there are factors which work in favour of new democratic institutions. Most importantly, new democracies experienced a 'honeymoon' period shortly after the transition (Mishler and Rose 1996; 1997). Like eastern Germans, publics were initially willing to endorse a new system because they expected it to perform better than the socialist system (Evans and Whitefield 1995). East-Central European publics are also aware of the greater efficiency of democracies, in particular, their ability to secure civil liberties (Weil 1989). Since a majority prefers a system providing freedoms (Chapter 5), democracies may be supported even if economic conditions are difficult.

Given these countervailing forces, analyses reveal the ambivalent support for new democracies in East-Central Europe. On the one hand, considerable support exists for basic democratic institutions as ideal types because East-Central Europeans link civil liberties to a democracy (Fuchs and Roller 1994). At the same time, when citizens indicate their trust in a range of existing institutions, support levels are modest at best. In the most comprehensive examination to date, Mishler and Rose (1997) suggest that East-Central Europeans hold sceptical views about a range of institutions, such as the police, parliament, or civil servants. They maintain that, although the vast majority of these institutions are distrusted by virtually every public in their study, the majority of citizens should be labelled sceptics: they neither fully accept nor reject them in 1994 when their survey was conducted. Mishler and Rose suggest that improving economic conditions are likely to enhance public's support for democratic institutions.

Given the fragile support-base for new democracies, one would expect publics' satisfaction with democratic systems not only to be mixed, but also to vary temporally, in view of the rapidly changing environment in many East-Central European countries. To examine publics' support for new democracies, the Central and Eastern Barometers asked respondents between 1990 and 1996 how satisfied they were with the way democracy was developing in their country (very, fairly, not very, or not all satisfied). I included the 'don't know' category in the calculation of the baseline percentage because this response may reflect genuine uncertainty about the development about democratic institutions.

Several patterns emerge consistent with the thrust of the studies

TABLE 9.4. *Satisfaction with democracy in East-Central Europe* (%)

	Bulgaria	Czech Republic	Slovakia	Hungary	Poland	Romania	Russia
1990	29.9	n/a	n/a	19.6	37.9	n/a	n/a
1991	38.3	n/a	n/a	30.6	26.6	44.1	14.9
1992	35.9	38.2	23.5	22.8	32.1	28.8	11.4
1993	21.1	48.2	20.0	20.3	37.8	29.7	14.7
1994	3.8	44.1	16.8	24.5	35.4	30.4	7.4
1995	13.2	46.3	26.8	19.9	50.4	37.0	6.0
1996	5.7	40.9	22.0	43.7	54.6	54.6	7.7

Note: Entries are percentages of respondents very or fairly satisfied with how democracy develops in their country. The 'don't-know' responses are included in the calculations of the baseline.

Source: Central and Eastern Barometers 1–7.

discussed in the preceding paragraphs (Table 9.4). The proportion of citizens satisfied (very or fairly) with how democracies develop constitutes a minority in almost all countries at virtually every time-point (the exceptions being the Romanian public in 1996 and the Polish public in 1995). Still, substantial segments are quite satisfied, in particular in the Czech Republic, Poland, Romania, and to a lesser degree in Hungary, which is consistent with Mishler and Rose's argument. Although Mishler and Rose use different measures, the basic message of their study and the analyses presented here converge: substantial minorities hold favourable views about the development of democratic institutions. Indeed, considering that my analyses include the 'don't know' category, the results tend to be conservative estimates of publics' satisfaction with democracies. Another important pattern is the increase in satisfaction in some countries, notably Poland, Romania, and the Czech Republic, while it either erodes (Bulgaria) or stagnates (e.g. Russia) in other nations.

It would go beyond the scope of this book to provide a detailed examination of the cross-national and temporal variations, but a few general observations are in order. First, it is no coincidence that those publics which are most satisfied with the development of democratic institutions are also among the publics believing that market reforms are on track (Table 8.8). Especially Romanians, but also the Polish and Czech publics, do not lose significant faith in market reforms. Since beliefs about the right course of market reforms constitute an important source of citizens' satisfaction with the political system,[10] the aggregate stability for market reforms undoubtedly helped to stabilize publics' satisfaction with the development of democratic institutions.

Another performance domain is located in the political realm. Given the yearning of East-Central Europeans for a system which secures civil liberties, the degree to which emerging democracies honour civil rights influences publics' satisfaction with democracies. Indeed, Evans and Whitefield find that political performance is one of the strongest predictors of satisfaction with democracies (see also Klingemann and Hofferbert 1998). In order to measure this aspect, East-Central Europeans were asked: 'How much respect is there for human rights nowadays in your country?' Table 9.5 displays the proportion believing that human rights enjoy a lot of or some respect.

In four nations there is a clear decline over time (Bulgaria, Hungary, Romania, and the Slovak Republic), although levels of support are still fairly high in Hungary in 1996. Responses in the other nations remain relatively stable between 1990 and 1996. In the Russian case, the stability is located at a low level—a stable but small minority believes that human rights are respected. Again, there is a general linkage between this aggregate pattern and publics' satisfaction with how democracies evolve. Publics believing that human rights are not respected also are the least satisfied (Bulgaria, Slovakia, Russia). Conversely, where evaluations are comparatively positive, levels of satisfaction are relatively high (e.g. Poland and the Czech Republic).

TABLE 9.5. *How well are human rights respected in East-Central Europe?* (%)

	Bulgaria	Czech Republic	Slovakia	Hungary	Poland	Romania	Russia
1991	66.4	n/a	n/a	75.2	45.0	51.7	16.1
1992	66.4	n/a	n/a	60.8	34.4	54.5	22.1
1993	57.0	54.7	63.9	60.8	38.9	42.2	20.9
1994	42.1	52.3	65.7	63.0	30.2	27.0	13.9
1995	43.6	49.2	43.3	60.3	44.9	28.2	12.8
1996	40.5	46.5	38.9	52.4	39.9	32.3	13.9

Note: Entries are percentages of respondents believing that human rights receive a lot or some respect.

Source: Central and Eastern Barometers 2–7.

One exception to this pattern concerns Romania, where the decline in political performance evaluations coincides with growing support for market reform. Overall, in three countries sceptical beliefs about market reforms coincide with declining evaluations along the political dimension (Bulgaria, Slovakia, Hungary)—and these are the nations where citizens' satisfaction with democratic development erodes. In sum, as in eastern Germany, the support base for existing institutions is limited to a substantial minority at best. And similar to eastern Germany, performance dimensions substantially influence citizens' satisfaction with emerging democratic institutions.

CONCLUSION

The analyses in this chapter support the logic of the ideological performance axiom. As institutionalists and culturalists maintain, distributional qualities exert the strongest direct influence on citizens' institutional trust. At the same time, the evidence indicates that ideological values indirectly and, in some cases, directly affect both mass and elites' institutional trust. On the whole, these processes operate similarly in the East and the West. There are, however, two East–West differences among MPs which deserve to be highlighted. First, the impact of performance evaluations on trust is stronger in the East than the West. This finding undoubtedly reflects western MPs' positive experience with democratic institutions, which reduces the impact of output factors on institutional support. Because eastern MPs lack this long-term experience, their trust in institutions is more contingent on the contemporary performance of institutions. Secondly, egalitarian and plebiscitarian ideals affect institutional support more strongly in the East than the West because eastern MPs frequently do not share the democratic and representative premises of Germany's constitution.

Importantly, the performance of institutions influences both eastern and western publics. While this pattern is expected for eastern citizens, it is surprising that western citizens make their trust to the same degree dependent on institutional performance as eastern Germans. After all, most students of western German public opinion conclude that support for democratic institutions has become insulated from performance aspects, at least over the medium-term

(Baker, Dalton, and Hildebrandt 1981). The similar pattern probably results from the economic strain created by Germany's unification in the West. Western Germans feel the pinch of economic problems through higher taxes or the enormous transfer of resources from the West into the East. Our time series indicates that western citizens' performance evaluations dropped significantly as a result of the revolutionary upheavals (Fig. 9.4). These results suggest that performance deficits, which occur over several years, may reduce citizens' diffuse support even in mature democracies.

Theoretically, it is appropriate to conclude that both institutionalists and culturalists underestimate the complex nature of these relationships. Both schools anticipate that the performance of institutions is crucial in explaining citizens' trust in them. However, the strong version of the congruence postulate is clearly inadequate in describing the link between ideological values and institutional trust. Institutionalists, in turn, underestimate the importance of societal ideals in shaping citizens' institutional trust and their measures for evaluating institutional performance. The confluence of these factors has important implications for democratic transitions in post-socialist nations which the next, and final, chapter will develop.

Conclusion

When Germans celebrated their country's formal union on 3 October 1990 most citizens did not realize that the onerous task of unification had but begun with the fallen Berlin Wall. Superficially, unification appeared complete when the GDR ceased to exist as an independent state. The same institutions now govern the territory of the two former German states; the same laws apply; the same parties compete in elections; and national television programmes are identical. Yet, despite this setting, this study documents that eastern and western Germans developed partially different ideological cultures between 1945 and 1989.

In order to highlight the degree to which ideological differences persist, Table 10.1 summarizes the broad empirical patterns found in this study. The summary focuses on MPs because information about their values is more complete than for the mass public. The first row summarizes how strongly MPs support democratic and market values. Except for the second column, the entries in the first row represent the average responses to those indicators measuring a value domain. For example, a majority of eastern (68 per cent) and western MPs (73 per cent) on average respond democratically to the six indicators measuring general democratic rights (Table 5.1). Note that the second row also indicates that the East–West coefficient is statistically significant in the multivariate analyses of the summary indicator. For this constellation—support for democratic values is strong in the East and the West, but higher in the latter than the former—the first and second rule of inference lead to the conclusion that democratic rights diffused into eastern Germany (Chapter 4).

In contrast to the scenario for general democratic rights, MPs' responses to the other ideological values—with the exception of pluralism—represent a different pattern. For example, tolerance prevails in the West, while intolerance prevails in the East. On average, 36 per cent of eastern MPs gave a tolerant response compared to 55 per cent

TABLE 10.1. *The effect of institutional learning: two ideological cultures*

Criterion	Democratic rights		Democratic ideals		Tolerance		Pluralism		Market ideals		Liberal-democratic institutions	
	East	West	East	West	East	West	East	West	East	West	East	West
Majority support exists for liberal-democratic indicators?	68%[a]	73%	39%[b]	89%	36%[c]	55%	70%[d]	81%	58%[e]	89%	54%[f]	72%
East–West coefficient is significant?	Yes		Yes		Yes		Yes		Yes		No	
Development of liberal-democratic values?	—[g]		21%[h]		12%		23%		9%		20%	
West/East MPs are more liberal-democratic than West/East public?	Yes		—[i]		Yes		Yes		Yes		Yes	

[a] Mean democratic responses to the indicators in Table 5.1 (1992 survey).
[b] 100 minus the percentage in Table 5.2 mentioning an egalitarian and direct democratic component (1992 survey).
[c] Mean tolerant response toward the first and second least-liked groups in Table 6.2 (1992 survey).
[d] Mean pro-pluralist response to indicators in Tables 7.2 and 7.3 (1992 survey).
[e] Mean pro-market response to the first and third indicator in Table 8.2 (1992 survey).
[f] Mean percentage trusting institutions in Table 9.3 (1992 survey).
[g] The mean could not be computed because of small cell entries in the conversion table.
[h] Average conversion toward a democratic or market values. Derived from chapter figures comparing MPs' responses in 1992 and 1995.
[i] Indicators at the mass and elite level could not be compared.

in the West. Likewise, a majority of western MPs endorse most market values (89 per cent), whereas a bare majority approve of market procedures in the East (58 per cent). The second row indicates that almost all East–West differences persist in the multivariate analyses when other influences on MPs' ideological values are considered simultaneously.

The 'Net-Liberal-Ideals' column highlights MPs' democratic ideals. Because there were no limits on how many components MPs could mention, the sum of these responses exceeds 100 per cent (Chapter 5). Since civil liberties were mentioned by virtually all MPs, I deducted the percentage of social-egalitarian and plebiscitarian responses in table 5.3 from 100. The resulting percentages—39.3 per cent in the East and 89 per cent in the West—reflect the different democratic visions. In the East, civil liberties are frequently mentioned along with social-egalitarian and plebiscitarian preferences. Western MPs, in contrast, prefer a liberal-representative system. Despite the consensus over general democratic rights, this configuration underlines the necessity to examine MPs' democratic rights *and* ideals in order to portray their ideological values accurately in their entirety.

Overall, the table highlights that the blend of ideological values held by eastern and western Germans differs considerably across the former East–West border. A majority of western MPs endorse most liberal-democratic rights, tend to hold liberal ideals, are relatively tolerant, favour pluralist competition, prefer market values, and support existing institutions. Western MPs thus approximate a classical democratic profile. In contrast, eastern MPs tend to endorse general democratic rights, support—with some reservation—pluralist competition, but also tend to be intolerant, have serious reservations about market mechanisms, and often hold social-egalitarian ideals, while a substantial minority distrust representative institutions. Each chapter shows that several East–West contrasts emerge especially within the post-war cohort, manifesting the generational effect of forty years of separate institutional learning.

The third row reviews the extent to which MPs' developed democratic values between 1992 and 1995. The entries represent average percentages of MPs expressing a democratic preference in 1995 but not in 1992. For example, in the context of MPs' democratic ideals (Fig. 5.3), on average 21 per cent expressed a democratic component in 1995 but not in 1992. Overall, the lack of substantial development of democratic values undercuts the conversion argument because the systemic transitions in eastern Germany occur under comparatively favourable conditions (however difficult they are for many individuals). Unlike many East-Central European nations, where democratic and market institutions are frequently incomplete, eastern MPs worked within a well-established democracy between the end of the first and the beginning of the second interview period (June 1992 and November 1994). Further, seasoned western MPs familiarize their eastern colleagues with institutional rules and parliamentary routines. The institutional learning effect—if driven by short-term value conversion —should be measurable under these conditions. And yet there is little systematic conversion toward a liberal-democratic profile. Indeed, this study revealed that social-egalitarian ideals are partially affirmed by 1995—a result which casts doubts on claims that individuals' ideological values adjust in a short time to the new institutions.

The final row indicates that elites in the West and the East are more likely to endorse democratic and market values than mass publics. Undeniably, the mass–elite comparison is hampered by the fact that directly comparable indicators are often unavailable. Still, the consistency of this pattern, where the same indicators are used, strongly suggests that elites are more committed than mass publics to democratic procedures in both parts of Germany. While this configuration is expected in the West, the pattern in eastern Germany suggests that higher education contributes to the development of democratic views within an authoritarian context. At the same time, one must recognize that eastern elites frequently lack a strong commitment to democratic ideals as well. Eastern MP's overall support for democratic values is lower than that of western MPs and often falls below the majority mark. The appropriate conclusion is that eastern German elites may possess the kernel of restraint, self-reliance, and corresponding ideals. But their lack of institutional learning in a democracy is also manifested in their equivocal support for several ideological values underlying a capitalist democracy.

IMPLICATIONS FOR GERMAN POLITICS

The lack of consensus over ideological values has implications for various aspects of political and social affairs in Germany. Three implications appear especially relevant, namely, that: (1) eastern

Germans' support for democratic procedures sets the situation apart from that in the immediate post-war years in the West; (2) eastern Germans' ideological values raise questions as to how willing they are to endorse liberal-representative institutions; and (3) the lack of a consensus may affect the ability of parties to represent voters equally well in the West and the East.

What Distinguishes Eastern Germany's Situation From the Western Post-war Years

The strong support for democratic rights in eastern Germany distinguishes the situation after 1989 from that in the immediate post-war years in the West. The undemocratic nature of western Germany's ideological culture after the Second World War ended is captured by surveys conducted between 1945 and 1955 by the western Allies (the OMGUS and HICOG surveys). Using these data, Richard Merritt (1995) documents the widespread authoritarianism and the reluctance of the western public to endorse the democratic process soon after the war (see also Merritt and Merritt 1970). Not only did a substantial proportion continue to endorse National Socialism as an ideal in the early 1950s—which is comparable in its level of abstraction to the strong support for the socialism-as-an-ideal indicator—western Germans endorsed several aspects of the actual political process in the Third Reich. A substantial proportion responded in the 1950s that Hitler was a great statesman, thereby endorsing the principle and practice of a one-party dictatorship. Likewise, many citizens agreed that a multi-party system is undesirable and a one-party system preferable over a parliamentary 'chatterbox'. The slow pace at which support for democratic rights developed in the post-war decades is documented by Max Kaase's analyses (1971) of the indicators measuring citizens' support for democratic rights (Chapter 5). His study suggests that the western German public remained ambivalent about abstract democratic rights even at the end of the 1950s; a pattern that also emerged in Conradt (1974) and Boynton and Loewenberg's (1973) longitudinal analyses of mass attitudes toward democracy. Equally important, elites from various societal sectors hesitated to endorse the democratic process in principle (Roth 1976; Hoffmann-Lange 1992). The fledgling democracy in western Germany thus faced considerable scepticism in the two decades following the Second World War.

The contemporary situation in eastern Germany is more promising, because the diffusion of democratic values increased eastern citizens' support for a political system that secures civil liberties. The exposure to information about the West undoubtedly explains why numerous studies, including this one, reveal strong support for general democratic rights. This is far from trivial. Given how long it took to develop this level of support for abstract rights in the West, the situation in eastern Germany compares rather favourably to the postwar years. Indeed, in terms of abstract democratic rights, eastern Germans appear to be model democrats when compared to western Germans in the 1950s. Thus, most eastern Germans do not prefer the return of the collapsed socialist state.

The near-consensual support for general democratic rights is one reason why the constitution especially is trusted by a large majority of eastern MPs (Table 10.1). Because it guarantees civil liberties, such as free elections and the right to demonstrate, the new system receives considerable support in the East. One must note, however, that eastern MPs' trust in the institutional framework is equivocal, because other institutions vital to the democratic system are distrusted by a majority of eastern MPs and, especially, the eastern public.

Socialist Ideals and Liberal-Representative Institutions

One reason why eastern Germans do not trust existing institutions to the same extent as western Germans is undoubtedly related to their democratic ideals. Germany's democracy presumes, for example, that some degree of economic inequality is acceptable, even desirable. As this study shows, however, many eastern Germans reject several ideals which Germany's constitution evinces. They often expect social-egalitarian outcomes of the economic and political process (Chapter 5), and they frequently favour a strong state which regulates economic and political activities in order to enhance citizens' social equality (Chapters 7 and 8). In addition, a substantial minority of eastern Germans prefer direct democratic procedures over representative ones. This incongruence of ideals and constitutional reality has two important consequences. First, there is a measurable reduction of trust—traceable to citizens' societal ideals—in existing institutions (Chapter 9). Secondly, citizens who disagree with the ideological premiss of the representative system also tend to be more dissatisfied with the outcomes it produces. Therefore, even if institutional performance is positive (according to those who accept representative and market institutions), citizens who prioritize egalitarian results may still harbour doubts about the desirability of a representative democracy.

This incongruence appears to be a long-term problem. The limited conversion of ideological values between 1992 and 1995 indicates that eastern Germans' democratic ideals persist, which is likely to lower their institutional trust for a longer time. Policy-makers partially tried to accommodate eastern Germans' preferences after unification. For example, a commission for constitutional reform debated adding plebiscitarian and social-egalitarian components to the federal constitution. However, the commission rejected the proposal, thereby maintaining the distance between eastern Germans' ideological values and Germany's constitution (Kommers 1995).

In addition, this study makes plain that it is a far cry from endorsing democratic principles to applying these principles in reality. Indeed, in so far as survey questions create a relatively pressure-free version of the political process, the degree of intolerance found among eastern elites is alarming. Although western Germans occupy most key positions in the institutional hierarchy (Bürklin 1996; Welzel 1997), the incomplete diffusion of democratic values again directs our attention to the possibility of authoritarian elites in the East. For example, although the relationship between procedural values and institutional trust is relatively weak (Chapter 9), intolerant elites may undermine the democratic process. When Jens Reich, a prominent member of the opposition movement in the GDR and a presidential candidate, proposes that some democratic procedures be suspended in order to protect the environment, his proposal reflects the view that democratic procedures be made secondary to his policy preferences.[1] Therefore, in a twist of historical irony, the remade western Germany now embarks on the task of remaking eastern Germany's ideological values.

Ideological Values and the Party System

The East–West dissent over ideological values not only affects formal institutions, but also the party system in Germany. Most important, it may reduce the ability of parties to represent western and eastern citizens' preferences equally, possibly lowering the quality of the representational process. Consider that parties intersect between citizens' interests and public policies. They must articulate citizens' interests and synthesize diverging preferences into manageable policy programs. This task is difficult to accomplish even within the confines of a liberal democracy, where most political actors agree on the basic institutional parameters. Given the lack of an ideological consensus, western German parties, which are accustomed to representing western voters only, must now represent a more ideologically diverse electorate. Indeed, because the East–West differences involve fundamental issues concerning the political process itself, it appears problematic whether western parties are able to represent the policy interests of voters equally well: how can parties satisfy the preferences of those who hold socialist or plebiscitarian preferences, if these ideals lead voters to challenge the representative process?

The resultant strain for the party system manifests itself in the growing success of the PDS and in the electoral behaviour of the unified electorate.

The PDS. One visible manifestation of the ideological East–West divergence is the growing success of the PDS in the East. After the Wall opened in November 1989, the ruling SED quickly changed its name, first to SED-PDS and, when Germany became unified in 1990, to PDS (Party of Democratic Socialism). By adopting a new name, the leadership tried to shed its Stalinist image and to develop a new profile, representing a more democratic socialism than existed in the GDR. One social group supporting the PDS comprises the old nomenclature of the GDR. Former party functionaries, former members of the secret police, and those who worked for the GDR bureaucracy disproportionately support the PDS. The electoral base reflects the PDS's past as the ruling party of the GDR, which explains why a high percentage of voters, who are typically classified as white-collar middle class, support the socialist left. A second constituency consists of the younger, postmaterialist, economically dissatisfied voters (Fuchs and Rohrschneider 1998). Although the membership of the PDS is ageing fast, it emphasizes the recruitment of younger voters. The PDS, for example, caters to the younger generation by giving protest-inspired party activists prominent positions in the party hierarchy.

Both constituencies are partially motivated by their ideological values in supporting the PDS. The analyses at the level of the mass public indicate that PDS-sympathizers value egalitarian ideals (see especially Chapters 5 and 8). The importance of ideological values is also manifested by the fact that the PDS receives nearly its entire support in the East, signifying that its socialist programme does not resonate well with western German voters. In the 1998 federal election the PDS received a total vote share of 5.1 per cent nationwide—1.1 per cent in the West and 19.5 per cent in the East. It would, of course, be implausible to suggest that ideological values are the only determinant of voters' electoral choice. Other factors, such as the condition of the economy or electoral strategies of other parties, influence voters' decisions. In addition, problems within the PDS may impair its ability to attract voters. The revelations about the involvement of various PDS leaders with the despised secret police limits its electoral success, as does the debate over the appropriate socialist programme. However, the PDS is likely to remain a significant competitor in the eastern states, because its programme resonates with the ideological predisposition of many eastern German voters.

Electoral Volatility. Another long-term implication concerns the electoral base of parties. In particular, the merger of the eastern and western electorates probably increases the volatility of voters' partisan choice. When eastern and western German voters cast their ballots in the 1990 election, there were actually two electorates participating in the 'unification' election (Rohrschneider and Fuchs 1995; Dalton 1996). In the West, voters arrive at partisan decisions in a manner which is well-established in the electoral behaviour literature (Baker, Dalton, and Hildebrandt 1981). The core of the working class disproportionately sides with the SPD; middle-class and religious voters tend to vote for the CDU; and younger, better-educated postmaterialists define the constituency of the Greens. Another characteristic of the western electorate is that each party's core constituency shrank over the past two to three decades because western voters increasingly base their electoral calculus on issues and less on deeply rooted cleavages (e.g. Kaase and Klingemann 1994; Dalton 1996). In the West, then, parties can rely on a core constituency for support in elections, although it has steadily eroded, which increases the importance of shorter-term issues in determining voters' partisan choice.

The eastern electorate exhibited a different base for partisan decisions especially in the 1990 and 1994 elections. Most importantly, the working class in the East disproportionately supports the CDU/CSU, whereas the SPD tends to be supported by the middle class. This pattern reverses the historical alignments between workers and leftist parties. Two factors contribute to this unexpected pattern. First, given the lack of opportunities to vote freely in the GDR, eastern German voters tend not to be influenced by long-standing partisan loyalties because they could not develop habitual or cleavage-based attachments to parties (Kaase and Klingemann 1994). In addition, the class structure was altered significantly during the reign of the socialist system. Secondly and relatedly, because the influence of long-standing attachments on voters' decisions are comparatively weak, eastern voters tend to rely on short-term issues in elections. For example, because economic issues dominated the 1990 and 1994 elections, a majority of the working class supported the CDU/CSU–FDP coalition, which is historically viewed as the most competent in creating economic growth and employment opportunities. By 1998, however, the heavy losses of the CDU in the East probably entail that the eastern alignment patterns more closely approximate those in the West. Thus, eastern German voters base their electoral choice more on material issues and less on long-standing loyalties to parties.

Against this backdrop, the ideological East–West differences within parties further erode the possibility that the eastern German electorate is smoothly integrated into the existing alignment structure. Since parties are for the most part controlled by western elites and substantially shaped by the western German context, there is frequently a mismatch between party programmes and the ideological values of many eastern voters. For instance, consider that a substantial majority of eastern CDU supporters view socialism as a positive ideal (Chapter 5). These voters are unlikely to develop close partisan attachments to the CDU over the long run and probably rely on shorter-term issues (primarily economic ones) when they determine their partisan preference. The context of the autumn 1994 election illustrates the fickle support-base of the CDU, when the governing coalition looked like a definite loser in the spring of 1994 (Rohrschneider and Fuchs 1995). However, when the economic situation appeared to improve in the summer of 1994, enough voters were swayed to endorse the governing coalition in the October election. Although this dynamic emerged in the West as well, it is especially noticeable in the eastern electorate because fewer voters hold long-term partisan attachments. Overall, then, ideological differences broaden the range of interests in the unified electorate that must be represented by (western) parties, placing greater strain on them to accomplish this goal.[2]

LOOKING BEYOND GERMANY:
THEORETICAL AND PRACTICAL IMPLICATIONS

A nation's ideological values reflect to some degree its idiosyncratic historical, cultural, and social context, which makes one cautious about generalizing the results from a single-nation study to other countries. At the same time, the comparative evidence strongly suggests that the results from the eastern German experience are generalizable to other post-socialist nations. Consequently, the Germany-based results offer important lessons for the democratic transition literature, fruitful avenues for comparative research and the practical management of democratic transitions.

Implications for Transition Studies

This study is in part motivated by the rift between culturalist and institutionalist approaches in the democratic transitions literature. As I argue in Chapter 2, however, both perspectives actually agree that institutions—once established—shape citizens' ideological values. The success of the democratization efforts in western Germany after 1949 is consistent with both perspectives, as is the effect of eastern Germany's regime on ideological values. One probable reason why this convergence is overlooked is the absence of a systematic framework that establishes how and why basic institutions shape ideological values.

The institutional learning perspective supplies such a micro-logic. It suggests that the central citizenship-qualities—restraint, self-reliance, and corresponding societal ideals—are developed predominantly when individuals have an opportunity to practise them. In the absence of such practice, individuals are unlikely to endorse a range of democratic values that are based upon these citizenship-qualities. By specifying how institutional structures affect ideological values, the institutional learning perspective places the 'institutions-to-values' process into the centre of analyses. The perspective thus separates systematically two issues which tend to be confused in the disputes between culturalists and institutionalists. The first issue is whether institutions shape ideological values; the second concerns the extent to which ideological values and distributional qualities affect citizens' institutional support. Separating the two issues clarifies a shared premiss, namely, that a nation's institutional framework may significantly affect citizens' ideological values.

There *are* genuine differences between institutionalists and culturalists. For one, the perspectives disagree over the pace of ideological value change after a new set of institutions is established. Institutionalists assume, but do not provide appropriate longitudinal data, that elites adjust their ideological values in relatively short-term periods (Chapter 2). In contrast, cultural analyses suggest that ideological values adjust predominately along generational lines. Although this study cannot conclusively resolve the debate, the ideological differences between individuals born before and after 1945 suggests the presence of significant generational effects. The stability of eastern MP's responses between 1992 and 1995 further points to a long-term process of developing restraint, self-reliance, and corresponding societal ideals, as does the continuity of aggregate responses of the eastern German public. Although this research does not refute the conversion argument once and for all, it casts doubts on its validity, thus challenging those who subscribe to it.

Another key difference between culturalists and institutionalists concerns the sources of institutional support. The former emphasize long-standing values (the congruence postulate), whereas the latter often emphasize performance evaluations. However, the ideological performance axiom suggests that this debate may be productively advanced by framing it as an empirical question, not as one to be decided a priori on normative grounds (see also Crawford and Lijphart 1995). I do not wish to play down the genuine differences between culturalists and institutionalists regarding the values-to-institutional support process. But the predominant focus on what divides these scholars may lead them to overlook their complementary contribution to this debate.

The institutional learning perspective also helps one determine which values are diffused and which are predominately acquired through democratic practice. The weak support for a range of democratic values in eastern Germany casts doubt on the optimistic premiss that democracies may spread globally to nations which have little experience with democratic rules. Because restraint and self-reliance underlie several democratic and market-based processes, eastern Germans frequently express authoritarian and anti-market sentiments. For these reasons, they also withhold support for liberal and market ideals which justify restraint and self-reliance. The fundamental lesson of the German case in terms of the diffusion argument is twofold: exposure to information about western democracies creates a *preference* for civil liberties and an efficient economy. But the *ability* to behave democratically, to follow market rules, and to develop corresponding ideals is substantially affected by citizens' exposure to appropriate institutions.

The mass–elite differences found in the East and the West further highlight the degree to which democratic values may develop within non-democratic nations through diffusion. Consistent with the diffusion argument is that elites in the East support liberal-democratic values more strongly than the eastern public. Indeed, eastern MPs tend to be more democratic than the western public. This pattern justifies analyses which view elites in transition countries as the most likely source of democratic support. At the same time, eastern German elites are relatively undemocratic when compared to western elites. This result is disheartening, because the new political elite in eastern Germany likely over-represents the democratic segments (Chapter 4). The substantial intra-German differences at the elite level thus raise the question of how supportive East-Central European elites are of procedures and ideals manifesting a capitalist democracy.

In sum, because the institutional learning perspective specifies the citizenship-qualities underlying democratic and market values, it helps to determine why some values diffuse while most ideological values are acquired through exposure to democratic and market institutions. This micro-logic reduces the danger of circular reasoning in 'learning' and diffusion arguments, for it provides analysts with conceptual criteria to specify a priori which ideological values are most likely to be supported in nations with little prior exposure to a capitalist democracy.

Avenues for Future Research. The discussion about the theoretical implications suggests several fruitful avenues for future research. First, we need considerably more research about citizens' ideological values. It is difficult to determine the prospects for liberal democracies if researchers primarily study individuals' support for abstract democratic rights to the detriment of other ideological values. In fact, because many studies focus on diffusible values they tend to lead to overly optimistic conclusions. Another implication of this book is to call for more empirical elite studies. To be clear, I do not favour abandoning studies of mass ideological values. I do suggest, however, that the relative balance of mass and elite studies in post-socialist nations should be changed in favour of the latter. Undoubtedly, post-socialist elites are more likely to endorse democratic values than publics in post-socialist countries. Yet, the substantial East–West differences among elites in Germany (and in the Ukraine, for example) indicates that *relatively* democratic elites may still be equivocating democrats. Just how committed post-socialist elites are to democratic ideals and procedures should therefore be examined in future studies.

This research also suggests the need for additional studies which determine how universal the linkage is between ideological values and citizens' performance evaluations. Similarly, more studies are needed to probe the effect of institutions' openness on the longevity of a new democracy. As mentioned above, it is possible that while exclusion from institutions may cause elites to reject a new system, access to decision-making may not automatically generate strong support *for* a new system. Inclusion may lower one's opposition, but not necessarily increase one's support. The degree to which this speculation accurately describes the context in East-Central Europe cannot be adjudicated on the basis of the available evidence.

Finally, future researchers might consider other sources of restraint and self-reliance. This book focuses on the institutional framework because Germany's quasi-laboratory conditions vary the institutional properties while keeping constant most societal characteristics. It is possible, however, that societal institutions also generate the seeds for restraint and self-reliance when one moves beyond Germany. One might, for example, investigate the degree to which individuals' participation in international economic sectors in, for example, Hungary, imbued market participants with those citizenship-qualities needed to develop democratic values. Future studies might also examine how participation of Central European elites in supra-national institutions affects their ideological values. There are a number of societal sectors that may develop restraint, self-reliance, and corresponding ideals, and we know little about how such sources may promote democratic values.

Managing Democratic Transitions. What practical lessons for East-Central Europe may we glean from Germany's multiple attempts to establish a democracy? Undoubtedly, there is no single, linear path leading from the central results of this study to its practical implications. It is possible, however, to outline a few recommendations for the

practitioner concerned with stabilizing a democracy. Most importantly, this study makes plain that managers of democratic transitions
must attempt: (1) to increase the odds that citizens evaluate the
performance of new institutions positively; (2) to reduce the distance
between pre-existing values and the ideological premisses of a new
regime; and (3) to maximize the inclusiveness of institutions to en-
compass key elites in the transition process. Although none of these
suggestions is novel when viewed in isolation, the crucial implication
of this study is that the three objectives must be pursued *simultaneously*.

The first recommendation is consistent with both institutionalist
and culturalist studies. Everything else being equal, positive performance evaluations increase one's willingness to support existing institutions. However, the overt simplicity of this recommendation vanishes
in light of the ideological performance axiom, which questions the
validity of the 'all-else-being-equal' premiss. If citizens disagree over
basic procedures and ideals, they may disagree over the proper yardstick one should use to assess institutions' performance (Chapters 2
and 9). To be sure, there is a minimal consensus across the ideological
spectrum in terms of what constitutes poor performance. Socialists
and market supporters would in all likelihood agree that rapid economic decline and widespread poverty are undesirable. Beyond this
minimal consensus, however, there is substantial room for disagreement over how institutional performance should be assessed. Because
of the confluence of performance evaluations and ideological values,
the issue of institutional performance cannot be completely separated
from citizens' ideological values—a key point that is all too often
ignored.

That is why the first recommendation must be considered simultaneously with the second one when new institutions are established: a
new democracy should minimize the distance between citizens' pre-
existing values and new institutions. This would help to stabilize a new
democracy by increasing the congruence between citizens' pre-
existing values and the new system. It would also increase the odds
that citizens evaluate the performance of a new system by using
criteria which match a system's underlying goals. The recommendation, therefore, is for a new democratic system to incorporate as many
pre-existing ideological preferences as are compatible with a democratic system. In the context of eastern Germany, for example, it would
be possible to enhance support for existing institutions if egalitarian

and plebiscitarian procedures are implemented selectively. In East-Central Europe, one might establish a market economy along with substantial welfare cushions in order to reduce the odds that citizens' reject market reforms. An economic reform strategy without conveying to citizens a sense of protection may be less successful than a reform strategy where citizens who are used to a paternalistic state feel protected from the worst repercussions of reforms. In the political realm, practitioners might, for example, follow Eckstein's (1996) suggestions to establish as many democratic procedures at the local level as possible, along with a centralized national system. This way, citizens would practice democracy locally while also being exposed to a system they are more likely to be accustomed to.

The third, and final, point is derived from institutionalist analyses. Key elites and their supporters must not feel permanently excluded from the decision-making structures of new institutions. The strong effect on trust of access to institutions reflects the importance of the process advanced by institutionalists (Chapter 9). However, the logic of the inclusion process unfolds primarily in the short term, because its positive effect does not exist independently of the daily, strategic interactions of elites. If their interests are no longer served by a democratic constitution in a changed strategic environment, elites by definition are likely to abandon their support for a democratic constitution—unless they internalize the beliefs that restraint and self-reliance are beneficial, and democratic and market ideals desirable. The long-term success of the inclusionary strategy in stabilizing a new democracy, therefore, hinges partly on the degree to which elites and mass publics are imbued with democratic values. Moreover, this study produces some evidence that is partly inconsistent with the inclusionary argument even in the short-term. For eastern MPs remain equivocal in their evaluations of democratic institutions between 1992 and 1995, even though most of them (especially from the CDU and SPD) have access to Germany's governmental structure.

Given the importance of ideological values for the long-term prospects of democracies, a central issue for the practitioner is how a congruent ideological culture might be created. Unfortunately, the lesson from eastern and western Germany's experience is that this is a long-term process indeed. It took western Germany's democracy almost two generations before a large majority of citizens unequivocally endorsed democratic values. The logic of the institutional learning axiom also suggests that core democratic qualities develop only slowly and over longer time-periods. Harry Eckstein echoes this sentiment when he writes 'the lesson is that *human beings do not have some natural affinity for democratic political orders*' (Eckstein 1996: 4; italics in original). At a minimum, the development of democratic values requires a considerable amount of time, perhaps even significant generational turnover. This conclusion is not comforting from the perspective of transition managers in the short term. Those with a longer-term perspective, however, may be consoled by Germany's experience, which indicates that ideological values can be remade in the long run.

This raises the intriguing question of how democratic institutions can be stabilized within a 'sceptical' or even 'hostile' ideological culture until democratic values emerge. Short of military occupation, it is challenging to consolidate democratic institutions in nations where publics and elites support them hesitantly (if at all). Although established wisdom would suggest that one way to stabilize democracies is through positive performance and the inclusion of most elites, this path is fraught with difficulties for the reasons just discussed. This dilemma highlights the crucial role supra-national institutions, such as the European Union, might play in supporting fledgling democracies. Through integration of elites into supranational institutions, elites may come to accept democratic systems even if they reject the ideas which a liberal democracy and market economy embody. Equivocating democrats may support democratic institutions, if, for instance, the EU provides the right incentives (subsidies, access to EU-institutions and markets). The basic idea, thus, is for supra-national institutions to mitigate the impact of incongruent ideological values and poor performance evaluations on national institutions. The fact that the EU will consider admitting several East-Central European nations in the near future may turn out to be one promising avenue to stabilize democratic institutions. From this vantage-point, the expansion of NATO to include Central European nations may also help to secure new democracies.

From the perspective of a social scientist, Germany's division created a unique quasi-laboratory where one may examine important theoretical and practical issues. Perhaps the study's single most important finding is that the process of institutional learning fundamentally shapes citizens' ideological values in partially predictable ways. The good news is that this process developed a democratic culture in western Germany. The troublesome implication is that eastern Germany and, by implication, most post-socialist nations now must undergo this long process toward democratic citizenship.

Appendix A Measuring Concepts

This appendix discusses the operationalization of variables in alphabetical order. The complete questionnaire used in the Berlin surveys is presented in Appendix C.

Political Elites

Authoritarianism. 'Here is another card with statements about political problems, but also about your personal situation. Would you tell much how much you agree or disagree with each statement?' MPs' expressed their agreement or disagreement with the following five statements using a seven-point indicator: (1) 'To compromise with political adversaries is dangerous because it frequently leads to the betrayal of one's own side'; (2) 'A country's general welfare should always override the special interests of groups and organizations'; (3) 'It will always be necessary to have a few strong, able individuals who know how to take charge'; (4) 'If we don't defend ourselves against rabble-rousers and troublemakers, our political order will be replaced by disorder and chaos'; (5) 'Discipline and obedience are essential in educating children into responsible citizenship.' High values represent authoritarian responses. The additive index ranges from 5 to 35.

Communist Party: A dichotomous variable coded '1' if the MP is a member of the reformed communist party (PS) and '0' if not.

Comparative Performance Evaluations (1995). 'If you think of the time in the GDR before the fall of the Berlin Wall, do you think people in the former GDR are, all in all, better off now, worse off, or does it make no difference?' MPs expressed their summary evaluation by means of a seven-point indicator. In addition to the overall evaluation, MPs also evaluated: (1) 'And when you just think of the personal freedom of people in the former GDR?'; (2) 'And when you think of the social conditions of people in the former GDR?'; (3) 'And when you think of the economic conditions of people in the former GDR?'

Conservative Ideology. 'In a number of studies, people have been asked to place themselves on a left–right scale indicating their overall political position. For purposes of comparison, would you please tell me where you would place your views on this scale?' MPs used a ten-point, left–right self-placement indicator to summarize their ideological views.

Contemporary Economic Problems. 'What are the two most important problems in Berlin?' For the most important problem, MPs received a score of '1' if they mentioned the general economic situation, unemployment, the budget deficit, or economic development. MPs received a score of '0' if they did not mention any of these problems. The same scoring procedure was applied to the second most important problems. I thus obtained two dummy variables. I then created an additive index, adding the two dummy variables and the unemployment category (#21) in Table A1 (see below).

Democratic Ideals: 'The term democracy is frequently used without further specifications these days. What seem to you personally the essentials of a democracy?' Based on detailed notes taken during the interview, I coded the responses into a maximum of five variables on the basis of a modified coding scheme developed by Putnam (1973). The categories presented in Table 5.3 consist of additive indicators summarizing more detailed code categories. The following description lists the general categories as used in Table 5.3 and their constituent categories (each is preceded by a letter). *Government by the People*: (a) government by the people, popular control, control by the people; (b) popular interest in and awareness of politics; (c) responsibility or answerability of the government to the people; government by consent; government based on electoral mandate. Most responses could actually be captured by two or three variables. That is, after coding MPs' responses into about three variables, the essence of most responses were captured. Each democratic component was coded only once so that repetitive answers do not influence the number of components coded. Thus, the 'government by the people' indicator has a range from 0 (a respondent did not mention any democratic component matching the three categories) to 3 (a respondent mentions components a, b, and c. *Social Equality*: (a) just standard of living; freedom from want; social and economic security for all; (b) classless society; less social distance; (c) fewer rich and poor; (d) social and economic security for all. *Active Participation*: (a) popular participation; an active role for the people, popular involvement in decision-making; direct democracy within the framework of parliamentary democracy. *Direct democracy*: (a) direct democracy; referenda for important decisions; public should be able to recall ministers at any time. *Equality of opportunity*: (a) equality in general; (b) political equality; one man, one vote; equality of opportunity; each person has the possibility of developing him/herself as far as possible; participation of citizens in all areas of society. *Civil Rights/Limited Government*: (a) liberty; freedom in general; (b) political or civic liberties in general; (c) freedom of expression (speech, free press); (d) minority rights; consideration of the minority; (e) limited government; checks and balances; no arbitrary power; (f) laissez-faire, socially and economically; freedom from government interference in socio-economic affairs; *Institutions*: (a) elections; (b) majority rule; (c) representative or parliamentary government in general; (d) parliamentary or legislative control over the executive; (e) rule of law; legal due process. *Political Competition*: (a) possibility of government changes; minority can become majority; (b) party competition; more than one party; (c) strong, critical opposition; (d) elite competition; ruling oligarchy; *Societal Competition*: (a) pluralism; variety of private associations and institutions; (b) consultation by the government with groups and organizations; *Citizens' responsibility*: (a) Mature educated, intelligent citizens; (b) freedom to do what is right; individual self-control; (c) assumption of responsibility and duties; (d) action in the interest of collective, not only of individual; reciprocal respect and tolerance.

The percentages in Table 5.3 represent the proportion of respondents mentioning at least one constituent component for each category. For the multivariate analyses (Table B1), I used an additive index of all the social-egalitarian responses. This indicator has a range from 0 to 4. Given the skewed distribution of this variable particularly in the West, I also analysed this model using probit, but the results generally lead to the same substantive conclusions (see Rohrschneider 1994 for details).

In order to examine the stability of responses (Fig. 5.3), I recoded the general categories into '0' (a respondent did not mention any component) and '1' (respondents mentioned at least one component). Then, the 1992 and 1995 responses were cross-tabulated.

Democratic Rights: 'In order to get a comparable picture of the distribution of opinion with earlier studies, I am now using a standardized format to simplify matters a little bit. I am aware that these statements capture your views only incompletely. Nevertheless, would you tell me for each of the statements whether you agree or disagree?' MPs evaluated the statements shown in Table 5.1 by means of a seven-point indicator. In Table 5.1 the percentages are based on respondents who agree (7, 6, 5) with statements A and B and who disagree (1, 2, 3) with the other statements. For the multivariate analyses, each statement was coded so that high values represent a democratic response; the original metric was used. The index ranges from 5 (undemocratic views) to 35.

Economic Values. 'What do you personally feel are the major advantages and disadvantages of establishing a social market economy in East Germany? [PROBE, IF NEEDED.] Some people argue that socialist economies, despite several limitations, offered certain advantages, such as social security, job security, or greater collegiality at the workplace. How would you evaluate this argument?' I coded the responses to the open-ended economy question in up to six variables on the basis of the coding scheme presented in Table A1.

TABLE A1. *Coding economic ideals*

'What do you personally feel are the major advantages and disadvantages of establishing a social market economy in East Germany? (PROBE, IF NEEDED). Some people argue that socialist economies, despite several limitations, offered certain advantages, such as social security, job security, or greater collegiality at the workplace. How would you evaluate this argument?'

Advantages
  11. Social market economies are generally superior (without specifying)
  12. Efficiency; productivity of market economies; emergence of competitive companies; achievement-based wages
  13. Surplus profits/superior technology can be used to fix major societal problems (e.g. pollution)
  14. Emphasis on individual capacity/freedom (e.g. responsibility, decision making; right to strike)
  15. Free enterprise system with all its facets; self-regulating and self-sufficient economy
  16. Social responsibility of entrepreneurs
  17. Higher living standards
  18. More jobs; higher social security
  19. Other

Short-term disadvantages
  21. Unemployment
  22. Pressure for people to adjust to new economic and social system
  23. 'Social' aspects of market economies isn't established yet
  24. Market economy doesn't function properly yet
  25. Speculation with property, (land; houses, etc)
  26. Fast pace/procedure with which market economy was established
  29. Other

Long-term disadvantages (coded here if characteristic is viewed as a serious disadvantage immanent to market economies i.e. these seem unfixable within systemic boundaries)
  31. Alienation of workers from product
  32. Collegiality among workers is lost
  33. Exploitation of workers under capitalist/market system
  34. Democracy in factories is lost since capitalist makes decisions
  35. High pressure environment, competition
  36. Humans are treated like products in market economy
  37. Workers have more freedom under a socialist system
  38. Market economy produces unfair results (living standards; income distribution, etc.)
  39. Profit motive redefines social norms and values negatively (e.g. how people treat each other)
  40. Social security is lost; no job security
  41. Destruction of the environment in new economic system

TABLE A1. (*cont.*)

42. Destruction of GDR industry
43. Large corporations control politics
49. Other

Positive aspects of GDR economy (coded here if GDR advantage is explicitly mentioned)
51. General positive aspects (without specification)
52. Social security; social net
53. Freedom of individuals; no exploitation
54. Globally, GDR economy was competitive/provided decent standards of living
55. Many good ideas in GDR society; implementation was faulty
56. Gender equality
59. Other

Miscellaneous Critique (coded here if market economies are principally accepted, but that fundamental reforms are needed)
61. Democratization of market economy is needed; anti-democratic character of large enterprises
62. Find new conceptualization of socialism within constraints of market economy
63. Market economy needs to be reformed in order to increase social security; social responsibility of industry must be increased
64. Ecological aspect needs to be incorporated in market economy
69. Other

Other
71.

98. Don't know
99. Not answered

The categories in Table 8.2 are based on the following recodes: *Systemic Advantages of Market Economies*: an additive index that counts how many elements from categories #11 through #16 are mentioned. *Systemic Disadvantages of Market Economies*: an additive index that counts how many elements from categories #31 through #40 and category #43 are mentioned. I omitted category #41 because of its New Politics content, and omitted characteristic #42 because of its possible short-term character. Including these categories does not affect the empirical results or substantive conclusions. *Positive Aspect of GDR Economy*: an additive index that counts how many elements from categories #51 through #56 are mentioned. *Reform Market Economy*: an additive index that counts how many elements from categories the #61 through #64 are mentioned. *Net Advantage Score*: a net score obtained by subtracting the systemic disadvantage score from the systemic advantage score. This indicator ranges from –4 to 4 (see Table 8.3).

For the stability analysis (Fig. 8.1), the net advantage scores were first recoded into three categories: below 0 (negative), 0 (neutral), and above 0 (positive).

MPs' views about welfare policies are measured by the following question: 'On this card is a list with statements regarding the economic system. Would you please tell me how much you agree or disagree with each of the following statements?' MPs then evaluated the statements shown in Table 8.1 by means of a seven-point indicator, ranging from agree completely (7) to disagree completely (1). The percentages in Table 8.1 represent MPs who agree (7, 6, 5) with a statement. For the multivariate analyses I constructed an additive indicator ranging from 7 (free market values) to 49 (welfare values).

Education: (1) Volkschule/8. Klasse; (2) Mittlere Reife/10. Klasse/Mittel Schule; (3) Abitur/EOS; (4) Fachhochschule/Fachschule; (5) Universität.

Future Personal Finances. 'In a few years, do you think that you will be better off, about the same, or worse off?'

Future National Economy. An additive index of characteristic #17 and #18 (Table A1).

Gender: Coded '1' for male MPs, and '0' for female MPs.

Income: (1) Below DM 4,000; (2) DM 4,000–5,999; (3) DM 6,000–7,999; (4) DM 8,000–9,999; (5) above DM 10,000.

Institutional trust: 'Here is a list with important political institutions in our society. Would you tell me how much trust you have in each of these institutions?' MPs' evaluated the five institutions shown in Table 9.1 on a seven-point trust–distrust indicator. The responses were collapsed into those trusting (7, 6, 5), ambivalent (4), and distrusting (3, 2, 1) institutions. For the OLS analysis I created an additive index using the original metric. The indicator ranges from a low of 5 (expressing distrust) to 35 (expressing trust).

Party Membership. A dummy variable of MPs' party membership. In the East the excluded parties are the PDS and the also Bündnis '90/Greens; in the West the excluded party is the Bündnis '90/Greens. When these dummy variables are used (because the theoretical argument requires a refined breakdown of respondents' party preference), I did not employ the PDS-party membership variable described earlier.

Plebiscitarian Views. 'Would you please indicate your opinion on the plebiscitarian involvement of citizens by indicating whether you find each of these [SHOW CARD] procedures involving citizens directly meaningful or not meaningful?' MPs evaluated the statement presented in Table 5.5. I used a dichotomous response format in order to keep the results comparable to the study of national-level East and West German MPs (Herzog *et al.* 1990;

Werner 1991): For the plebiscitarian index used in multivariate analyses, I first included the small number of missing values as a neutral middle category, and then created an additive index, ranging from 3 (reject all procedures) to 15 (endorse all procedures).

Pluralism. 'You mentioned earlier —— as the most important problem in Berlin. There are a number of conflicts of interests involved in solving this problem, since different groups and people have different conceptions of how to solve it. Do these conflicts of interests have a positive or negative effect on the governability of Berlin? [PROBE, IF NEEDED.] Why? [OR] Why not?' Table A2 presents the coding scheme used to code MPs' responses to this question. The following recodes were used to prepare the frequency distribution in Table 7.2. *Positive Views*: categories #11, 12, 13, 14, 15 in Table A2; *Statist Aversion*: #31, 32, 44; *Socialist Aversion*: #35, 45, 46.

The statements in Table 7.1 were evaluated by political elites by means of a seven-point indicator ranging from agree strongly (7) to disagree strongly (1).

The pluralism index employed in the multivariate analyses is composed of two indicators. First, I recoded indicator B in Table 7.1 into three categories (5–7 = 0; 4 = 1; 1–3 = 2). Secondly, the pluralism score in Table 7.3 is collapsed into three categories (0 = 0; 1 = 1; else = 2). This recoding entails that high scores reflect pluralist orientations. I then combined both indicators into an additive index ranging from 0 (anti-pluralist views) to 4 (pro-pluralist views).

Post-war Generation: A dichotomous variable where '1' represents MPs born in 1945 or later, and '0' represents MPs born in 1944 and earlier. I chose this cut-off point for generations because it is theoretically meaningful *and* because it leaves enough cases within each cohort to conduct the cohort analyses. The decision to divide MPs into two groups—those born in 1944 or before and those born later—means that MPs reaching the age of 15 before 1960 are coded as a pre-war cohort. This cut-off point parallels the degree to which the quasi-laboratory conditions had been established in Germany, because the Berlin Wall was not built until 1961. Before that time East and West Germany were less insulated from each other. I have conducted a sensitivity analysis using eleven adjacent cut-off points for the cohort definition. For example, I first defined a pre-war cohort by combining MPs born in 1938 and before into the pre-war category. A second pre-war variable includes those born in 1939 and before, a third contains MPs born in 1940 and before, etc. I then conducted the analyses presented in Table B1 (Appendix B), using these different cohort variables in separate analyses. The results parallel the historical reality in Germany: the largest cohort differences within the East emerge when the post-war cohort contains predominately MPs who grew up after the construction of the Berlin Wall. While a more refined breakdown of cohorts would undoubtedly be desirable, these analyses suggest that the

You mentioned earlier (Most Important Problem) as an important problem in Berlin. There are a number of conflicts of interests involved in solving this problem since different groups and people have different conceptions of how to solve the problem. Do these conflicts of interests have a positive or negative effect on the governability of Berlin? (PROBE, IF NEEDED) Why? (OR) Why not? (CODE UP TO FOUR MENTIONS OF WHY OR WHY NOT PROBLEMS REDUCE GOVERNABILITY).

Positive effect of conflicts of interest on governability
11. Conflicts of interest are essence of democracy (code here if R mentions this explicitly)
12. Suppressing conflicts of interest leads to dictatorship/prevents social progress
13. Conflicts of interest need to be articulated in order to find a policy compromise
14. Conflicts of interests make needs of citizens visible/add new perspective to MPs' viewpoints
15. Conflicts are positive, but conflicts must stay within peaceful means of conflict resolution; conflicts must be resolved undogmatically
29. Other positive

Negative effect on governability
31. Conflicts of interest often prevent governments from achieving the best policy (code here if this disadvantage is central to R's response)
32. Conflicts of interest slow down the political process (code here if this disadvantage is central to R's response)
33. Strong groups have an unfair advantage over weaker groups; (code here if rules of conflict resolution are still accepted by R; R still values conflict)
34. Not all relevant societal interests are properly organized (code here if rules of conflict resolution are still accepted by R)
35. Problems are too severe to be solved within existing rules of conflict resolution; parties have no solution
36. Conflicts are artificially magnified (e.g. unnecessary debate between parties; interest groups are too dogmatic).
38. Other negative

No effect on governability
41. No effect (not specified)
42. Problems are under control; not severe enough
43. Parliamentary majority is large enough to handle problems
44. Governments should act principally independent from interest groups
45. Owners of production/powerful economic groups dominate conflicts of interest (code here if existing rules of conflict resolution are rejected
46. Real conflicts of interests are not discussed (e.g. between rich and poor).

Other
51.

97. Refused
98. Don't know
99. Not asked

cohort analyses presented here are robust and do not depend on an arbitrary birth-date cut-off point.

Postmaterialism: I used a slightly modified coding procedure of the original items Inglehart developed. While materialists and postmaterialists are coded as Inglehart suggests, I distinguish between mixed materialists and mixed postmaterialists, depending on whether respondents first mention the materialist or the postmaterialist item. This coding procedure uses more information than the three-point indicator. (The results are almost identical when the mixed categories are combined.)

Political Tolerance. 'I would like to ask you a few questions about social groups and movements which are viewed by some people as threatening to the political and social order in the united Germany. Would you please select from this list [SHOW CARD] the group or organization that you like the least?' After selecting the first group, I asked: 'What is your second least-liked group?' After selecting the groups: 'I would like to know your personal opinion on the following statements regarding the activities of each group. Let us begin with [LEAST-LIKED GROUP]. Independent of the existing legal framework, would you tell me, how strongly you agree or disagree with the following statements?' MPs used a seven-point scale to express their views about the political activities contained in Table 6.1. Entries in Table 6.1 represent agreement (7, 6, 5) with indicators 1 and 3 and disagreement (1, 2, 3) with the other indicators. For the multivariate analyses, I first recoded each of the indicators so that high values represent a tolerant response. I then combined the four questions about each group into two separate indices. Each of the two tolerance indicators thus ranges from 4 (representing intolerance) to 28.

For the stability analyses (Fig. 6.4), I first recoded the two summary indicators into three categories: intolerant (4–13); ambivalent (14–18); tolerant (19–28). These recodes reflect the intuitively accessible original metric where 1–3 reflects rejection of a statement, 4 represents undecided views, and 5–7 reflects supportive views. Then the 1992 and 1995 responses were cross-tabulated. *Reasons for Intolerance* (based on code categories presented in Table A3). Percentages in Table 6.2 represent MPs who mention at least one category. Historical reasons, first group (the focus in Table 6.2 is on fascists): categories 11, 12, 13, 14, 15, 16, 17; Historical reasons, second group: categories 11, 12, 13, 14, 16, 18. (2) Defendable democracy (first and second groups): categories 21, 22, 23, 24, 25. *Reasons for Tolerance*. (1) Principle-based tolerance: categories 41 and 44; (2) Control-based tolerance: category 42; (3) Group is harmless: categories 43, 45, 46, 47.

Religiosity: 'How often do you attend church? Would you say: At least every Sunday; almost every Sunday; sometimes; once a year; less than once a year; never.' High values represent religious responses.

Table A3. *Coding reasons for/against tolerance*

Historical reasons for refusing to grant rights
11. General reference to history without specifying the time-period
12. Group violates human rights; group is unwilling to respect the political opponent as history shows
13. History documents the inhumane goals of group
14. Group does not respect basic civil liberties, as history shows
15. Explicit reference to Holocaust
16. Explicit reference to Weimar Republic
17. Explicit reference to Third Reich
18. Experience of GDR citizens with communism
19. Other

Contemporary conditions
21. A democracy must defend itself against the ideological enemy (code here if R mentions this explicitly)
22. A group which denies rights to other viewpoints, should not enjoy basic political rights
23. Group pursues the physical destruction of the political enemy/group violates basic human rights
24. Group is violent
25. Group tries to overthrow the constitution
26. Extremist groups should not be subsidized with public funds
27. Young people are too receptive to extremist ideas
29. Other

Miscellaneous
31. Group hurts image of Federal Republic in other countries
32. Distinction between disagreeable reform and revolutionary movements
33. R disagrees with goals
34. Group produces international tension/instability
39. Other

Reasons for tolerance
41. A true democrat must extend political rights to extremist groups (code here if mentioned explicitly)
42. Group can be better controlled if it is out in the open; its true character can be revealed if it is out in the open
43. Democracy is firmly established; group is not dangerous politically at present
44. Ideas need to be argued out in the public realm/freedom of speech must be extended to extremist groups
45. Group does not intend to overthrow the constitution
46. Group does not deny human rights to others
47. Group pursues humanitarian goals
48. Group goals are legitimate (from R's viewpoint).
49. Other

Other
51.
98. Not asked
99. Not answered

Right-wing Target Group. A dichotomous variable where '1' represents the choice of right-wing groups (fascists, anti-abortionists, and displaced peoples' organizations) and '0' any other group.

Satisfaction with democracy's performance: 'On the whole, are you very satisfied, fairly satisfied, not very satisfied, or not satisfied at all with the way democracy works in Germany?'

Social Change. 'Here is another card with statements about political problems, but also about your personal situation. Would you say how much you agree or disagree with each statement?' MPs expressed their views on a seven-point indicator when evaluating the following statements measuring social change: (1) 'Everything is changing so fast these days that it is difficult to find firm reference points'; (2) 'Everything is so uncertain these days that one has to be ready for anything.' An additive index was created ranging from 2 to 14.

Threat Perception. 'Please evaluate the two groups you selected in terms of the following characteristics [SHOW CARD]. Please select a 7 if you feel the characteristics mentioned on the left side is most accurate. A 1 means that you think the characteristics mentioned on the right side is most accurate. (Members of Group): (1) 'are violent or nonviolent'; (2) 'are democratic or non-democratic'; (3) 'partially employ illegal methods or only employs legal methods.' The responses were recoded to represent the same polarity and then combined into two additive indexes. High values represent high threat perceptions.

Mass Publics

Age: Measured in years.

Democratic Ideals. 'In your opinion, what is most important about democracy. Which things on this list are absolutely necessary for one to be able to say of a country, This is a democracy?' Multiple responses were allowed. Percentages in Table 5.4 are based on the number of respondents which selected a statement. The number of cases in the Allensbach surveys is between N = 1,000 and N = 1,100.

Democratic Rights. 'On this card, there are several statements about politics, state, and society. We would like to ask you to indicate your views about these statements.' Respondents were shown the statements presented in Table 5.2. Respondents evaluated these statements by means of a six-point scale which runs from +3 to –3 without a neutral category. Entries in Table 5.2 are either those agreeing with a statement (1, 2, 3) or disagreeing with a statement (–1, –2, –3). For the summary index, each statement was coded so that high values represent a democratic response.

Economic Values. The eastern and western German public were asked in the 1991 and 1994 Allbus surveys (foreign nationals are excluded from the Allbus-based analyses in every chapter): 'Here is a list with different opinions about social status differences in Germany in terms of existing ones as well as how it ought to be. Please tell me for each statement whether you agree completely, agree somewhat, disagree somewhat, or disagree completely.' Respondents were then shown the statements presented in Table 8.4. After including the small number of missing data as a neutral middle category, I summed the responses to create an overall welfare economic indicator for mass publics. This indicator is used in the analyses presented in Table 8.6. *Opinion about the Market Economy*: 'Do you have a positive or negative opinion about the economic system in Germany.' Response categories are: (1) A good opinion; (2) A bad opinion; (3) Undecided. *Welfare versus Socialist Views*: The International Social Justice Surveys asked respondents to respond to two statements (Tab. 8.7): 'The government should guarantee everyone a minimum standard of living' and 'The government should place an upper limit on the amount of money any one person can make.' The response categories are: (1) Agree completely; (2) Agree somewhat; (3) Neither agree nor disagree; (4) Disagree somewhat; (5) Disagree completely.

Education: Higher values represent a higher degree. The few respondents who still attend school, gave no answer, or who obtained other school degrees, are excluded.

Freedom versus Equality: 'Two people are talking about what is ultimately more important, freedom or as much equality as possible. Would you please read this and tell me which of the two comes closest to saying what you also think?'

A. 'I think that freedom and equality are equally important. But if I had to choose between the two, I would say personal freedom is more important; that is, for people to be able to live in freedom and not be restricted in their development.'

B. 'Certainly both freedom and equality are equally important. But if I had to choose between the two, I would consider as much equality as possible to be more important; that is, for no one to be underprivileged and class differences not to be so strong.'

Gender: Male '1' and female '0'.

Income: I used a finely graded scale ranging from '1' (income is between DM 400 and 600) to 22 (respondents' income is more than DM 15,000). In the OLS analysis I replaced missing data for eastern respondents with the mean for the East (mean = 11) and missing data for western respondents with the mean for the West (mean = 13).

Institutional trust: 'I am going to mention several institutions. Please tell me how much you trust each of them?' Citizens evaluated the constitutional court, the federal parliament, the local administration, the justice system, and the federal government by means of a seven-point scale which is identical to the one used by MPs. In Table 9.1 responses were recoded to reflect trust (7, 6, 5) ambivalence (4), and distrust (3, 2, 1). The combined indicator ranges from 5 (representing distrust) to 35.

Party preference: 'If there were a federal election next Sunday, which party would you vote for?' I created three dummy variables representing the CDU, FDP, and SPD supporters. The excluded reference groups are the voters who would support the Bündnis '90/Greens, PDS, Republikaner, non-voters, and voters of other parties. This variable is used in Chapter 9 because the theoretical argument requires a refined breakdown of respondents' party preference.

PDS Party preference: 'If there were a federal election next Sunday, which party would you vote for?' I created a dummy variable where '1' represents those who would support the PDS and '0' for supporters of other parties CDU, FDP, SPD, Bündnis '90/Greens, and Republikaner. This variable was used in Chapter 8.

Pluralism: The statements for mass publics lack the neutral middle category, but the statements are identical to those used in the Berlin surveys.

Political Tolerance. Respondents in eastern and western Germany were asked in the *Times/Mirror* survey (1991) 'Here are some statements on different topics. Please tell me how much you agree or disagree with each of these statements': (1) 'Freedom of speech should not be granted to fascists'; (2) 'Books that contain ideas dangerous to society should be banned from public school libraries'; (3) 'Homosexuals should not be permitted to teach school.' Response categories are: (1) Strongly agree; (2) Agree; (3) Disagree; (4) Disagree strongly. Entries in Figure 6.3 are respondents who disagree (3, 4) with each statement. About undemocratic parties, respondents were asked: 'Some people feel that in a democracy all political parties should be allowed, even those that don't believe in the democratic system. Others feel that even in a democracy certain political parties should be outlawed. Which comes closer to your view?' Response categories are: (1) Allow all; (2) Outlaw some; (3) Can't say. Entries are respondents who would allow all parties. The common characteristic of these statements is that they ask respondents to consider civil liberties with reference to specific circumstances.

Respondents in the World Values survey 1995–7 were presented with a list of groups closely resembling the list in the Berlin parliamentarian surveys: 'Now I want to know something about various groups in this society. On this card, there are various groups. Please select the groups which you like the least.' Respondents evaluated the following statements: (1) Members of [GROUP] should not occupy a public office; (2) [GROUP] should not be allowed to hold demonstrations; (3) Members of [GROUP] should not be allowed as teachers in schools. Response categories are dichotomous (allow or not allow). Percentages in Figures 6.3 represent respondents who would allow an activity. Although the mass survey includes the problematic category 'criminals' on the list of groups, this category was fortunately chosen by only about 10 per cent in the surveys in Germany. I did not exclude this group from the analyses, for lack of access to the original data set at the time of this writing.

Positive expectations about future personal finances: 'How is your personal financial situation?' (1) Very good; (2) Good; (3) Mixed; (4) Bad; (5) Very bad.

Positive Evaluations of the contemporary economy: 'How would you evaluate the contemporary economic situation in Germany?' (1) Very good; (2) Good; (3) Mixed; (4) Bad; (5) Very bad.

Positive expectations about the future economy: 'How well do you think the economy will do in a year?' (1) Much better than today; (2) A little better than today; (3) The same; (4) A little worse than today; (5) Much worse than today.

Postmaterialism: Inglehart's postmaterialism indicator with four categories.

Socialism as an Ideal: In the Allensbach surveys, upon which Figure 5.2 is based, respondents were asked to respond to the statement: 'Socialism is a good idea that was poorly implemented.' Response categories are 'yes' and 'no'. In the Allbus 1994 survey, used in Figure 5.5, respondents were given the same statement, but then either agreed (completely or somewhat) or disagreed (completely or somewhat).

Appendix B Multivariate Analyses

This appendix presents the complete multivariate analyses discussed in the various chapters. The central results are highlighted in the text, but the quantitatively inclined reader may find these full results useful.

TABLE B1. *Predicting MPs' democratic values*

Predictors	Democratic rights			Egalitarian democracy			Direct democracy		
	East	West	Combined	East	West	Combined	East	West	Combined
West Berlin	a	a	.17**	a	a	-.30***	a	a	-.28***
			(1.8)			(-.41)			(-1.50)
Communist party	-.12	a	-.01	.25*	a	.21***	.21	a	.13
	(-1.40)		(-.21)	(.53)		(.47)	(1.40)		(1.20)
Post-war generation	.26**	.04	.13*	.08	-.13	.04	.05	.08	.06
	(2.60)	(.46)	(1.40)	(.15)	(-.070)	(.05)	(.25)	(.38)	(.34)
Postmaterialism	.41***	.30***	.35***	.01	.17	.07	.18	.06	.11
	(2.40)	(1.80)	(1.90)	(.01)	(.040)	(.05)	(.56)	(.14)	(.32)
Religiosity	-.18	-.03	-.05	-.12	-.01	-.06	-.01	-.20*	-.14
	(-.60)	(-.11)	(-.16)	(-.07)	(-.01)	(-.03)	(-.01)	(-.32)	(-.19)
Education	.13	.32***	.24***	-.12	.05	.06	-.08	-.08	-.10
	(.77)	(1.40)	(1.20)	(-.13)	(.03)	(.04)	(-.29)	(-.17)	(-.25)
Income	.08	-.12	-.02	-.01	.06	-.01	-.02	-.02	-.01
	(.45)	(-.62)	(-.10)	(-.01)	(.01)	(-.01)	(-.07)	(-.04)	(-.01)
Gender (high = male)	.10	-.04	.02	-.17	-.12	-.14	-.15	-.11	-.11
	(1.00)	(-.51)	(.26)	(-.34)	(-.07)	(-.21)	(-.87)	(-.56)	(-.68)
Adjusted R-square	.19	.18	.20	.03	.01	.17	.09	.04	.17
(N)	(76)	(85)	(161)	(76)	(85)	(161)	(76)	(85)	(161)

Note: Entries are standardized regression coefficients (OLS); unstandardized coefficients appear in parenthesis. The democratic rights index is an additive index based on items presented in Table 5.1. (The appendix contains details about the construction of the indicators). The egalitarian indicator is an additive indicator of the number of egalitarian responses to the open-ended democracy question. The direct democracy index is an additive index based on items presented in Table 5.5. *, **, and *** indicate significance on the .10, .05, and .01 level respectively. a = Indicator not included.

TABLE B2. *Predicting mass publics' socialist ideals*

Predictors	East	West	Combined
West Germany	a	a	−.31***
			(−.98)
Communist party	.21***	.03	.10***
	(.73)	(.92)	(.71)
Age	.10***	.04*	.06***
	(.01)	(.01)	(.01)
Postmaterialism	.01	−.06***	−.03
	(.01)	(−.08)	(.14)
Education	.01	.01	.01
	(.01)	(.01)	(.01)
Income	−.10***	−.10***	−.10***
	(−.03)	(−.04)	(−.01)
Gender (high = male)	−.04	−.07	−.03*
	(−.13)	(−.21)	(−.01)
Adjusted R-Square	.08	.03	.20
(N)	(792)	(1660)	(2452)

Source: Allbus (1994). The dependent variable is the response of mass publics to the statement 'Socialism is a good idea that was poorly implemented.' *, **, and *** indicate significance on the .10, .05, and .01 level respectively. a = indicator not included.

TABLE B3. *The influence of institutional learning on MPs' tolerance*

Predictors	Least-liked group			Second least-liked group		
	Com-bined	East	West	Com-bined	East	West
West Berlin MP	.17**	a	a	.14*	a	a
	(2.00)			(1.90)		
Communist party MP	−.24***	−.31***	a	−.08	−.08	a
	(−4.70)	(−4.00)		(−1.70)	(1.30)	
Democratic rights	.10	.13	.09	.15*	.08	.18
	(.11)	(.13)	(.09)	(.18)	(.10)	(.20)
Threat perception	−.31***	−.50***	−.29**	−.42***	−.50***	−.31***
	(−.82)	(−1.80)	(−.59)	(−.53)	(−.66)	(−.36)
Right-wing target group	−.01	−.07	−.06	.18**	.14	.27**
	(−.06)	(−1.60)	(−1.00)	(2.40)	(1.90)	(3.50)
Authoritarianism	−.34***	−.33**	−.44***	−.24***	−.25*	−.19
	(−.35)	(−.29)	(−.47)	(−.27)	(−.28)	(−.22)
Conservative self-placement	.10	.11	.12	.20**	.34**	.05
	(.27)	(.27)	(.32)	(.59)	(1.00)	(.14)
Social change	.14**	.23**	.07	.15**	.22**	.05
	(.27)	(.39)	(.14)	(.33)	(.49)	(.11)
Postmaterialism	−.04	−.15	−.03	.08	.18	.02
	(−.29)	(−.90)	(−.18)	(.56)	(1.40)	(.14)
Religiosity	−.02	−.01	−.06	−.09	−.05	−.07
	(−.09)	(−.04)	(−.22)	(−.38)	(−.21)	(−.29)
Gender (male)	.10	.06	.16	.03	.12	.01
	(1.40)	(.64)	(2.10)	(.48)	(1.80)	(.15)
Age	.05	.13	.08	−.05	−.15	−.01
	(.05)	(.07)	(.05)	(−.04)	(−.11)	(−.01)
Education	−.02	.04	−.06	.02	.10	.01
	(−.11)	(−.22)	(−.27)	(.13)	(.84)	(.06)
Income	−.03	−.10	−.01	−.01	.06	−.05
	(−.15)	(−.58)	(−.04)	(−.07)	(.44)	(−.25)
Adjusted R-square	.35	.39	.14	.44	.46	.37
(N)	(159)	(76)	(83)	(159)	(75)	(83)

Note: Entries are standardized regression coefficients; unstandardized coefficients appear in parentheses. *, **, and *** indicate significance on the .10, .05, and .01 level respectively. a = variable is not included.

TABLE B4. *The influence of institutional learning on pluralist views*

Predictors	East	West	Combined
West Berlin	a	a	.25***
			(.63)
Egalitarian democracy	−.22*	−.04	−.14*
	(−.30)	(−.17)	(−.25)
Liberal-democratic rights	.08	.17	.13
	(.02)	(.03)	(.03)
Post-war cohort	−.16	−.03	−.05
	(−.40)	(−.06)	(−.12)
Communist party	−.05	a	−.11
	(−.16)		(−.45)
Postmaterialism	.09	.23*	.21**
	(.14)	(.26)	(.28)
Religiosity	.05	.07	.05
	(.04)	(.05)	(.05)
Income	−.17	−.02	−.10
	(−.23)	(−.02)	(−.11)
Education	−.16	.16	.04
	(−.24)	(.14)	(.05)
Gender (male)	−.21	−.08	−.04
	(−.57)	(−.19)	(−.11)
R-Square	.15	.19	.24
(N)	(77)	(84)	(161)

Note: Entries are standardized regression coefficients; unstandardized coefficients appear in parentheses. *, **, and *** indicate significance on the .10, .05, and .01 level respectively. a = variable is excluded from the analyses.

TABLE B5. *Predicting MPs' performance evaluations, 1992*

Predictors	East	West	Combined
West Berlin	a	a	.29***
			(.47)
Egalitarian ideals	−.14*	−.05	−.13**
	(.13)	(.10)	(−.15)
Market ideals	.24***	.32***	.25***
	(.13)	(.17)	(.13)
Plebiscitarian ideals	−.10	−.10	−.01
	(−.20)	(−.02)	(−.01)
CDU	.16	.60***	.39***
	(.32)	(.66)	(.65)
FDP	.09	.23*	.15**
	(.29)	(.41)	(.43)
SPD	.25*	.38***	.31***
	(.46)	(.42)	(.52)
Post-war cohort	−.16**	−.22	−.12**
	(−2.40)	(−.23)	(−.19)
Negative future personal finances	−.41***	.06	−.23***
	(−.42)	(.06)	(−.24)
Postmaterialism	−.09	−.03	.07
	(−.09)	(−.02)	(.06)
Gender (male)	.12	.20*	.13***
	(.24)	(.23)	(.09)
Income	−.03	.31***	.13***
	(−.03)	(.14)	(.09)
Education	−.02	.12	.05
	(−.02)	(.05)	(.04)
Adjusted R-square	.58	.38	.58
(N)	(77)	(84)	(161)

Note: Entries are standardized regression coefficients with unstandardized coefficients appearing in parentheses. *, **, *** indicate significance of coeffients at the .10, .05, and .01 level, respectively. a = the exclusion of a variable from the analysis.

TABLE B6. *Predicting institutional trust, mass publics*

Predictors	East	West	Combined
Western Germany	a	a	.17***
			(2.10)
Socialism is a positive ideal	−.06**	−.06***	.07***
	(.30)	(.22)	(.25)
Market ideals	.01	.07***	.05***
	(.01)	(.07)	(.05)
CDU	.15***	.21***	.19***
	(2.20)	(2.40)	(2.50)
FDP	.07**	.09*	.08***
	(1.50)	(1.70)	(1.70)
SPD	.14***	.12***	.13***
	(1.80)	(1.40)	(1.60)
Democracy functions well	.29***	.25***	.26***
	(2.60)	(2.00)	(2.20)
Age	.01	.09***	.06***
	(.01)	(.03)	(.02)
Positive views about contemporary economy	.11**	.12***	.11***
	(.93)	(.77)	(.81)
Positive personal finances	.06***	.07***	.07***
	(.37)	(.48)	(.45)
Positive expectations about future economy	.16***	.07***	.08***
	(1.10)	(.48)	(.51)
Postmaterialism	−.01	−.04***	.04**
	(−.07)	(−.26)	(.23)
Gender (Male)	.03	.06	.03
	(.41)	(.31)	(.04)
Education	.01	.03	.05***
	(.12)	(.28)	(.27)
Income	.02	.03	.02
	(−.02)	(.04)	(.20)
Adjusted R-square	.28	.24	.31
(N)	(743)	(1568)	(2311)

Note: Entries are standardized regression coefficients with unstandardized coefficients appearing in parentheses. *, **, *** indicate significance of coeffients at the .10, .05, and .01 level respectively. a = the exclusion of a variable from the analysis.

Source: Allbus (1994).

TABLE B7. *Predicting positive performance evaluations, mass publics*

Predictors	East	West	Combined
Western Germany	a	a	.15***
			(.25)
Socialism is a positive ideal	−.06**	−.03	.02
	(.04)	(.22)	(.01)
Market ideals	.20***	.11***	.15***
	(.03)	(.01)	(.02)
CDU	.27***	.27***	.27***
	(.45)	(.38)	(.41)
FDP	.01	.12***	.09***
	(.03)	(.28)	(.21)
SPD	.20***	.12***	.15***
	(.28)	(.16)	(.21)
Age	.05	.02	.01
	(.01)	(.01)	(.01)
Positive views about contemporary economy	.11***	.16***	.14***
	(.10)	(.13)	(.13)
Positive personal finances	.08**	.07***	.07***
	(.06)	(.06)	(.06)
Positive expectations about future economy	.16***	.10***	.12***
	(.13)	(.08)	(.09)
Postmaterialism	−.01	−.01	.02
	(−.01)	(−.01)	(.01)
Gender (Male)	.03	.09***	.06***
	(.04)	(.12)	(.09)
Education	.06*	.02	.03
	(.04)	(.02)	(.02)
Income	.07*	.04*	.01
	(.01)	(.01)	(.01)
Adjusted R-square	.27	.17	.24
(N)	(757)	(1549)	(2351)

Note: Entries are standardized regression coefficients with unstandardized coefficients appearing in parentheses. *, **, *** indicate significance of coeffients at the .10, .05, and .01 level respectively. a = the exclusion of a variable from the analysis.

Source: Allbus (1994).

Appendix C Questionnaire

Democracy and Political Elites in the United Berlin

Thank you for taking the time to participate in this study. I would like to assure you that I will protect the confidentiality of your answers.

Section I: Political Equality

1. I would like to start by asking you about some of the problems which are currently debated in Berlin. What are the two most important problems in Berlin today? (PROBE IF NEEDED): How would you rank the problems in order of importance?

1. ——   2. ——

2. One problem in Germany these days concerns the question of what to do with refugees who try to obtain political asylum. What are, in your view, the main sources of tension between some German citizens and asylum seekers?

3. Would you support or oppose the direct involvement of citizens, for example through a referendum, in deciding between different policies concerning asylum seekers?

1. Support   2. Depends   3. Oppose

4. Would you give me the most important reason why you (SUPPORT/OPPOSE) it? (IF RESPONSE IS 'It DEPENDS'): What does it depend upon?

5. Would you please indicate your opinion on the plebiscitarian involvement of citizens by indicating whether you find each of these (SHOW CARD) procedures involving citizens directly meaningful or not meaningful?

Card 1-5
1. Meaningful   2. Not Meaningful

1. A legally non-binding referendum initiated by the parliament.
2. A legally non-binding referendum initiated by the executive.
3. A referendum initiated by a minority in parliament.
4. A referendum initiated by a majority in parliament.
5. A referendum initiated by the executive.
6. A referendum initiated by the people.

6. Are there any gaps in the commitment of East and West Germans to play the proper role of a democratic public? (PROBE, IF NEEDED): What is the proper role of a public in politics?

7. In order to get a picture of the distribution of opinion comparable with earlier studies, I am now using a standardized format to simplify matters a little bit. I am aware that these statements capture your views only incompletely. Nevertheless, would you tell me for each of the statements, whether you agree or disagree?

Card 1-7

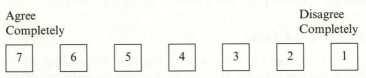

Agree
Completely

Disagree
Completely

| 7 | 6 | 5 | 4 | 3 | 2 | 1 |

A. Every democracy requires a political opposition.
B. It is the primary duty of the political opposition to support the government, and not to criticize it.
B. Every citizen has the right to demonstrate.
C. Freedom of opinion and discussion must be limited by moral and ethical considerations.
E. A citizen forfeits the right to demonstrate and to strike when s/he threatens the political order.
D. The freedom of political propaganda is not an absolute freedom, and the state should carefully regulate its use.

8. The term democracy is frequently used without further specifications these days. What seem to you personally the essentials of a democracy?

Section II: Pluralism

1. You mentioned earlier —— (MIP) as an important problem in Berlin. There are a number of conflicts of interests involved in solving this problem since different groups and people have different conceptions of how to solve the problem. Do these conflicts of interests have positive or negative effects on the governability of Berlin? (PROBE, IF NEEDED.) Why? (OR) Why not?

2. Would you please summarize your experience about the scope of conflicts of interests in East and West Berlin by selecting the statement which most accurately reflects your experience? Please separate your evaluation for East and West Berlin.

Card 2-2
   A. Consensus among social groups is the rule; serious conflicts rarely occur.
   B. Consensus is more typical, although there are some serious conflicts.
   C. Serious conflict of interest is far more typical, but there is some shared interest.
   D. Serious conflict is the rule; there is hardly any shared interest among social groups.

East Berlin   West Berlin

3. Considering your work as a politician and parliamentarian, do conflicts of interests among social groups or among people have a positive or negative influence on your work? (PROBE, IF NEEDED.) In what ways?

4. For comparability, here is again a list with statements concerning the relations among social groups. Please indicate how much you agree or disagree with the following statements. (SHOW CARD.)

Card 2-4

Agree   Disagree
Completely   Completely

| 7 | 6 | 5 | 4 | 3 | 2 | 1 |

   A. To compromise with political adversaries is dangerous because it frequently leads to the betrayal of ones own side.
   B. The general welfare and interests of the Federal Republic are seriously endangered by the continual clash of and demands posed by interest groups.
   C. Even if one is right in a controversy, one should look for a compromise.
   D. It will always be necessary to have a few strong, able individuals who know how to take charge.
   E. A country's general welfare should always override the special interests of groups and organizations.
   F. An intense discussion or controversy is often necessary in order to arrive at a workable policy compromise.

Section III: Minority Groups

1. I would like to ask you a few questions about social groups and movements which are viewed by some people as threatening to the political and social

order in the united Germany. Would you please select from this list (SHOW CARD) the group or organization that you like the least?

Card 3-1
- A. Environmentalists
- B. Fascists/extreme right-wing groups/neo-Nazis
- C. Lesbians
- D. Jews
- E. Feminists
- G. Sinti/Roma
- H. Peace Movement
- I. Anti-abortionists
- J. Communists/extreme Left-wing groups
- K. 'Expelled' [*Vertriebenenverbände*]
- L. Pro-choice
- M. Turks
- N. Homosexuals
- O. Other (please specify) ——

—— (1ST GROUP).

2. What is your second least-liked group?
—— (2ND GROUP)

3. I would like to know your personal opinion on the following statements regarding the activities of each group. Let us begin with —— (LEAST-LIKED GROUP). Independent of the existing legal framework, would you tell me, how strongly you agree or disagree with the following statements?

Card 3-3

Agree   Disagree
Completely   Completely

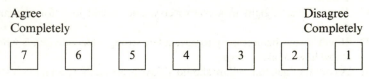

| 7 | 6 | 5 | 4 | 3 | 2 | 1 |

- A. —— (GROUP) should be allowed to hold demonstrations.
- B. Political parties primarily representing —— (GROUP) should be declared unconstitutional.
- C. —— (GROUP) should be allowed to teach in schools.
- D. —— (GROUP) should not be allowed to appear on television and state their views.

4. Now about —— (2ND LEAST-LIKED GROUP). How strongly do you agree or disagree with the following statements?

Card 3-4

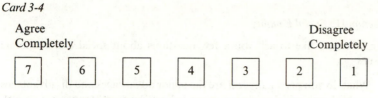

Agree
Completely

Disagree
Completely

| 7 | 6 | 5 | 4 | 3 | 2 | 1 |

A. —— (GROUP) should be allowed to hold demonstrations.
B. Political parties primarily representing —— (GROUP) should be declared unconstitutional.
C. —— (GROUP) should be allowed to teach in schools.
D. —— (GROUP) should not be allowed to appear on television and state their views.

5. Please evaluate the two groups you selected in terms of the following characteristics (SHOW CARD). Please select a 7 if you feel the characteristics mentioned on the left side is most accurate. A 1 means that you think the characteristics mentioned on the right side is most accurate. The numbers in between can be used to differentiate between these two polar ends. Again, I would like to begin with (LEAST-LIKED GROUP). How would you rate (1ST GROUP) in terms of the following adjective pairs?

Card 3-5

| 7 | 6 | 5 | 4 | 3 | 2 | 1 |

—— (GROUP)
A. is violent   is non-violent
B. is democratic   is undemocratic
C. partially employs illegal methods   only employs legal methods

6. Would you please rate —— (2ND LEAST-LIKED GROUP):

Card 3-6

| 7 | 6 | 5 | 4 | 3 | 2 | 1 |

—— (GROUP)
A. is violent   is non-violent
B. is democratic   is undemocratic
C. partially employs illegal methods   only employs legal methods

7. Could you give me the reasons behind your responses? I am particularly interested in why you (SUPPORT/OPPOSE) limiting the political activities of (GROUPS).

Section IV: Social Equality

I now would like to ask you a few questions about social and economic issues.

1. What do you personally feel are the major advantages and disadvantages of establishing a social market economy in East Germany? (PROBE, IF NEEDED). Some people argue that socialist economies, despite several limitations, offered certain advantages, such as social security, job security, or greater collegiality at the workplace. How would you evaluate this argument?

2. Here is a list with characteristics (SHOW CARD) which some people find desirable for economic systems. Would you please rank them in order of importance to you.

Card 4-2

	Rank
A. An ideal economic system should make efficient use of human and material resources.	——
B. An ideal economic system should minimize differences in living standards as much as possible.	——
C. In an ideal economic system, all spheres of economic activities are democratized.	——
D. An ideal economic system should be undisturbed from government regulations as much as possible.	——

3. On this card is a list with statements regarding the economic system. Would you please tell me how much you agree or disagree with each of the following statements? (SHOW CARD).

Card 4-3

Agree   Disagree
Completely   Completely

| 7 | 6 | 5 | 4 | 3 | 2 | 1 |

A. Social market economies generally lead to acceptable differences in income distribution.

B. The profit motive often brings out the worst in human nature.

C. Democracy is only possible if individuals not only participate in general elections, but can also participate in important management decisions at their workplace.

D. The poor are poor because they often don't make use of available opportunities which the economic system provides.

E. The national government should play a greater role in the management of the economy.

F. There are limits to growth beyond which our society cannot expand.

G. Unions should have more power in our society.

H. When private industry is allowed to make as much money as it can, everyone profits in the long run.

Section V: Personal Views

In this last section, I would like to ask a few questions about your work as a parliamentarian and about your personal circumstances.

1. Let me start with your work as a parliamentarian. How often do you meet with MPs from other parties to work out political agreements outside of regular sessions?

Card 5-1

1. Very often   2. Often   3. Occasionally   4. Rarely   5. Never

1. CDU
2. SPD
3. PDS
4. Bündnis '90/Greens (AL)/UFV
5. FDP
6. Gruppe Neues Forum/Bürgerbewegung

2. There has been some discussion about the different political cultures in East and West Germany. Considering your contacts with other MPs, how is the different experience with political systems reflected in the behaviour of MPs from East and West Berlin?

3. Here is another card with statements about political problems, but also about your personal situation. Would you tell me how much you agree or disagree with each statement?

Card 5-3

Agree Completely						Disagree Completely
7	6	5	4	3	2	1

A. It should be legal to have an abortion within the first three months of a pregnancy.

B. Everything is changing so fast these days so that it is difficult to find firm reference-points.

C. If we don't defend ourselves against chaos and troublemakers, our political order will be replaced by disorder and chaos.

D. In order to meet Germany's growing need for energy, one should also use nuclear energy.

E. Stronger measures should be taken to ensure the equality of men and women.

F. Discipline and obedience are essential in educating children into responsible citizenship.

G. In earlier days, people were better off because they knew what their duties were.

H. Every foreigner who would like to live in Germany should be welcome.

I. Everything is so uncertain these days that one has to be ready for anything

4. Here is a list with important political institutions in our society. Would you tell me how much trust you have in each of the institutions?

Card 5-4

Trust very much   No trust at all

| 7 | 6 | 5 | 4 | 3 | 2 | 1 |

A. Courts
B. Constitution
C. Federal parliament
D. Bureaucracy
E. Executive

5. There has been a discussion recently on how to treat former employees of the state security police (MfS). Would you please indicate for each statement listed on this card whether you support or oppose it?

Card 5-5

1. Support   2. Oppose

1. All former employees should be granted a general amnesty.
2. Only employees at middle and lower levels should be granted an amnesty.
3. Each case should be investigated individually.
4. None of the former MfS employees should receive an amnesty.
5. The leadership of the MfS should be penalized through an international tribunal.

6. In a number of studies, people have been asked to place themselves on a

left–right scale indicating their overall political position (SHOW CARD). For purposes of comparison, would you please tell me where you would place your views on this scale?

Card 5-6

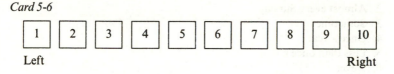

Left   Right

7. And in terms of the general political orientations of your political party in Berlin where would you locate it on this same left–right scale?

Card 5-7

Left   Right

8. There is a lot of talk these days about what the aims of this country should be for the next ten years. On this card (SHOW CARD) are listed some of the goals which different people would give top priority. Would you please say which of these you, yourself, would consider the most important, and which would be your second choice?

Card 5-8

                                                        Rank

A. Maintaining order in the nation.   ——
B. Giving people more say in important government decisions.   ——
C. Fighting rising prices.   ——
D. Protecting freedom of speech.   ——

9. On the whole, are you very satisfied, fairly satisfied, not very satisfied, or not at all satisfied with the way democracy works in Germany?
        1. Very   2. Fairly   3. Not Very   4. Not at all

10. If you compare your financial situation today with that one year ago, are you better off, about the same, or worse off?
        1. Better off   2. About the same   3. Worse off

11. In a few years, do you think that you will be better off, about the same, or worse off?
        1. Better off   2. About the same   3. Worse off

12. Which denomination do you belong to?

13. How often do you attend church? Would you say:

Card 5-13
　　1. At least every Sunday
　　2. Almost every Sunday
　　3. Sometimes
　　4. Once a year
　　5. Less than once a year
　　6. Never

14. Between 1949 and 1989, did you live anywhere other than in (WEST/EAST) Germany?
　　　　　　　1. No　　2. Yes (PROBE) Where and for how long?

15. Would you please tell me which category best reflects your monthly income?
　　1. Above DM 10,000
　　2. DM 8,000–9,999
　　3. DM 6,000–7,999
　　4. DM 4,000–5,999
　　5. Below DM 4,000

16. What is the highest degree your father and mother obtained?

Thank you for participating in the study.
(Information about MPs' socio-demographic background was obtained from the handbook of parliamentarians published by the Berlin parliament.)

Notes

1. Schabowski's account of the press conference suggests that it went as planned (1991: 304 ff.), which conflicts with accounts that his announcement was misinterpreted. However, he also notes that the leadership of the Politburo had no idea that eastern Germans would immediately rush to western Berlin. He attributes the confusion at the intra-German border during that night to a breakdown of communication between state authorities and border guards.

1. Perhaps the clearest expression of Almond and Verba's belief in the reciprocity of the values–institutions causality is contained in the following passage: 'The most productive research on political psychology in the future will treat childhood socialization, modal personality tendencies, political orientations, and political structure and process as separate variables in a complex, multidirectional system of causality' (Almond and Verba 1963: 35). Furthermore, the chapter on socialization clearly expresses their belief that institutions may influence cultural values.

2. In this review, I am excluding historical analyses of national political cultures. Although such studies provide rich information, they are included in this discussion only if they are directly concerned with the institutions–values nexus.

3. These studies suggest that although cultural traits are not easily remoulded by a new institutional environment, the creation of democratic institutions may lead to ideological convergence over time.

4. Other elite studies document the relatively weak influence of socio-demographics on elites' attitudes (Edinger and Searing 1967; Beyme 1971; Crewe 1974; Herzog 1975).

5. Additional systemic factors mentioned are the socio-economic composition

of elite sectors when modern political systems formed, or the outcome of political competitions between social groups.

6. Barnes (1994: 60) also agrees with this perspective when he suggests that institutions 'instill beliefs and reinforce them and hence are major influences on both childhood and life-long socialization'.

7. The degree to which various elite sectors were included in the transition process in southern Europe and Latin America influenced elites' readiness to endorse democratic institutions (O'Donnell and Schmitter 1986; Higley and Gunther 1992).

8. A systematic analysis of this question requires a multiple country approach where public support for existing institutions and other national level factors (GNP, type of system, etc.) are considered simultaneously (e.g. Inglehart 1997).

9. This figure is not to imply that liberal democracies and socialism represent the only conceivable ideological alternatives. Instead, given Germany's historical context, these are the two main ideological alternatives.

CHAPTER 3. INSTITUTIONAL LEARNING IN GERMANY

1. Unless noted otherwise, this historical overview is largely based upon Krisch 1974; Sandford 1983; Weber 1986; Dennis 1988; Schneider 1988; Glässner 1989; Rüschemeyer and Lemke 1989; Göckel 1990; Fulbrook 1991, 1995; Turner 1992; Kocka 1993; Merkl 1993; Jarausch 1994; Orlow 1995; Pulzer 1995; Kopstein 1997.

2. This acronym represents the first letters of the German version of the term Soviet-Military-Administration-Germany.

3. SED stands for *Sozialistische Einheitspartei Deutschlands*.

4. See, for example, the biographies of Rainer Eppelmann (1993) and Irene Kukutz and Katja Havemann (1990).

5. To this end, private property was catalogued on three lists. List A contained all economically important enterprises which were nationalized. List B contained unimportant private factories; these were left in the hands of private entrepreneurs for the time being; and List C contained property without owners at that time. Property on List C initially produced goods destined for exportation to the Soviet Union. In addition to these measures, large farms were divided into smaller units and distributed among small farmers or peasants who did not own land. Other economic resources also came under the control of the centralized administration. For example, the government confiscated bank accounts of over DM 3,000.

6. This discussion about the nature of opposition in eastern Germany greatly

relies on Mary Fulbrook's splendid *The Anatomy of a Dictatorship* (1995), especially chapters 4 through 8.

7. 'Stasi' is based on the German name Ministerium für Staatsicherheit (Ministry for State Security).

8. This change in objectives of the demonstrations from liberalization to unification is nicely captured by the change in the two slogans that dominated the theme of the demonstrations. Initially, the main thrust was directed against the SED by chanting 'Wir sind das Volk' (We are the people), which later changed to 'Wir sind ein Volk' (We are one people).

9. The growing tension between the Soviet Union and the West made it increasingly less desirable to turn western Germany into an agricultural state, as Morgenthau, for example, advocated.

CHAPTER 4. RESEARCH DESIGN

1. I focused on East Berlin MPs in the second wave due to time constraints.

2. The city parliament is called the Berliner Abgeordnetenhaus. For reasons of simplicity, I refer to it as the Berlin parliament.

3. In the case of the PDS, its leader invited me to present the project to the parliamentary group in order to secure MPs' participation. My presentation of the project led very quickly to an intriguing discussion about the value of 'bourgeois science' which, however, did not reduce the willingness of PDS-MPs to participate in the project—if anything, it stimulated MPs' curiosity.

4. I refer to the first survey as the 1992 study even though the interviews were conducted from October 1991 through June 1992. A similar logic applies to the 1995 survey.

5. For example, because western CDU-MPs are slightly under-represented, I also conducted all the analyses using a weighted data set. However, the results do not differ from the ones presented in the analyses. Furthermore, the intra-party group analyses presented throughout the book also document that the East–West split emerges *within* different parties.

6. In addition, the mere fact that the study's arguments and their implications travel across levels of analyses does not invalidate them as long as one does not commit an individual or ecological fallacy. As Barnes, Kaase, *et al.* observe (1979: 528): '[W]hile we are cautious not to commit the individualistic fallacy . . . we nevertheless maintain that the collective character of political action and its increasing facilitation through processes we have discussed before have a direct bearing on the quality of political life in advanced industrial societies.'

7. Indirect evidence for the presence of diffusion may also be adduced by cohort analyses at the mass and elite level. I discuss this in Chapter 5.
8. In the West, the greater exposure to institutional norms is a second reason;
   this process does not apply to the first wave of interviews with eastern
   MPs.

CHAPTER 5. DEMOCRATIC IDEALS

1. This theoretical discussion relies primarily on Sartori (1967); Pateman
   (1970); Dahl (1971; 1989); MacPherson (1977); Pennock (1979); Barber
   (1984); Held (1987; 1993); Cronin (1989).
2. The term 'plebiscitarian' expresses this confidence in citizens' ability to
   judge their own affairs: while *plebs* refers to the people, the Latin *scire*
   means to know.
3. One might argue that the GDR leadership unintentionally created a democratic citizenry by emphasizing egalitarianism or by giving democratic
   rights a prominent position in the earlier GDR constitutions. Against this
   interpretation speaks, however, that civil liberties were downplayed in
   subsequent versions and explicitly subordinated to the principle of party
   leadership; and that citizens experienced a system void of the guarantees
   written into the constitution. Available evidence, for example, suggests
   that GDR students believed that what was taught in schools about the
   GDR did not accurately represent their experience (Schubarth 1991).
   Finally, given the slow cultural changes in western Germany after the war,
   it seems unlikely that this overt written support for democratic rights had
   a significant effect on democratic citizenship-qualities.
4. If MPs, like mass publics, had not been offered the middle category, those
   who chose this category would have had to select the support or disagree
   side, which in all likelihood would have further increased the percentages
   of MPs supporting these rights.
5. Dalton (1994) also includes two pluralism indicators in his democratic-
   rights index, whereas I will examine mass and elite views on pluralism
   separately (Chapter 7). The exclusion of these indicators does not affect
   the conclusions reached; Dalton finds the same age-related differences I
   do.
6. Although one should not overly emphasize these cohort differences,
   they are useful in so far as they contradict the institutional learning axiom.
   They also tend to be consistent with the diffusion axiom if one assumes
   that value diffusion became increasingly prevalent after the Second World
   War.
7. Throughout the fieldwork I tried to obtain additional information about

eastern MPs' involvement in various GDR organizations. It turned out to be extraordinarily difficult to find this information in archives. In addition, the published biographies of eastern MPs frequently do not mention membership in GDR organizations. Although a more complete measure of the extent of regime involvement would undoubtedly be desirable, this information could not be found.

8. In another model I included several variables measuring respondents' perception of the economy. While some of these variables are significant, the conclusions reported here remain unaffected.

9. On the contrary, when I discussed the results from the first wave with the parliamentary president in 1995, her reaction was: 'They told you the truth.'

CHAPTER 6. POLITICAL TOLERANCE

1. I created a summary index based on the responses of eastern and western Germans concerning fascists, homosexuals, and dangerous books. This indicator correlates weakly with years of schooling in the East (r = .07) and the West (r = .07). Based on the 1988 Eurobarometer, the weak correlation between education and tolerance also emerges in Duch and Gibson's study of intolerance in Europe (1992).

2. Naturally MPs' responses must be interpreted cautiously. After all, western MPs in particular are frequently experienced politicians and likely to be image-conscious. At a minimum, however, such an analysis enables one to investigate what type of justifications MPs overtly associate with tolerant and intolerant responses. Further, the initial evidence presented below indicates that the different reasoning is associated with predicted differences of tolerance levels. This suggests that the open-ended question offers meaningful insights into MPs' democratic beliefs.

3. A tolerant MP primarily specifies reasons for being tolerant, while an intolerant MP focuses on explaining intolerance. Since eastern MPs are less tolerant than western MPs, the East–West differences of absolute frequencies partially reflect the different levels of tolerance.

4. The results are similar when these relationships are analysed separately for East and West MPs. One exception concerns the relationship between a principal toleration of the first group and the tolerance score towards the second group which is weak in the East (r = .13) and considerably stronger in the West (r = .35).

5. The results are virtually identical when those few MPs who do not select fascists as their first least-liked group are excluded. Likewise, these relationships do not depend on the choice of the second group.

CHAPTER 7. PLURALISM

1. Democratic variants of conflicts are constructive and peaceful clashes of interests, while socialist and right-wing interpretations of conflicts typically involve revolutionary, frequently violent, changes.

2. Because I rely largely on published sources about mass data for these indicators, I cannot reverse the polarity of responses. I therefore present the percentage agreeing with one indicator while the disagreement to the other indicator is presented.

3. One might also suggest that agreement with the two pluralism indicators represents an Olsonion critique of interest groups. However, as the responses to an open-ended question will make plain below, this interpretation is implausible in light of MPs' responses.

4. I created an additive index based on the two indicators using the April 1990 German identity survey. In the East, the correlation between education and the index is r = .13; in the West the relationship is r = .12. This relationship also appears in a multivariate analysis where this pluralism index is regressed on education and several predictors of citizens' economic perceptions. Thus, the relationship between education and pluralism is not simply a function of one's economic well-being. These findings corroborate the argument that cognitive processes associated with education contribute to the observation that the better educated, especially elites, are more likely than the less educated, especially mass publics, to hold pluralist views.

5. Further, a majority of eastern (65.8 per cent) and western MPs (69.7 per cent) agree that a compromise is necessary even if one is 'right' in a controversy. Still, post-war MPs from the East are less willing to search for a compromise than eastern pre-war MPs if they believe they hold the 'right' view, while such cohort-based differences do not emerge in the West.

6. The same increase emerges when I examine the 1992 figure for only those sixty-five MPs I re-interviewed in 1995.

7. Surprisingly, however, the proportion of younger western MPs who mention a statist aversion to conflicts is larger among the post-war than the pre-war cohort, and there is no ready explanation for this unexpected finding. I have examined various possibilities. For example, I examined the proportion of CDU-MPS among the post-war cohort of western MPs on the grounds that CDU-MPs are more likely than others to express a statist aversion as part of their 'strong-state' ideology. I suspected that they might be concentrated among post-war western MPs because CDU-MPs are more likely than other MPs to hold a statist aversion to conflicts. However, this is not an evident source for this result. Overall, this result is clearly inconsistent with the generation-based hypothesis.

8. This procedure entails that both indicators weigh equally in the additive index.

9. For example, religiosity typically correlates with a conservative political outlook, such as limited interference of citizens in the governmental process. The income variable is included because MPs with lower economic resources may view the pluralist process as unfairly biased toward those who are endowed with economic resources. Since eastern MPs, on average, are less well off and less religious than western MPs, these differences must be controlled for. I included MPs' education because, as I discussed in previous chapters, school systems transmit the values of a political system. Finally, I included the gender variable in order to control for the possibility that the different opportunities for women in the East and the West lead to the observed East–West divergence.

10. These conclusions about the influence of institutional learning on pluralist views are confirmed when this analysis is repeated within the pre- and post-war cohort. Within the pre-war cohort the East–West coefficient is insignificant ($b = .31$; beta $= .11$). Eastern and western MPs' views on pluralism among pre-war MPs do not differ systematically across the East–West boundary. In contrast, the East–West coefficient is highly significant within the group of post-war MPs ($b = .73$; beta $= .32$). The increase in East–West differences as one moves from the pre- to the post-war cohort matches the cohort-based predictions of the institutional learning argument: those MPs who experienced the most different political circumstances are also the ones who evidence the largest value differences. Furthermore, the egalitarian democracy coefficient exerts the strongest influence among post-war MPs ($b = -.19$; beta $= -.27$). In sum, these results corroborate the argument that western Germany's parliamentary institutions created a pluralist outlook among western MPs, while the socialist institutions reinforced anti-pluralist orientations.

CHAPTER 8. ECONOMIC VALUES

1. Roller (1994) also finds that East–West differences tend to be larger for indicators that measure ceilings to economic activities as opposed to social floors. However, her study is also hampered by the fact that the indicators she has at her disposal are less than ideal.

2. I conducted all the analyses with and without this indicator. They confirm that the East–West coefficient increases in magnitude if the PDS-indicator is excluded. Likewise, the egalitarian-democracy and the post-war indicators increase in magnitude and statistical significance.

3. One advantage of using the open-ended question is that I may attribute the cause for the anticipated economic performance unequivocally to market or socialist systems. In contrast, a closed-ended prospective indicator of the expected economic performance may not allow one to judge whether negative economic expectations result from a belief that the socialist system prevents the market system from blossoming, or whether individuals believe that a market economy is undesirable (see Duch 1993 for a discussion of the problems associated with the closed-ended question).

4. I included postmaterial values as a predictor of economic values because the New Left advocates both political and social equality (Inglehart 1990). Postmaterialists may therefore be more likely than materialists to endorse egalitarian goals. Furthermore, levels of postmaterialism are lower in the East than in the West. I included a measure of MPs' religiosity because religious values tend to be related to centre-conservative political orientations. Since eastern Germans are considerably less religious than western Germans (Dalton 1992), one must control for this East–West difference. MPs' gender is included in order to examine the possibility that eastern MPs are more supportive of welfare values than western MPs because the unification eradicated numerous services for women which the GDR supposedly provided (Rueschemeyer and Lemke 1989). On the whole, controlling for these factors allows one to examine the extent to which MPs' institutional learning affects their economic values independent of their social values and perceptions of the economy.

5. Recall that the open-ended question on the economy constitutes the basis for both the prospective indicator and the net advantage scores of market systems. Detailed analyses of recorded interviews and the data suggest that western MPs who are favourably disposed to market principles *either* mention the economic advantages of market systems (categories 17 and 18 in Appendix A, Table A1) *or* they tend to focus on other systemic advantages (categories 11 through 16). Those who mention the economic performance aspect did not mention other systemic aspects (e.g. about individual freedom) and vice versa. Since both indicators are based upon the same question, this unwittingly produced a negative relationship between MPs' future economic expectations and the systemic advantage scores ($r = -.32$) among western MPs. In contrast, the relationship is (moderately) positive among eastern MPs ($r = .17$), probably because they were very concerned with giving a complete response. If we employ the disadvantage score (Table 8.3) instead of the net-advantage score in the multivariate analyses, then the prospective economic indicator among western MPs is statistically insignificant.

6. If I repeat this analysis for the advantage and disadvantage scores separately, the East–West coefficient continues to be a highly significant and

strong predictor for both indicators. However, changes in the magnitude of the prospective economic indicator suggest that while the advantages are recognized independent of economic expectations among eastern MPs (beta = .08; b = .13), MPs' perception of the disadvantages of market forces are substantially influenced by economic expectations (beta = .43; b = .93).

7. A panel analysis of the 1992–5 elite data also confirms the strong effect of prior learning on economic values. MPs' initial economic values in 1992 are the strongest determinant of MPs' 1995 economic values, independent of their evaluations of current economic performance.

8. I repeated the analyses for CDU-MPs and SPD-MPs separately in order to keep MPs' partisan affiliations constant. The results indicate that East–West differences generally persist within party groups. Furthermore, when the analysis is limited to the CDU, FDP, and SPD only, the results are similar to the one presented for the entire data set.

CHAPTER 9. THE SOURCES OF INSTITUTIONAL SUPPORT

1. An additional reason why institutionalists and culturalists ignore their common objectives is that citizens' institutional support and ideological values are merged conceptually in *The Civic Culture* (Pateman 1972; see also Shin, Chey, and Kim 1989). Almond and Verba initially distinguish between institutional support and value predispositions when they speak, for instance, of the self-as-an-object (e.g. citizens' views on their participatory roles) and the political system as an object. However, a civic culture is defined as a mix of orientations towards value predispositions and institutional support (Almond and Verba 1963: 31). This conceptualization of a civic culture makes it difficult to disentangle the relationship between institutional support and ideological values, because both dimensions constitute core elements of a civic culture.

2. The propensity of eastern Germans to distrust political institutions also emerges at other time-points. When asked in the 1990 World Values survey 'How much confidence do you have in the following institutions: A great deal, quite a lot, not very much at all, or none at all?', 50.2 per cent of western and 40.8 per cent of eastern citizens trust parliament a great deal or quite a lot, for example. Likewise, trust in the civil service reaches 38.2 per cent in the West and 18.2 per cent in the East. These figures are higher than in the 1994 Allbus survey, partly because the response format in the 1994 survey contains seven points whereas the 1990 survey offers only four categories. Still, the overarching conclusion remains unchanged: trust in

institutions is in short supply in eastern Germany and it is not over-whelming in the West either. To put these findings in a European-wide perspective, one must recognize that levels of trust in western Germany are by no means an anomaly compared to other western European countries. Support for government institutions in Western Germany hovers roughly at the European-wide average (Listhaug and Wiberg 1995). Eastern Germans, in contrast, trust parliament about as much as Italians do (30.6 per cent of Italians trust the Italian parliament in 1990).

3. This result raises a difficult question similar to the ones discussed in Chapter 6: what are we to make of the fact that MPs who are most willing to limit the rights of ideological extremists are also the strongest supporters of democratic institutions? I already discussed in Chapter 6 how political tolerance is shaped by Germany's post-war context. Again, I stress that the results point to the unique circumstances in Germany's post-war history with respect to the treatment of ideological extremists.

4. In the autumn of 1990 eastern and western Germans were asked about the performance of eastern and western institutions separately.

5. The 1991 and 1992 Allbus surveys contain a question measuring citizens' satisfaction with democracy. Unfortunately for my purpose, these surveys have three shortcomings. First, the response categories differ across the two surveys. Secondly, and more important, the institutional trust questions in these two surveys contains fewer institutional objects for publics to evaluate. Thirdly, these surveys contain fewer indicators for publics' economic ideals.

6. This indicator generates the same pattern as the analyses of the Eurobarometer surveys. Satisfaction with the performance of the political system is greater in the West than in the East. As in the Eurobarometer series, however, the economic difficulties of Germany's unification reduces the level of positive performance evaluations among the western public. In 1991 84.5 per cent respond that the system functions well and only needs some changes (the first and second response options). This percentage declines to 68 per cent in 1992 and 63.4 per cent in 1994. However, the percentages for eastern Germans are 64.2 per cent in 1991, 49.2 per cent in 1992, and 41 per cent in 1994. Thus, a majority of western Germans continue to hold positive views about institutions, whereas eastern Germans' evaluations dropped below the 50 per cent threshold. The time series is too short to determine whether performance evaluations become more positive during 1994 as they did in the Eurobarometer series. But the levelling decline between 1992 and 1994 may indicate the beginning of a reversal toward more positive evaluations.

7. I included MPs' age in order to gauge the socialization efforts of the western system. Western MPs born in the post-war years experienced only a democracy and may therefore be more supportive of these institutions

than older MPs. Citizens' education is included in the model because better educated citizens are disproportionately exposed to the democratic messages of western Germany's institutions (Baker, Dalton, and Hildebrandt 1981). Since most MPs are well educated, I anticipate this variable to be more important at the mass than the elite level. Postmaterial values, in turn, may shape institutional trust—or distrust— because they are more critical of purely representational institutions than materialists (Inglehart 1990). Because western German society underwent a broad transformation in the post-war decades, the force of postmaterialism should be especially palpable in the West. In contrast, gender may be especially important in the East, because women may blame the new institutions for the eradication of social services that presumably existed in eastern Germany. Finally, I included several variables gauging citizens' economic evaluations in order to examine the degree to which institutional support depends on citizens' perceptions of the economic context. These variables include citizens' personal income and their evaluations of their future personal finances. Another measure gauges citizens' assessment of the present economic situation and their expectations about how well the economy will do in the near future.

8. I also conducted these analyses for the procedural values—democratic rights, tolerance, and pluralism. Most of them turn out to be statistically insignificant. This result further corroborates the argument that the relationship between these values and institutional trust is less relevant for institutional trust than citizens' societal ideals.

9. If a dummy variable is included for the Bündnis '90/Greens in the East, this variable is statistically insignificant. Evidently, MPs of this party and PDS-MPs equally distrust western institutions, independent of other characteristics.

10. For example, when satisfaction with democratic development is regressed on several predictors, including beliefs about market reforms, views about reforms are often stronger than perceptions of economic conditions; a pattern that corroborates Evans and Whitefield's (1995) conclusions.

CHAPTER 10. CONCLUSION

1. The interview with Jens Reich, a prominent member of the opposition movement in the GDR, was published in *Der Spiegel* 1995 (3 April), 42–9, a few months after Reich lost the presidential election to Roman Herzog. His preference for a limited suspension of parliamentary sovereignty becomes transparent at various places, including the following passage

(p. 46), where he explains how he wants to 'kick the legislature in the butt' in order to motivate it to pass environmentally friendly legislation:

Reich: In addition to the federal parliament, we need an ecological committee of the highest level (*mit Verfassungsrang*) which must be consulted concerning questions of our survival. This committee should be able to introduce legislation in the federal parliament and advise the federal government (*der Regierung Beschlussinitiativen vorlegen dürfen*); it also should have a veto right and should be able to initiate or prevent things.

Spiegel: First you demanded the right for free elections in the GDR and now you don't want voters to decide any longer?

Reich: Of course, such institutions as the House of Lords, which aren't up for elections, represent a danger from the perspective of a radical democrat. This country must function in a democratic and civilized way. That's why I support the idea that this club, which is going to change how we live, has to be elected, but not every four years.

Spiegel: How long should the time between elections be?

Reich: The committee ought to be able to work without any disturbance for at least ten, possibly fifteen years . . .

2. For a comprehensive study of East-Central European party systems, see Kitschelt *et al.* (forthcoming).

References

Aberbach, Joel D., Putnam, Robert D., and Rockman, Burt A. 1981. *Bureaucrats and Politicians in Western Democracies*. Cambridge, Mass.: Harvard University Press.

Almond, Gabriel A. 1956. 'Comparing Political Systems.' *Journal of Politics* 18: 391–409.

—— 1983. 'Communism and Political Culture Theory.' *Comparative Politics* 15: 127–38.

—— 1990. *A Discipline Divided. Schools and Sects in Political Science*. Newbury Park: Sage.

—— and Verba, Sidney. 1963. *The Civic Culture*. Princeton: Princeton University Press.

—— —— (eds.). 1980. *The Civic Culture Revisited*. Boston: Little, Brown, and Co.

Anderson, Christopher J., and Guillory, Christine A. 1997. 'Political Institutions and Satisfaction with Democracy: A Cross-National Analysis of Consensus and Majoritarian Systems.' *American Political Science Review* 91: 66–81.

Arzheimer, Kai and Klein, Markus. 1997. 'Die friedliche und stille Revolution,' pp. 37–59 in Oscar W. Gabriel (ed.), *Politische Einstellungen und politisches Verhalten im Transformationsprozess*. Opladen: Leske + Budrich.

Bahry, Donna, Boaz, Cynthia, and Gordon, Stacy Burnett. 1997. 'Tolerance, Transition, and Support for Civil Liberties in Russia.' *Comparative Political Studies* 30: 484–510.

Baker, Kendall, Dalton, Russell J., and Hildebrandt, Kai. 1981. *Germany Transformed*. Cambridge, Mass.: Harvard University Press.

Barber, Benjamin. 1984. *Strong Democracy*. Berkeley: University of California Press.

Barnes, Samuel H. 1994. 'Politics and Culture,' pp. 45–64 in Frederick Weil (ed.). *Research on Democracy and Society*, vol. 2. Greenwich, Conn.: JAI Press.

—— McDonough, Peter, and Lopez-Pina, Antonio. 1985. 'The Development of Partisanship in New Democracies.' *American Journal of Political Science* 29: 695–720.

—— Kaase, Max, *et al.* 1979. *Political Action*. Beverly Hills: Sage.

Barry, Brian. 1970. *Sociologists, Economists, and Democracy*. London: MacMillan Company.

Bauer, Petra. 1991. 'Politische Orientierungen im Übergang. Eine Analyse politischer Einstellungen der Bürger in West- und Ostdeutschland.' *Kölner Zeitschrift für Soziologie und Sozialpsychologie* 43: 433–53.

Bauer-Kaase, Petra and Kaase, Max. 1996. 'Five Years of Unification: The Germans on the Path to Inner Unity.' *German Politics* 5/1: 1–25.

Beyme, Klaus von. 1971. *Politische Eliten*. München: Piper.

Bollen, Kenneth A. and Jackman, Robert W. 1989. 'Democracy, Stability, and Dichotomies.' *American Sociological Review* 54: 612–21.

Boynton, G. R. and Loewenberg, Gerhard. 1973. 'The Development of Public Support for Parliament in Germany.' *British Journal of Political Science* 3: 169–89.

—— —— 1974. 'The Decay of Support for Monarchy and the Hitler Regime in the Federal Republic of Germany.' *British Journal of Political Science* 4: 453–488.

Bracher, Karl-Dietrich. 1970. *The German Dictatorship*. New York: Praeger.

Bürklin, Wilhelm. 1996. 'Kontinuität und Wandel der deutschen Führungsschicht. Ergebnisse der Potsdamer Elitestudie 1995.' Potsdam: University of Potsdam.

Childs, David, Baylis, Thomas A., and Rueschemeyer, Marilyn. 1989. *East Germany in Comparative Perspective*. New York: Routledge.

Chong, Dennis, McClosky, Herbert, and Zaller, John. 1983. 'Patterns of Support for Democratic and Capitalist Values in the United States.' *British Journal of Political Science* 13: 401–40.

Conradt, David P. 1974. 'West Germany: A Remade Political Culture?' *Comparative Political Studies* 2: 222–38.

—— 1980. 'Changing German Political Culture,' pp. 212–72 in Gabriel A. Almond and Sidney Verba (eds.). *The Civic Culture Revisited*. Boston: Little, Brown, and Co.

Crawford, Beverly and Lijphart, Arend. 1995. 'Explaining Political and Economic Change in Post-Communist Eastern Europe.' *Comparative Political Studies* 28: 171–99.

Crewe, Ivor. 1974. 'Introduction: Studying Elites in Britain,' pp. 9–51 in Ivor Crewe (ed.). *Elites in Western Democracy*. New York: Wiley.

Cronin, Thomas E. 1989. *Direct Democracy. The Politics of Initiative, Referendum, and Recall*. Cambridge, Mass.: Harvard University Press.

Dahl, Robert. 1966. *Political Opposition in Western Democracies*. New Haven: Yale University Press.

—— 1971. *Polyarchy*. New Haven: Yale University Press.

—— 1989. *Democracy and its Critics*. New Haven: Yale University Press.

Dahrendorf, Ralf. 1967. *Society and Democracy in Germany.*' Garden City, NY: Doubleday and Co.

Dalton, Russell J. 1987. 'Generational Change in Elite Political Beliefs: The Growth of Ideological Polarization.' *Journal of Politics* 49: 976–97.

—— 1992. *Politics in Germany*. 2nd edn. New York: HarperCollins.

—— 1994. 'Communists and Democrats: Attitudes Towards Democracy in the Two Germanies.' *British Journal of Political Science* 24: 469–93.

—— (ed.). 1996. *Germans Divided. The 1994 Bundestag Elections and the Evolution of the German Party System*. Washington, DC: Berg.

Dennis, Mike. 1988. *German Democratic Republic*. New York: Pinter Publisher.

Di Palma, Guiseppe. 1990. *To Craft Democracies*. Berkeley: University of California Press.

Dohlus, Ernst. 1991. 'Augen und Ohren nach Westen gerichtet? Zuschauer- und Höhrerverhalten in den neuen Bundesländern.' *Publikum* 23: 80–95.

Downs, Anthony. 1957. *An Economic Theory of Democracy*. New York: Harper & Row.

Duch, Raymond. 1993. 'Tolerating Economic Reform: Popular Support for Transition to a Free Market in the Former Soviet Union.' *American Political Science Review* 87: 590–608.

—— 1995. 'Economic Chaos and the Fragility of Democratic Transition in Former Communist Regimes.' *Journal of Politics* 57/1: 121–58.

—— and Gibson, James L. 1992. 'Putting up with Fascists in Western Europe: A Comparative, Cross-level Analysis of Political Tolerance.' *Western Political Quarterly* 45: 237–74.

Dyson, Kenneth. 1980. *The State Tradition in Western Europe*. Oxford: Martin Robertson.

Easton, David. 1965. *A Systems Analysis of Political Life*. New York: John Wiley.

Eckstein, Harry. 1966. *Division and Cohesion in Democacy*. Princeton: Princeton University Press.

—— 1988. 'A Culturalist Theory of Political Change.' *American Political Science Review* 82: 789–804.

—— 1996. 'Lessons for the "Third Wave" from the First: An Essay on Democratization.' University of California, Irvine: Center for the Study of Democracy.

Edinger, Lewis. 1960. 'Post-Totalitarian Leadership: Elites in the German Federal Republic.' *American Political Science Review* 54: 58–82.

—— and Searing, Donald. 1967. 'Social Background in Elite Analysis.' *American Political Science Review* 61: 428–45.

Ellwein, Thomas. 1983. *Das Regierungssystem der Bundesrepublik Deutschland*, 5th edn. Opladen: Westdeutscher Verlag.

Elkins, David J. and Simeon, Richard E. B. 1979. 'A Cause in Search of Its Effect, or What does Political Culture Explain?' *Comparative Politics* 11: 127–46.

Eppelmann, Rainer. 1993. *Fremd im Eigenen Haus*. Köln: Kiepenheuer and Witsch.

Evans, Geoffrey and Whitefield, Stephen. 1995. 'The Politics and Economics of Democratic Commitment: Support for Democracy in Transition Societies.' *British Journal of Political Science* 24: 485–514.

Falter, Jürgen and Klein, Markus. 1994. 'Die Wähler bei der Bundestagswahl 1994.' *Aus Politik und Zeitgeschichte* B51–52/94: 22–34.

Finifter, Ada. 1996. 'Attitudes Toward Individual Responsibility and Political Reform in the Former Soviet Union.' *American Political Science Review* 40: 138–52.

—— and Mickiewicz, Ellen. 1992. 'Redefining the Political System of the USSR.' *American Political Science Review* 86: 857–74.

Fishbein, Sterling and Martin, Lothar. 1987. *Education and Society in the Two Germanys*. New York: Praeger.

Fiske, Susan T. and Taylor, Shelley E. 1991. *Social Cognition*. 2nd edn. New York: McGraw-Hill.

Flora, Peter and Heidenheimer, Arnold J. 1981. *The Development of Welfare States in Europe and America*. New Brunswick: Transaction Book.

Friedrich, Walter. 1990. 'Mentalitätswandlungen der Jugend in der DDR.' *Aus Politik und Zeitgeschichte* 16/17: 25–37.

Fuchs, Anweiler and Dornemann, Peter (eds.). 1992. *Bildungspolitik in Deutschland, 1945–1990. Ein historisch-vergleichender Quellenband*. Opladen: Leske + Budrich.

Fuchs, Dieter. 1997. 'Welche Demokratie wollen die Deutschen? Einstellungen zur Demokratie im vereinigten Deutschland,' pp. 91–113 in Oscar W. Gabriel (ed.). *Politische Einstellungen und politisches Verhalten im Transformationsprozess*. Opladen: Leske + Budrich.

—— and Roller, Edeltraud. 1994. 'Cultural Requisites of the Transition Process to Liberal Democracies in Central and Eastern Europe.' Discussion Paper FS III 94-202. Wissenschaftszentrum Berlin (WZB).

—— and Rohrschneider, Robert. 1998. 'Postmaterialism and Electoral Choice before and after German Unification.' *West European Politics* 21: 95–116.

—— Klingemann, Hans-Dieter, and Schöbel, Carolin. 1991. 'Perspektiven der politischen Kultur im vereinigten Deutschland.' *Aus Politik und Zeitgeschichte* B32/91: 35–46.

—— Roller, Edeltraud, and Weßels, Bernhard. 1997. 'Die Akzeptanz der Demokratie des vereinigten Deutschland.' *Aus Politik und Zeitgeschichte* B51/97: 3–12.

Fukuyama, Francis. 1989. 'The End of Liberty.' *The National Interest* 16: 3–18.

Fulbrook, Mary. 1991. *The Divided Nation: Germany 1918–1990*. London: Fontana.

—— 1995. *Anatomy of a Dictatorship. Inside the GDR 1949–1989*. New York: Oxford University Press.

Gabriel, Oskar. 1987. 'Demokratiezufriedenheit und demokratische Einstellungen in der Bundesrepublik Deutschland.' *Aus Politik und Zeitgeschichte* Band 22/87 (30 May): 32–45.

Geissler, Gert and Wiegmann, Ulrich. 1996. *Pädagogik und Herrschaft in der DDR.* Frankfurt a. M.: Peter Lang.

Geddes, Barbara. 1995. 'A Comparative Perspective on the Leninist Legacy in Eastern Europe.' *Comparative Political Studies* 28: 239–274.

Gibson, James L. 1988. 'Political Intolerance and Political Repression during the McCarthy Red Scare.' *American Political Science Review* 82: 511–29.

—— 1992. 'Alternative Measures of Political Tolerance: Must Tolerance be Least-Liked?' *American Journal of Political Science* 36: 560–77.

—— 1993. 'Political and Economic Markets: Connecting Attitudes Towards Political Democracy and a Market Economy within the Mass Culture of the USSR.' Paper prepared for delivery at the 1993 annual meeting of the APSA, 2–5 Sept. 1993.

—— 1998. 'A Sober Second Thought. An Experiment in Persuading Russians to Tolerate.' *American Journal of Political Science* 42: 819–50.

—— and Duch, Raymond M. 1993. 'Political Intolerance in the USSR: The Distribution and Etiology of Mass Opinion.' *Comparative Political Studies* 26: 286–329.

—— —— and Tedin, Kent L. 1992. 'Democratic Values and the Transformation of the Soviet Union.' *Journal of Politics* 54: 329–71.

Glässner, Gert-Joachim. 1989. *Die Andere Deutsche Republik.* Opladen: Westdeutscher Verlag.

Göckel, Robert. 1990. *The Lutheran Church and the East German State: Political Conflict and Change under Ulbricht and Honecker.* Ithaca, NY: Cornell University Press.

Greiffenhagen, Martin and Greiffenhagen, Silvia. 1993. *Ein schwieriges Vaterland.* München: List Verlag.

Heath, Anthony, Evans, Geoffrey, and Martin, Jean. 1994. 'The Measurement of Core Beliefs and Values: The Development of Balanced Socialist/ Laissez Faire and Libertarian/Authoritarian Scales.' *British Journal of Political Science* 24: 115–32.

Held, David. 1987. *Models of Democracy.* Stanford: Stanford University Press.

—— (ed.). 1993. *Prospects For Democracy: North, South, East, West.* Stanford: Stanford University Press.

Hesse, Kurt R. 1990. 'Fernsehen und Revolution: Zum Einfluß der Westmedien auf die politische Wende in der DDR.' *Rundfunk und Fernsehen* 38: 328–42.

Herzog, Dietrich. 1975. *Politische Karrieren.* Opladen: Westdeutscher Verlag.

—— Rebenstorf, Hilke, Werner, Camilla, and Wessels, Bernhard. 1990. *Abgeordnete und Bürger.* Opladen: Westdeutscher Verlag.

Higley, John and Burton, Michael G. 1989. 'The Elite Variable in Democratic Transitions and Breakdowns.' *American Sociological Review* 54: 17–32.

—— and Gunther, Richard (eds.). 1992. *Elites and Democratic Consolidation in Latin America and Southern Europe.* New York: Cambridge University Press.

Hoffmann-Lange, Ursula. 1985. 'Structural Prerequisites of Elite Integration in the Federal Republic of Germany,' pp. 45–96 in Gwen Moore (ed.). *Studies of the Structure of National Elite Groups.* Vol. 1 in Research in Politics and Society Series. Greenwich, Conn.: JAI Press.

—— 1992. *Eliten, Macht, und Konflikt in der Bundesrepublik.* Leske + Budrich.

Huntington, Samuel P. 1984. 'Will More Countries Become Democratic?' *Political Science Quarterly* 99/2: 193–218.

—— 1991. 'How Countries Democratize.' *Political Science Quarterly* 106/4: 579–616.

Inglehart, Ronald. 1977. *The Silent Revolution.* Princeton: Princeton University Press.

—— 1988. 'The Renaissance of Political Culture.' *American Political Science Review* 82: 1,203–30.

—— 1990. *Culture Shift.* Princeton: Princeton University Press.

—— 1997. *Modernization and Postmodernization.* Princeton: Princeton University Press.

—— and Abramson, Paul. 1994. 'Economic Security and Value Change.' *American Political Science Review* 88: 336–54.

Jarausch, Konrad. 1994. *The Rush to German Unity.* New York: Oxford University Press.

Jervis, Robert. 1976. *Perception and Misperception in International Politics.* Princeton: Princeton University Press.

Kaase, Max. 1971. 'Demokratische Einstellungen in der Bundesrepublik Deutschland.' In Rudolf Wildenmann (ed.). *Sozialwissenschaftliches Jahrbuch für Politik*, vol. 2. München: Günter Olzog Verlag.

—— 1983. 'Sinn oder Unsinn des Konzepts "Politische Kultur" für die vergleichende Politikforschung oder auch: Der Versuch, einen Pudding an die Wand zu nageln,' pp. 144–71 in Max Kaase and Hans-Dieter Klingemann (eds.). *Wahlen und Politisches System-Analysen aus Anlass der Bundestagswahl 1980.* Opladen: Westdeutscher Verlag.

—— 1990. 'Mass Participation,' pp. 23–64 in M. Kent Jennings and Jan W. van Deth (eds.). *Continuities in Political Action.* New York: Walter de Gruyter.

—— 1994. 'Political Culture and Political Consolidation in Central and Eastern Europe,' pp. 233–74 in Frederick Weil (ed.). *Research on Democracy and Society*, vol. 2. Greenwich, Conn.: JAI Press.

—— and Klingemann, Hans-Dieter. 1994. 'Der mühsame Weg zur Entwicklung von Parteiorientierungen in einer "neuen" Demokratie: Das Beispiel der früheren DDR,' pp. 365–96 in Hans-Dieter Klingemann and Max Kaase (eds.). *Wahlen und Wähler. Analysen aus Anlaß der Bundestagswahl 1990*. Opladen: Westdeutscher Verlag.

—— and Newton, Kenneth. 1995. *Beliefs in Government*. Oxford: Oxford University Press.

Kitschelt, Herbert. 1986. 'Political Opportunity Structures and Political Protest.' *British Journal of Political Science* 16: 57–85.

—— Mansfeldova, Zdenka, Markowski, Rodek, and Toka, Gabor. forthcoming. *Post-Communist Party Systems. Competition, Representation, and Inter-Party Cooperation*. New York: Cambridge University Press.

Klingemann, Hans-Dieter and Kaase, Max. 1994. *Wahlen und Wähler*. Opladen: Westdeutscher Verlag.

—— and Fuchs, Dieter (eds.). 1995. *Citizens and the State*. New York: Oxford University Press.

—— and Hofferbert, Richard I. 1998. 'Remembering the Bad Old Days: Human Rights, Economic Conditions, and Democratic Performance in Transitional Regimes.' Discussion Paper FS III 98–203: Wissenschaftszentrum Berlin für Sozialforschung (WZB).

Kocka, Jürgen (ed.). 1994. *Die DDR als Geschichte*. Berlin: Akademie Verlag.

Kommers, Donald P. 1995. 'The Basic Law and Reunification,' pp. 187–205 in Peter H. Merkl (ed.). *The Federal Republic of Germany at Forty-Five*. New York: New York University Press.

Kopstein, Jeffrey. 1997. *The Politics of Economic Decline in East Germany, 1945–1989*. Chapel Hill: University of North Carolina Press.

Krisch, Henry. 1974. *German Politics Under Soviet Occupation*. New York: Columbia University Press.

—— 1985. *The German Democratic Republic*. Boulder, Col.: Westview.

Küchler, Manfred. 1992. 'The Road to German Unity: Mass Sentiment in East and West Germany.' *Public Opinion Quarterly* 56: 53–76.

Kukutz, Irena and Havemann, Katja. 1990. *Geschützte Quelle*. Berlin: Basis Druck.

Lewis-Beck, Michael. 1986. 'Comparative Economic Voting: Britain, France, Germany, Italy.' *American Journal of Political Science* 30: 315–46.

Linz, Juan and Stepan, Alfred. 1978. *The Breakdown of Democratic Regimes*. Baltimore: Johns Hopkins University Press.

Lijphart, Arend. 1980. 'The Structure of Inference,' pp. 37–56 in Gabriel A. Almond and Sidney Verba (eds.). *The Civic Culture Revisited*. Boston: Little, Brown, and Co.

Lipset, Seymour M. 1959. *Political Man*. Baltimore: Johns Hopkins University Press.

Listhaug, Ole and Wiberg, Matti. 1995. 'Confidence in Political and Private Institutions,' pp. 298–322 in Hans-Dieter Klingemann and Dieter Fuchs (eds.). *Citizens and the State*. New York: Oxford University Press.

Ludz, Peter C. 1972. *The Changing Party Elite in East Germany*. Cambridge, Mass.: MIT Press.

McCauley, Martin. 1983. *The German Democratic Republic Since 1945*. New York: St Martin's Press.

McClosky, Herbert. 1964. 'Consensus and Ideology in American Politics.' *American Political Science Review* 58: 361–82.

——and Zaller, John. 1984. *The American Ethos. Public Attitudes Toward Capitalism and Democracy*. Cambridge, Mass.: Harvard University Press.

McDonough, Peter. 1995. 'Identities, Ideologies, and Interests: Democratization and Cultures of Mass Politics in Spain and Western Europe.' *Journal of Politics* 57: 649–76.

——Barnes, Samel H., and Lopez-Pina, Antonio. 1986. 'The Growth of Democratic Legitimacy in Spain.' *American Political Science Review* 80: 735–60.

McGregor, James P. 1991. 'Value Structures in a Developed Socialist System: The Case of Czechoslovakia.' *Comparative Politics* 23: 181–99.

MacKuen, Michael B., Erickson, Robert S., and Stimson, James A. 'Peasants or Bankers? The American Electorate and the US Economy.' *American Political Science Review* 86/3: 597–611.

MacPherson, C. B. 1977. *Democratic Theory*. Oxford: Clarendon Press.

Marcus, George E., Sullivan, John L., Theiss-Morse, Elizabeth, and Wood, Sandra L. 1995. *With Malice Toward Some. How People Make Civil Liberties Judgements*. New York: Cambridge University Press.

Mason, David. 1995. 'Justice, Socialism, and Participation in the Postcommunist States,' pp. 49–80 in James R. Kluegel, David S. Mason, and Bernd Wegener (eds.). *Social Justice and Political Change*. New York: Aldine De Gruyter.

Merkl, Peter H. 1993. *German Unification in the European Context*. University Park, Pa.: Pennsylvania State University Press.

Merritt, Richard. 1995. *Democracy Imposed*. New Haven: Yale University Press.

Merritt, Anna and Merritt, Richard. 1970. *Public Opinion in Semisovereign Germany*. Urbana, Ill.: University of Illinois Press.

Miller, Arthur H. and Checcio, Regan. 1996. 'Comparing Mass and Elite Conceptions of Social Justice in Post-Soviet Societies,' paper presented at the annual meeting of the APSA, 29 Aug.–1 Sept., San Francisco.

——Hesli, Vickie L., and Reisinger, William M. 1997. 'Conception of Democracy Among Mass and Elites in Post-Soviet Societies.' *British Journal of Political Science* 27: 157–90.

Minkenberg, Michael. 1993. 'The Wall After the Wall: On the Continuing Division of Germany and the Remaking of Political Culture.' *Comparative Politics* 1/26: 53–68.

Mishler, William and Rose, Richard. 1996. 'Trajectories of Fear and Hope.

Support for Democracy in Post-Communist Europe.' *Comparative Political Studies* 28: 553–81.

—— —— 1997. 'Trust, Distrust, and Skepticism: Popular Evaluations of Civil and Political Institutions in Post-Communist Societies.' *Journal of Politics* 59: 418–51.

Muller, Edward N. and Seligson, Mitchell A. 1994. 'Civic Culture and Democracy: The Question of Causal Relationships.' *American Political Science Review* 88: 635–52.

Nagle, John D. 1994. 'Political Generation Theory and Post-Communist Youth in East-Central Europe,' pp. 25–52 in Louis Kriesberg, Michael Dobkowski, and Isidor Wallimann (eds.). *Researching Social Movements, Conflicts, and Change*, vol. 7. Greenwich, Conn.: JAI Press.

Noelle-Neumann, Elisabeth. 1991. 'The German Revolution: The Historical Experiment of the Division and Unification of a Nation as Reflected in Survey Research Findings.' *International Journal of Public Opinion Research* 3: 238–59.

—— 1994. 'Problems with Democracy in Eastern Germany after the Downfall of the GDR,' pp. 213–31 in Frederick Weil (ed.). *Research on Democracy and Society*, vol. 2. Greenwich, Conn.: JAI Press.

—— 1995. 'Das demokratische Defizit.' Dokumentation des Beitrags in der *Frankfurter Allgemeinen Zeitung* Nr. 219 vom 20 September 1995.

—— 1998. 'Was ist Anders als 1994?' Dokumentation des Beitrags in der *Frankfurter Allgemeinen Zeitung* Nr. 47 vom 25 Februar 1998.

Norpoth, Helmut and Roth, Dieter. 1996. 'Timid or Prudent? The German Electorate in 1994,' pp. 209–32 in Russell J. Dalton (ed.), *Germany Divided*. New York: Berg.

O'Donnell, Guillermo A. and Schmitter, Philippe C. 1986. *Transitions from Authoritarian Rule. Tentative Conclusions About Uncertain Democracies*. Baltimore: Johns Hopkins University Press.

Olson, Mancur. 1982. *The Rise and Decline of Nations*. New Haven: Yale University Press.

Orlow, Dietrich. 1995. *A History of Modern Germany 1871 to Present*. Englewood Cliffs, NJ: Prentice Hall.

Pateman, Carole. 1972. 'Political Culture, Political Structure, and Political Change.' *British Journal of Political Science* 1: 291–305.

—— 1980. 'The Civic Culture: A Philosophical Critique,' pp. 57–102 in Gabriel A. Almond and Sidney Verba (eds.). *The Civic Culture Revisited*. Boston: Little, Brown, and Co.

Pennock, Roland J. 1979. *Democratic Political Theory*. Princeton: Princeton University Press.

Peffley, Mark and Sigelman, Lee. 1990. 'Intolerance of Communists During the McCarthy Era: A General Model.' *Western Political Quarterly*: 94–111.

Pescosolido, Bernice A., Boyer, Carol, and Tsui, Wai Ting. 1986. 'Crisis in the

Welfare State: Public Reactions to Welfare Policies,' in Norman Furniss (ed.). *Futures for the Welfare State*. Bloomington: Indiana University Press.

Prothro, James W. and Grigg, Charles M.. 1960. 'Fundamental Principles of Democracy.' *Journal of Politics* 22: 276–94.

Przeworski, Adam. 1991. *Democracy and the Market. Political and Economic Reforms in Eastern Europe and Latin America*. New York: Cambridge University Press.

—— and Teune, Henry. 1970. *The Logic of Comparative Social Inquiry*. New York: Wiley.

Pulzer, Peter. 1995. *German Politics 1945–1995*. New York: Oxford University Press.

Putnam, Robert D. 1973. *The Beliefs of Politicians*. New Haven: Yale.

—— with Leonardi, Roberto and Nanetti, Raffaella Y. 1993. *Making Democracy Work*. Princeton: Princeton University Press.

———— and Pavoncello, Franco. 1983. 'Explaining Institutional Success: The Case of Italian Regional Government.' *American Political Science Review* 77: 55–75.

Pye, Lucian W. 1990. 'Political Science and the Crisis of Authoritarianism.' *American Political Science Review* 84: 3–20.

Rogowski, Ronald. 1974. *Rationale Legitimacy*. Princeton: Princeton University Press.

Rohrschneider, Robert. 1994. 'Report from the Laboratory: The Influence of Institutions on Political Elites' Democratic Values in Germany.' *American Political Science Review*, Dec. 1994 (88/4): 927–41.

—— 1996*a*. 'Cultural Transmission versus Perceptions of the Economy: The Sources of Political Elites' Economic Values in the United Germany.' *Comparative Political Studies*, Feb. 1996 (29/1): 78–104.

—— 1996*b*. Institutional Learning versus Value Diffusion: The Evolution of Democratic Values Among Parliamentarians in Eastern and Western Germany.' *Journal of Politics*, May 1996 (58/2): 442–66.

—— 1996*c*. 'Pluralism, Conflict, and Legislative Elites in the United Germany.' *Comparative Politics* 29: 43–67.

—— and Fuchs, Dieter. 1995. 'A New Electorate? Economic Trends and Electoral Choice in the 1994 Federal Election in Germany.' *German Politics and Society*, Spring 1995 (13/1): 100–22.

Roller, Edeltraud. 1994. 'Ideological Basis of the Market Economy: Attitudes Toward Distributional Principles and the Role of Government in Western and Eastern Germany.' *European Journal of Sociology* 10: 105–17

—— 1997. 'Sozialpolitische Orientierungen nach der deutschen Vereinigung,' pp. 115–46 in Oscar Gabriel (ed.). *Politische Orientierungen und Verhaltensweisen im vereinigten Deutschland*. Opladen: Leske + Budrich.

Roth, Dieter. 1976. *Zum Demokratieverständnis von Eliten in der Bundesrepublik Deutschland*. Frankfurt am. M.: Peter Lang.

Rüschemeyer, Marylin and Lemke, Christiane. 1989. *The Quality of Life in the German Democratic Republic.* Armonk, NY: M. E. Sharpe.

Rustow, Dankwart A. 1970. 'Transition to Democracy. Toward a Dynamic Model.' *Comparative Politics* 3: 337–63.

Sandford, Gregory. 1983. *From Ulbricht to Hitler: The Communist Reconstruction of East Germany, 1945–1946.* Princeton: Princeton University Press.

Sartori, Giovanni. 1967. *Democratic Theory.* New York: Praeger.

Schabowski, Günther. 1991. *Der Absturz.* Reinbeck: Rowolt.

Schneider, Otmar. 1988. *Rechtsgedanken und Rechtstechniken totalitärer Herrschaft aufgezeigt am Recht des öffentlichen Dienstes im 3. Reich under der DDR.* Berlin: Duncker + Humblot.

Schweigler, Gebhard. 1975. *National Consciousness in Divided Germany.* Beverly Hills, Calif.: Sage.

Searing, Donald. 1985. 'The Role of the Good Constituency Member and the Practice of Representation in Great Britain.' *Journal of Politics* 47: 348–81.

—— 1994. *Westminster's World.* Cambridge, Mass.: Harvard University Press.

Shamir, Michal. 1991. 'Political Intolerance among Masses and Elites in Israel: A Re-evaluation of the Elitist Theory of Democracy.' *Journal of Politics* 53: 1,018–43.

Shin, Doh Chul, Chey, Myung, and Kim, Kwang-Wong. 1989. 'Cultural Origins of Public Support for Democracy in Korea.' *Comparative Political Studies* 22: 217–38.

Sigel, Roberta S. (ed.). 1989. *Political Learning in Adulthood.* Chicago: Chicago University Press.

Smith, Tom W. 1987. 'The Welfare State in Cross National Perspective.' *Public Opinion Quarterly* 51: 401–21.

Sniderman, Paul M. 1975. *Personality and Demcoratic Politics.* Berkeley: University of California Press.

—— Tetlock, Philip E., Glaser, James M., Green, Donal Philip, and Hout, Michael. 1989. 'Principled Tolerance and the American Mass Public.' *British Journal of Political Science* 19: 25–45.

—— Fletcher, Joseph, Russell, Peter H., Tetlock, Philip E., and Gaines, Brian J. 1991. 'The Fallacy of Democratic Elitism: Elite Competition and Commitment to Civil Liberties.' *British Journal of Political Science* 21: 349–70.

Starr, Harvey. 1991. 'Democratic Dominoes. Diffusion Approaches to the Spread of Democracy in the International System.' *Journal of Conflict Resolution* 35: 356–81.

Sullivan, John, Piereson, James, and Markus, George E. 1982. *Political Tolerance and American Democracy.* Chicago: Chicago University Press.

—— Shamir, Michal, Walsh, Patrick, and Roberts, Nigel S. 1985. *Political Tolerance in Contex.* Boulder, Col.: Westview Press.

Sullivan, John, Welsh, Pat, Shamir, Michal, Barnum, David G., and Gibson, James L. 1989. 'Why Politicians Are More Tolerant.' *British Journal of Political Science* 23: 51–76.

Turner, Henry A. 1992. *Germany from Partition to Reunification.* New Haven: Yale University Press.

Veen, Hans-Joachim. 1997. 'Innere Einheit—aber wo liegt sie?' *Aus Politik und Zeitgeschichte* 40/41:19–28.

Verba, Sidney. 1965a. 'Germany: The Remaking of Political Culture,' pp. 130–70 in Lucian W. Pye and Sidney Verba (eds.). *Political Culture and Political Developments.* Princeton: Princeton University Press.

—— 1965b. 'Conclusion: Comparative Political Culture,' pp. 512–60 in Lucian W. Pye and Sidney Verba (eds.). *Political Culture and Political Developments.* Princeton: Princeton University Press.

—— et al. 1987. *Elites and the Idea of Equality.* Cambridge, Mass.: Harvard University Press.

Ward, Benjamin. 1979. *The Ideal Worlds of Economics: Liberal, Radical, and Conservative Economic World Views.* New York: Basic Books.

Watts, Meredith W. 1994. 'A "Participatory" Revolution Among the German "Unification" Generation? Youth Attitudes Toward Noninstitutional Participation After the East German Revolution.' *European Journal of Political Research* 25: 187–206.

Weber, Hermann. 1986. *Die DDR 1945–1986.* München: Oldenbourg Verlag.

Weil, Frederick. 1985. 'The Variable Effect of Education on Liberal Attitudes.' *American Sociological Review* 50: 458–74.

—— 1989. 'The Sources and Structure of Legitimation in Western Democracies.' *American Sociological Review* 54: 682–706.

—— 1993. 'The Development of Democratic Attitudes in Eastern and Western Germany in a Comparative Perspective.' *Research on Democracy and Society*, vol. 1: *Democratization in Eastern and Western Europe.* Greenwich, Conn.: JAI Press.

Welzel, Christian. 1997. *Demokratischer Elitenwandel.* Opladen: Leske + Budrich.

Welsh, Helga. 1994. 'Political Transition Processes in Central and Eastern Europe.' *Comparative Politics*, July: 379–94.

Werner, Camilla. 1991. 'Direktdemokratische Entscheidungsverfahren in der Bundesrespublik Deutschland? Zum Diskussionsstand und zu den Meinungen der Abgeordneten des 11. Bundestages und der Volkskammer,' pp. 405–34 in Hans-Dieter Klingemann, Richard Stöss, and Bernhard Weßels (eds.). *Politische Klasse und politische Institutionen.* Opladen: Westdeutscher Verlag.

Westle, Bettina. 1994. 'Demokratie und Sozialismus. Politische Ordnungsvorstellungen im vereinten Deutschland zwischen Ideologie, Protest, Nostalgie.' *Kölner Zeitschrift für Soziologie und Sozialpsychologie* 46/4: 571–96.

Index

unification, events leading to 41–2
United States, citizens' views about
economic values 194–5
citizens' views about tolerance 133–5

Veen, H-J. 9, 104
Verba, S. 2, 3, 8, 10, 26, 162, 201–3,
281 n.
voting behaviour in Germany 237–41

Ward, B. 162
Watts, M. 36
Weber, H. 282 n.
Weil, F. 2, 9, 13, 22, 29, 104, 109,
216

welfare state, *see* market economy
Welsh, H. 26
Welzel, C. 237
Werner, C. 91, 224–5
Wessels, B. 9
Western Europe, orientations about:
income ceilings 195
welfare policies 195
Westle, B. 86
Whitefield, S. 226
Wiberg, M. 289 n.
Wiegman, U. 36
winners of competition, *see* restraint

Zaller, J. 162, 195